Caribbean Certificate History

Development and Decolonisation

Book 3

R. Greenwood
S. Hamber

MACMILLAN CARIBBEAN

© R. Greenwood and S. Hamber 1980

All rights reserved. No part of this publication
may be reproduced or transmitted, in any form or
by any means, without permission.

First published 1981
Reprinted 1982 (three times), 1983, 1984

Published by
Macmillan Publishers
London and Basingstoke
*Companies and representatives in Lagos, Zaria,
Manzini, Gaborone, Nairobi, Singapore, Hong Kong,
Delhi, Dublin, Auckland, Melbourne, Tokyo,
New York, Washington, Dallas*

ISBN 0 333 30570 1

Printed in Hong Kong

Contents

Introduction vii

1 The United States in the Caribbean 1
Foreign policy of the United States 1
position in 1783; becoming a Caribbean power; 'Manifest Destiny'; the Monroe Doctrine
The United States and Cuba to 1902 5
attempts to purchase Cuba; the Ostend Manifesto
The Cuban War of Independence, 1895–1898 7
United States investment in Cuba; the causes of the war; United States intervention; the Spanish-American War, 1898; Cuban independence; the Platt Amendment, 1901
United States involvement in the Caribbean before 1900 10
Hispaniola; Puerto Rico; the Venezuelan border dispute, 1895

2 The United States in the Caribbean in the twentieth century 11
The Panama Canal 11
early history; diplomatic moves; the Panama revolution; the Canal and the Caribbean; the Roosevelt Corollary
'Dollar Diplomacy' 14
the Dominican Republic; Haiti; Nicaragua; the Danish Virgin Islands; factors influencing United States policy

'Good Neighbour Policies' 17
The United States and Cuba, 1902 to 1959 17
The United States and the British Caribbean after 1939 19
naval bases; other American interests

3 Trade unions in the British Caribbean 22
Introduction to trade unions 22
Unions in the British West Indies before 1938 23
the early unions; working class difficulties
Riots and strikes, 1935–1938 25
new unions, new powers; the 1938 Labour Congress
Four outstanding labour leaders 27
Hubert Critchlow; Arthur Andrew Cipriani; Uriah 'Buzz' Butler; Sir Alexander Bustamante
Trade unions and politics 30
how union-political party links arose; in Barbados; in Jamaica
Trade unions in the 1960s 32
achievements; procedure in disputes

4 Constitutional developments in the British Caribbean, 1866 to 1944 34
Breakdown of the representative system of government 34
the representative system; non co-operative assemblies; the judiciary; local government; status of British Guiana, St Lucia and Trinidad

The Morant Bay Rebellion 39
the hardships of the 1850s and 1860s; two key
personalities; events leading to the rebellion;
the Morant Bay Rebellion; the repression;
judgement on Eyre
The change to Crown Colony 44
government
how Crown Colony government was
established; Bahamas, Bermuda and Barbados;
Crown Colony government at work
Modifications to Crown Colony 46
government, 1884 to 1944

5 Movements towards independence I 48
Self-governing British Territories 48
decolonisation; attitude to Empire; external
pressures for self-government; internal
pressures for self-government
Constitutional progress to 52
independence
explanation of terms
Typical stages to independence 54
Independence in the 1960s 55
Jamaica; Trinidad and Tobago; British Guiana;
Barbados
The non-self-governing British 61
Territories
constitutional development; associated statehood;
remaining colonies
Independence in the 1970s 62
Post-independence problems 64
political problems; economic problems

6 Movements towards independence II 68
The French Caribbean 68
changes in 1946; political movements in the French
Caribbean; the future
Puerto Rico 71
the Spanish-American War and its results; 1917
to 1952; the Commonwealth of Puerto Rico,
1952; politics

7 Regional co-operation 76
Early attempts at unification 76
Stapleton and the Leewards; the Leeward Islands
Federation, 1871 to 1956; the Windward Islands;
other associations
Unifying forces, 1897 to 1947 81
tendency to disunity; forces contributing
unity; signs of growing unity; the attitude of the
British government

8 Federation and after 85
Progress to federation 85
the Montego Bay conference; other conferences;
the Constitution
The federation at work 88
politics; finance and other affairs; constitutional
revision, 1959
Breakdown of the federation 90
general reasons for the breakdown; specific
causes of breakdown; British account of the
breakdown
Inter-regional co-operation 92
after 1962
CARIFTA; CARICOM; other inter-regional
bodies

9 Colonial churches 96
Amerindian religion 96
Spanish Catholicism 97
the Church and the Indians; Montesinos
and las Casas; the Roman Catholic church
and slavery
Protestant churches in the British 101
West Indies
the organisation of the Church of England;
weakness of the Church of England before
1800; Church of England missions
The Nonconformist churches 104
the Quakers; the Moravians; the Wesleyan
Methodists; the Baptists; persecution of
Nonconformist churches

10 Religion after emancipation 108
Preparation for emancipation 108
nonconformist missions; conclusion
Reforms in the Church of England 109
the creation of two dioceses; post-emancipation
period
The disestablishment of the 113
Church of England
reasons for disestablishment; procedure for
disestablishment; Barbados
Immigrant religions 114
Hinduism; Islam
American revivalism 116
Afro-Caribbean religions 118
voodoo in Haiti; other Afro-Caribbean cults;
Rastafarians

11 Social life 120
After emancipation 120
Colour 121
Society divided 122

Social patterns	123

marriage; matri-focal families; segregation of the sexes; kinship; 'the yard'

Social change in the twentieth century	125
White élite/urban blacks – a study in contrast	125

the white élite; urban blacks

Newspapers	129

newspapers in political and social conflicts; newspapers and party politics

Cricket	130

national prestige in cricket

12 Social conditions and the Moyne commission — 135

Social conditions prior to the Moyne Commission	135

working conditions; unemployment; food; health; conclusion

The Moyne Commission	141
Social and economic recommendations of the Moyne Commission	141

conclusion

Comparison with Puerto Rico	143

in the 1930s; remedies for social distress

Reactions to poor social conditions	145

popular movements

13 Art forms in the Caribbean — 146

Art and architecture	146

archaeological discoveries

Art tradition in the Caribbean	147

art in Trinidad; art in Jamaica; art in Haiti

Architecture	153

Spanish architecture; British architecture; French architecture; Dutch architecture; Haiti

Music	163

instruments

The importance of carnival	163
Steel band music	163

origins; history of the bands

Other Caribbean musical forms	167

the Calypso; Reggae, Cadence, Soca

Revision questions	169
Further reading	175
Index	177

Acknowledgements

The author and publishers wish to acknowledge the following photograph sources:

Associated Press   p 68
BBC Hulton Picture Library   pp 1; 3; 8; 11; 13; 15; 17; 18 top; 34; 39; 43; 104; 106
Stephen Benson   pp 98; 154; 161
Anne Bolt   pp 35; 37; 89; 91; 96; 110; 115; 126; 128; 135; 152; 156; 157; 158; 160; 164; 165
J. Allan Cash   pp 101; 142
Church Missionary Society   p 124
Commonwealth Institute   p 151
Commonwealth Institute and Collection of the National Gallery of Jamaica   pp 150; 151 top
Patrick Eagar   p 132
Len Garrison   p 119
Stanley Gibbons   pp 22; 42; 52
Institute of Jamaica   p 76
Keystone   pp 18 bottom; 48; 63; 74; 85; 168
G. W. Lennox   p 146
Popperfoto   pp 59; 108
Virginia Radcliffe   p 159
Royal Commonwealth Society   p 140
Royal Geographical Society   p 155
J. Rudin   p 148
David Saunders   p 153
The Times   p 49
Trinidad High Commission   pp 57; 166; 167
United Nations   p 50
West India Committee   p 86
Cover by kind permission of Edna Manley and the National Gallery of Jamaica

The publishers have made every effort to trace the copyright holders of all illustrations, but, where they have failed to do so they will be pleased to make the necessary arrangements at the first opportunity.

Introduction

This is the third and final book of the Caribbean Certificate History series. The first two books were written before the Caribbean Examinations Council had produced their first public examination papers in June, 1979. Thus we only had their proposed syllabus and specimen papers to follow. However, the third book could be approached more confidently since the 1979 papers showed that the CXC examiners were following their proposed syllabus very closely and their questions indicated the level of factual knowledge required. We were pleased to see that our first two books met the requirements of the examination satisfactorily and we hope that Book 3 will do the same.

This book covers the more innovative parts of the syllabus where there was no traditional approach because the themes had not been tackled before at this level of school history. Such topics as Trade Unionism in the British Caribbean; Religion in the Caribbean; Art Forms in the Caribbean; Independence Movements and Social Life and Conditions were not parts of the colonial syllabi nor were they examined at 'O' level. Book 3 covers these themes, extensively in the case of trade unionism, independence movements and religion, and more selectively in the case of art forms and social life.

Other topics such as The United States in the Caribbean, Constitutional Developments prior to 1944 and Regional Co-operation have been dealt with at greater length than required by the old syllabi to cover the detailed study required by the CXC syllabus. Finally, Book 3 covers the non-British areas of the Caribbean which the British colonial syllabi neglected. Where the proposed syllabus specifically requires an understanding of a non-British territory, or a comparison to be made with one, we have endeavoured to satisfy it; for example, the United States and Cuba, the constitutional position of the French Caribbean and Puerto Rico and social conditions in Puerto Rico, have been given considerable attention.

Special mention must be made of three areas of the new syllabus in particular: Social Conditions in the Twentieth Century; Art Forms in the Caribbean; and Religion as a Social Force. These are very broad themes and could constitute separate subjects in a discipline other than history. It was not possible to deal with these areas in depth. We hope that teachers and pupils who are especially interested in these topics will feel encouraged to study them more fully from their own sources.

Once again we have adopted a factual approach whenever possible to satisfy the Cambridge syllabus and the in-depth study required by the CXC. However, recent issues are still sometimes controversial and a completely factual approach is no longer possible. We have tried to avoid expressing personal opinions on delicate issues such as Jamaica's socialism, relations with Cuba and the United States or the recent coups in the Eastern Caribbean. However, some well-known views have been stated, for example, that of the Third World on the constitutional position of Puerto Rico. We are very conscious that domestic political issues, international relations and non-alignment are inflammatory topics amongst school teachers and senior pupils in developing countries.

As in the first two books in the series, revision questions are given at the end of the book. In the traditional areas of the syllabus where many sample questions are available, our questions try to bring out evidence of intelligent study. In the new themes the questions are attempting to anticipate the expectations of the examiners.

Acknowledgements

I wish to thank my wife, Margaret, for her encouragement and understanding during the writing of this book.

Robert Greenwood

1
The United States in the Caribbean

John Quincy Adams

Foreign policy of the United States

Position in 1783

From 1775 to 1783 the British North American colonies had been fighting for their independence. By 1783 they had achieved this and by the Treaty of Paris a new country was established – the United States of America. The thirteen colonies had had close links with the British West Indies, having had not only the same colonial master but also a thriving mutual trade which Britain had never been able to control completely. Relations between the United States and the Caribbean were obviously going to be of very great importance in the future.

The United States found herself in a hostile world. Britain restricted American trade with the British West Indies, refused to abandon forts on the north-western frontier and disputed territories to the north. France and Spain, who had sided with the North American colonies during the War of Independence in order to defeat Britain, were also colonial powers. They feared the effects that a successful colonial revolt might have on their own colonies. They had both wanted the United States to be confined to the east of the Appalachians even though the Treaty of 1763 had established the Mississippi as her western boundary.

France also restricted American trade with her West Indian colonies. Even more serious was the

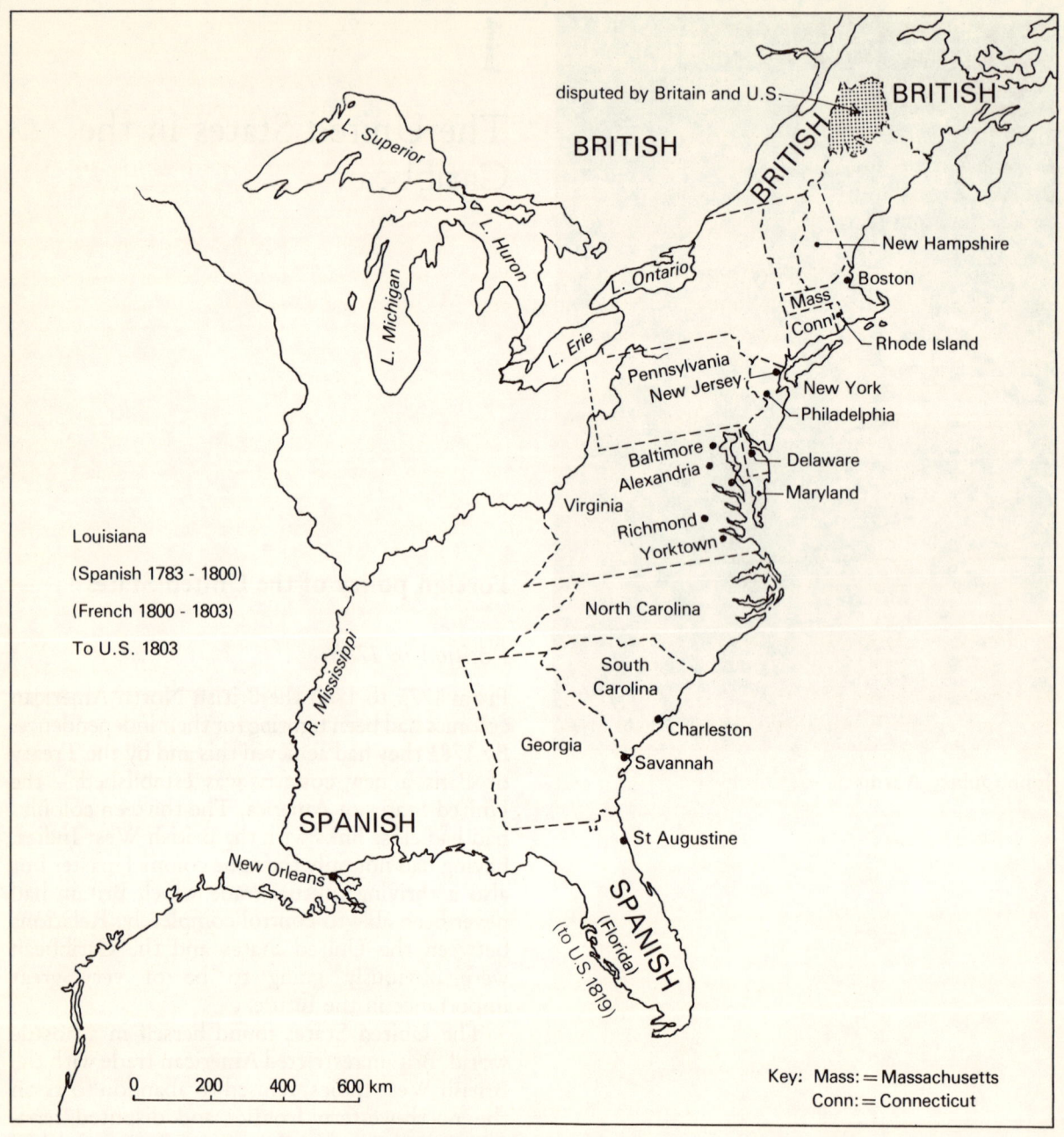

Map 1 The independent United States in 1783

hostile attitude of Spain. In 1783 the United States had no outlet into the Gulf of Mexico and, hence, the Caribbean. Louisiana and Florida were Spanish. The Spanish closed the port of New Orleans to the United States although they had accepted that the Mississippi was her western boundary. The vast area from the Appalachians to the Mississippi was open to American expansion, but it would do little good if these lands could not transport their goods down the Mississippi. The United States could not play a bigger role in the Caribbean until her boundaries extended to the Gulf of Mexico.

Nationalism in a newly-independent country is strong and in the United States there was certainly a desire to show the world that she was a force to be reckoned with. An adventurous and aggressive foreign policy would demonstrate this.

It would also have other advantages:
1 The thirteen disunited colonies had united to achieve independence. Peace might bring back disunity but war would ensure the maintenance of unity in the face of a common danger.
2 The United States was a republic and hated the idea of monarchy. European monarchies still dominated the western hemisphere and should be opposed.
3 The United States had shaken off colonialism, but this still held sway over most of America. Moreover, the colonial powers were checking the expansion of the United States.
4 There were many specific quarrels which the United States had to settle with Britain, France and Spain. Peace would imply weakness; aggression might bring success in boundary disputes.

There were, however, other factors which favoured a peaceful policy:
1 After a long, hard-fought war the country was very poor and needed peace for recovery and consolidation.
2 There was westward expansion to be undertaken within North America while keeping peace with foreign countries.
3 The United States had much to gain from peace and neutrality. The commercial prospects for a neutral trading nation were particularly attractive in the Caribbean if Britain and France were fighting each other.
4 The United States would benefit from peace with Britain in particular. As Thomas Jefferson said later: '... with her (Britain) on our side we need not fear the whole world'.

Peace was the policy adopted by the first two Federalist Presidents, George Washington and John Adams. Of course, the Republicans were aggressive and wanted war with the monarchies of Europe on any pretext, but generally peace was popular in the new nation, especially amongst New Yorkers and New Englanders who were anxious to extend commerce and trade.

Becoming a Caribbean power

The United States entered the Caribbean sphere geographically as well as commercially by obtaining a long coastline on the Gulf of Mexico. This was achieved in three stages.
1 *Pinckney's Treaty* When the French Revolutionary Wars broke out in 1793, France expected the United States to support her in accordance with the alliance of 1778. However, the latter remained neutral, concluding minor treaties with either side. One of these was Pinckney's Treaty with Spain in 1795. Spain agreed to open the Mississippi and the port of New Orleans to the United States and in return the United States accepted latitude 31 degrees north as the northern boundary of Florida. The United States had her first outlet into the Gulf of Mexico and the Caribbean.

New Orleans at the beginning of the nineteenth century

2 *The Louisiana Purchase* Thomas Jefferson, a Republican, became President in 1801 and adopted an openly expansionist policy. His greatest success was to buy Louisiana from France in 1803 for $15,000,000. This established the United States on the west bank of the Mississippi and gave her a coastline on the Gulf of Mexico to the west of New Orleans.

3 *The acquisition of Florida* Spain still held the coastline to the east of New Orleans. Jefferson had tried, unsuccessfully, to obtain it in 1805 because it would enable the United States to become involved in the Caribbean, particularly in Cuba. In the decade after the 1812–1814 war, nationalism was strong. Andrew Jackson pursued a very aggressive policy towards Spain over Florida, forcing her to hand it over in 1819 in return for the United States' government agreeing to take over the payment of $5,000,000 compensation which Spain had owed to American merchants.

'Manifest Destiny'

Jefferson spoke of expansion not only within the North American continent, but also in other parts of the Americas. In 1801 he said:

> However our present interests may restrain us within our limits, it is impossible not to look forward to distant times, when our rapid multiplication will expand beyond those limits and cover the whole northern, if not the southern, continent with a people speaking the same language, governed in similar forms and by similar laws.

This was the first expression of the idea which was later called 'Manifest Destiny'. Put simply, it was the idea that it was natural and inevitable that the United States would dominate the Americas in wealth, power and territory. It was nationalistic, expansionist and aggressive, and was based on a feeling of the racial and cultural superiority of the American people. Thus the United States expected in time to dominate the Caribbean. To many the first step towards this would be to control Cuba.

The Monroe Doctrine

The Monroe Doctrine was also directly relevant to the Caribbean. The United States, being a republic and an ex-colony herself, supported colonial uprisings in Latin America. In 1818 the revolutionary governments in Argentina. Venezuela and Chile asked for, and expected to receive, American recognition. However, the United States was trying to obtain Florida from Spain and did not want to upset her, so she remained neutral during the uprisings. By 1822 Peru and Mexico had become independent of Spain, and Brazil had become independent of Portugal. The European powers began to consider restoring the Latin American colonies to their former masters. This threat of European intervention made the United States act as if she had already recognised the independence of most of these new countries.

Britain was interested in trade with Latin America and considered she had a claim on it since most of the money for the revolutions had come from Britain. George Canning, the British Foreign Minister, proposed that the United States and Britain should co-operate to stop the recolonisation of Latin America. Many people in the United States favoured this, but John Quincy Adams felt that Canning's proposal would allow Britain to stop the United States expanding into any territory once held by Spain, particularly Cuba. He advised the rejection of co-operation and President Monroe followed his advice. These words from his Presidential Address became known as the Monroe Doctrine:

> ... we should consider any attempt on their (European powers) part to extend their system to any portion of this hemisphere as dangerous to our peace and safety. With the governments who have declared their independence and maintained it, and whose independence we have acknowledged, we could not view any interposition by any European power in any other light than as the manifestation of an unfriendly disposition toward the United States.

Later he added: '... The American continents are henceforth not to be considered as subjects for future colonisation by any European powers.'

President Monroe was telling Europe to keep its hands off America. The doctrine had little immediate effect, but European countries considered it was very arrogant. Since all the Caribbean islands belonged to colonial powers, the doctrine applied there.

The United States and Cuba to 1902

Once the United States had reached the Gulf of Mexico, her nearest neighbour to the south was Cuba which was ruled by Spain. Its strategic importance to the United States was obvious. Cuba, a long island straddling the entrance to the Gulf of Mexico, could effectively block American outlets to the south. It also commanded the Florida Channel which was the passage from the Gulf to the Atlantic. The port of Havana at the entrance to the Gulf was the key port in the Spanish trade system in the Caribbean.

At the beginning of the nineteenth century Spain was weak and was finding it increasingly difficult to control her American empire. The United States could have conquered Cuba at any time from the beginning of the nineteenth century onwards. However, she could not justify conquest while championing the ideas of self-determination and anti-colonialism.

Jefferson first stressed the importance of Cuba to the United States in 1809. He felt that if Cuba was not strong enough to stand by herself once she had obtained her freedom from Spain, her independence could be maintained in a federation of West Indian islands. The obvious federation for Cuba, as was suggested later, was with Hispaniola and Puerto Rico. This federation would naturally turn towards the United States for protection.

John Quincy Adams followed the Manifest Destiny ideas of Jefferson. He too felt that there was no need for conquest, because Cuba would gravitate towards the United States. Subsequent American statesmen looked for ways to hasten the process.

Attempts to purchase Cuba

In the first half of the nineteenth century the United States adopted the idea of purchasing territories as an alternative to conquest or

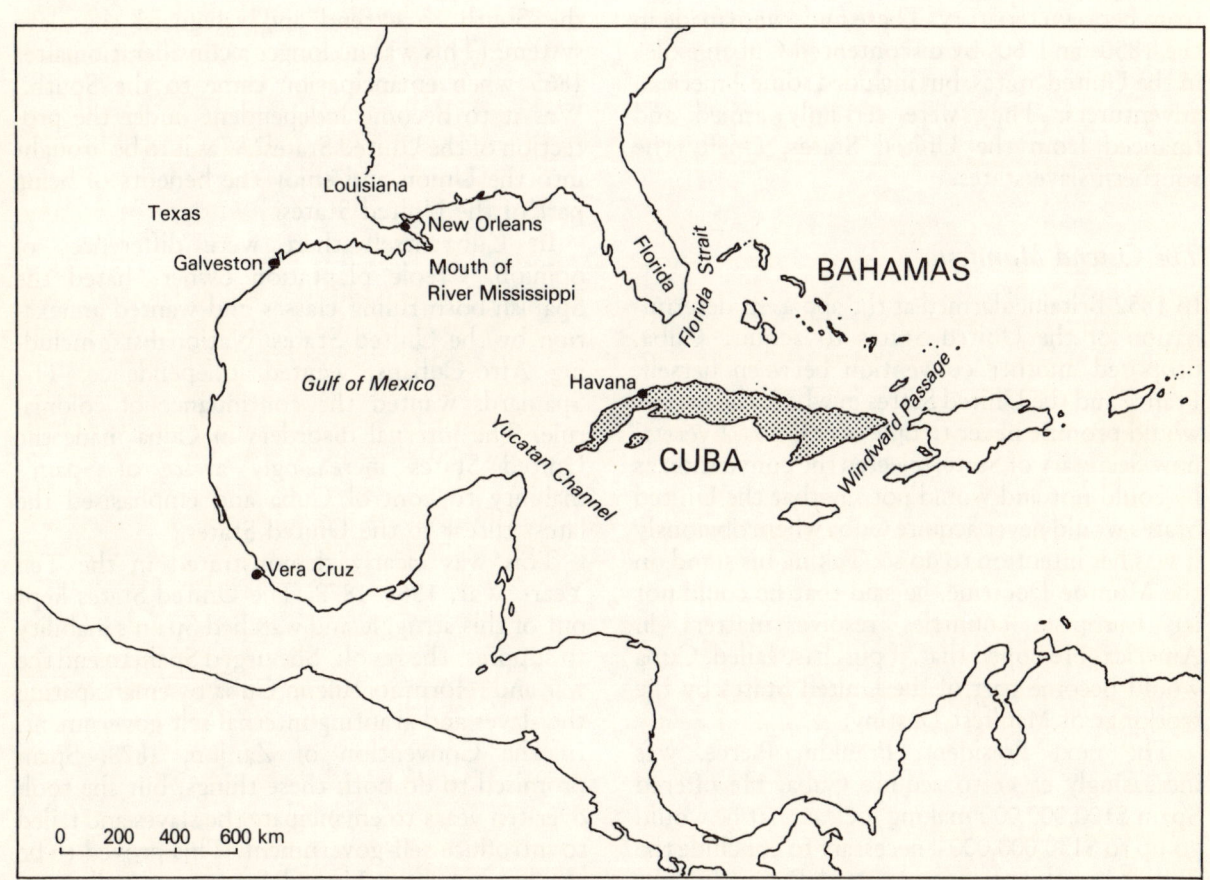

Map 2   The strategic importance of Cuba to the United States

exchange by treaty. This was frowned upon by traditional diplomacy.

Monroe's Presidential Address in 1823 was couched in general terms, but it was aimed at Cuba. Two years later Edward Everett, Minister to Spain, suggested that Cuba should be the security for a large loan to Spain. If the debt was not repaid by a fixed date, the United States would take Cuba. This suggestion was not adopted.

Britain became concerned about the American interest in Cuba and George Canning proposed that Britain, France and the United States should agree to preserve Spanish rule in Cuba, but the United States would not agree. In the 1840s Lord Palmerston made a further attempt to stop American designs on Cuba.

Nevertheless politicians in the United States did not hide their designs on Cuba. In 1848, President James K. Polk offered $100,000,000 for Cuba, but Spain refused to consider this as she did all subsequent offers. The United States did not help by allowing filibustering raids to be made from her own territory. These raids were made in the 1850s and '60s by discontented Cuban exiles in the United States, but included some American adventurers. They were certainly armed and financed from the United States, chiefly the southern slave states.

The Ostend Manifesto

In 1852 Britain, alarmed at the apparent determination of the United States to acquire Cuba, proposed another convention between herself, France and the United States in which the parties would promise never to take over Cuba. Everett, now Secretary of State, rejected the convention as he could not and would not say that the United States would never acquire Cuba when, obviously it was her intention to do so. Taking his stand on the Monroe Doctrine, he said that he could not let European countries resolve matters in America. He hoped that, if purchase failed, Cuba would become part of the United States by the workings of Manifest Destiny.

The next President, Franklin Pierce, was increasingly eager to acquire Cuba. He offered Spain $100,000,000 making it clear that he would go up to $130,000,000 if necessary to conclude the deal. When this offer was rejected, Pierce thought about conquest.

He asked Pierre Soulé, the American Minister in Madrid, to call together the Minister to Britain, James Buchanan, and the Minister to France, John Mason, to assess European reaction to the conquest of Cuba by the United States. After meeting in Ostend in Belgium in October 1854, they suggested another attempt to purchase Cuba on the grounds that Spain's rule over Cuba was dangerous to 'our internal peace and the existence of our cherished Union'. They recommended an offer of $120,000,000. The opponents of the administration insisted on the publication of the three diplomats' advice to the Secretary of State. It was published as the 'Ostend Manifesto'. Its implied aggression caused such alarm in the country that the Pierce Aministration had to reject it.

In 1859 the Senate made a further attempt to purchase Cuba. Once again Spain rejected the offer. The idea of purchase was not abandoned in the 1860s, but was no longer pursued so vigorously. The reasons for acquiring Cuba became rather confused. Was it to be acquired for the South to extend and safeguard the slave system? (This was no longer a consideration after 1865 when emancipation came to the South.) Was it to become independent under the protection of the United States? Was it to be brought into the Union and enjoy the benefits of being part of the United States?

In Cuba itself there were differences of opinion. Creole plantation owners hated the Spanish-born ruling classes and wanted annexation by the United States. Nationalists, including Afro-Cubans, wanted independence. The Spaniards wanted the continuance of colonial rule. The internal disorders in Cuba made the United States increasingly aware of Spain's inability to control Cuba and emphasised the latest threat to the United States.

This was clearly demonstrated in the Ten Years War, 1868–1878. The United States kept out of this struggle and watched Spain's inability to suppress the revolt. She urged Spain to end the war and reform its rule in Cuba by emancipating the slaves and granting internal self-government. In the Convention of Zanjon, 1878, Spain promised to do both these things, but she took over ten years to emancipate the slaves and failed to introduce self-government. This proved to be the last time the United States was willing to stand aside.

The Cuban War of Independence, 1895-1898

United States investment in Cuba

Until the mid-nineteenth century the United States had been a predominantly agricultural economy, but by 1865 she had experienced a vast industrial revolution stimulated by the Civil War which led to considerable economic growth in the 1870s and 1880s. Many fortunes were made and people were looking for profitable channels for investment. As early as 1868 the United States dominated the Cuban economy, in that eighty-three per cent of the latter's exports went to the United States (only six per cent went to Spain). With the help of American investment, Cuban sugar production became mechanised in the 1880s and production soared to nearly 1,100,000 tonnes in 1894. Since nearly all this extra production was taken by the American market, Cuba was dangerously dependent on the United States.

By 1895 American investments in Cuba were worth $50,000,000 and the annual trade between the two countries reached $100,000,000. This investment ranged from about ninety per cent of Cuba's transport system to about forty per cent of the sugar industry. The investors expected protection from their government and any disturbance which threatened them and their property caused concern in the United States and made intervention likely.

The causes of the war

The main cause of the war was that Cuban nationalists wanted independence. They were encouraged and supplied with money and arms by Cuban exiles in the United States. The widespread discontent in Cuba, especially among Afro-Cubans, ensured that thousands would support a war for independence.

The spark which turned this nationalist discontent into war in 1895 was a result of the stranglehold which the United States had on the Cuban economy through the sugar market. In 1894, when Cuban sugar production reached a record level of over a million tonnes, the production of European beet sugar was also very high. The world price of sugar fell. The Wilson Tariff in the United States placed a forty per cent duty on imported sugar. The effect on the Cuban economy was catastrophic and there was unemployment and poverty in the canefields.

The war began in February 1895. Spain sent an army of 200,000 but was unable to suppress the revolt because of the guerilla tactics of the Cubans, aimed at securing American involvement. Within three years, sugar production slumped to one-fifth of its 1894 level. Both sides killed civilians. The United States could not remain aloof when the lives and property of its citizens were in danger.

Furthermore, in January, 1896, Spain sent a new general to Cuba, Valeriano Weyler, who soon became known as 'Butcher'. He divided Cuba into concentration camps in which he confined the entire population of the area. More than 200,000 innocent citizens died of starvation and disease in these camps. This increased anti-Spanish propaganda in the United States.

United States intervention

Americans, earlier in the nineteenth century, had felt that the United States should keep out of world affairs and set an example of peace, self-determination and democracy, but after 1880 this feeling changed. The amazing economic growth brought about by the industrial revolution had made her a world power and some politicians felt that she should take a major part in world affairs. There were also expansionist groups in the United States. Finding that the continental frontiers of the United States had been reached (the 'frontier' was officially closed in 1890), they looked overseas for new markets for agricultural and industrial products. Admiral Mahan led a group who argued that the national security and greatness of the United States in the future depended on a large navy with coaling stations and bases throughout the world.

As a result of the aggressive behaviour of Britain, France and Germany in imperial affairs in the 1880s, the attitude of the United States changed. For example, she attended the Berlin Conference for the partition of Africa in 1884-5. Nearer home, France had begun a project to build a canal across the Isthmus of Panama in 1881. The United States felt this endangered her position in the Caribbean and the Pacific. France could not be allowed to take over Cuba if Spain was too weak to hold on to it. The 'Social Darwinists' became increasingly influential in the United

States. They held that countries would inevitably quarrel and fight with each other and only the strong nations would survive. Thus government owed it to its citizens to be strong and aggressive. Albert Beveridge and Theodore Roosevelt said that it was the duty of the United States to make itself strong in order to preserve its national life.

Thus the American attitude towards foreign involvement and imperialism changed and there was an increasing demand for intervention in the Cuban War. However, President Grover Cleveland, resisted this demand in spite of American losses and appeals from the rebels. The 'yellow press', chiefly Joseph Pulitzer of the New York *World* and William Randolph Hearst of the New York *Journal*, exaggerated the reports of Spanish brutality to stir up pro-war feeling. Cleveland countered this propaganda by saying that there were atrocities on both sides.

The Spanish-American War, 1898

Then in March, 1897, William McKinley, who had campaigned for Cuban independence, became President. The United States still did not intervene immediately because Spain again promised reform in Cuba, and replaced 'Butcher' Valeriano Weyler. However, chance played its

The loss of the USS *Maine*

General Shafter's attack on Santiago

part. In January, 1898, a battleship, the USS *Maine*, blew up in Havana harbour with the loss of 260 lives. A United States Naval Court of Inquiry said that the explosion had been caused by a Spanish mine, but Spain rejected this. She did not want war and offered concessions, but the United States demanded immediate withdrawal from Cuba. This was refused and in April the United States declared war.

There was fighting in the Philippines, Cuba and Puerto Rico. In Cuba itself, Spain was defeated in ten weeks. The large Spanish army of 200,000 was tired of the war by the time the Americans entered. The main battle was at Santiago where Admiral Sampson sunk the Spanish fleet which was still composed of wooden ships. The city of Santiago surrendered to General Shafter's army. Spanish resistance was over by July. A preliminary peace was signed in Washington in August and formal peace was made in Paris in December.

In under four months fighting, the Americans had lost about 5,500 men, but only about 400 were killed in the fighting, the rest died from disease. The war cost the United States $250,000,000. Spain's losses were much greater. It was the end of an era. Spain had finally lost the empire which she had held since 1493.

Cuban independence

The treaty of Paris was signed on 10 December 1898. Spain formally recognised the independence of Cuba. The United States was to take over Guam, Puerto Rico and the Philippines on payment of $20,000,000. The Senate still had to ratify the treaty. The biggest controversy was over the Philippines which marked the beginning of an American Empire. The anti-imperialists were furious, feeling that it was the end of all that the United States stood for – liberty, self-determination, democracy and justice. However, the treaty was ratified by fifty-seven votes to twenty-seven, just two votes above the required two-thirds majority.

Cuban freedom was not achieved immediately and the military occupation continued. The purpose of this was to 'americanise' Cuba so thoroughly that, when independence was handed over, Cuba would be just like a part of the United States. The military occupation began very badly for the Cubans. General John Brooke, the first military governor, disbanded the Cuban army and tried to keep Cubans out of the government. He was succeeded by General Leonard Wood whose governorship brought lasting benefits to Cuba. Although the Cubans appreciated these benefits, they were suspicious of American intentions and impatient to be rid of them. They felt, rightly, that General Wood was prolonging the American presence in Cuba deliberately.

Wood restored normal life in Cuba and the military government carried out many improvements. Havana harbour was deepened and the streets of the city were paved. The telegraph and telephone systems were repaired and extended. Throughout the island, schools, roads and bridges were built. The United States was very conscious of the ease with which diseases could spread from Cuba to the mainland and insisted on a public health programme. A sewage system was begun. Yellow fever was almost completely eradicated.

To fulfil the American promise made at the Treaty of Paris to guarantee Cuban independence, Wood passed an electoral law enabling the Cubans to elect a convention which could draft a constitution for an independent Cuba. In the United States Congress, the Teller Amendment was passed to reassure the Cubans that the United States was not going to annex Cuba. The United States was torn between her promise to give Cuba independence and her unwillingness to hand over until americanisation had advanced further. This dilemma was solved by the Platt Amendment.

The Platt Amendment, 1901

The Platt Amendment gave the United States close control over Cuban affairs after the withdrawal of the military government. Cuba could not:
a) conclude treaties with foreign powers;
b) borrow money in excess of what its normal revenues could repay;
c) completely control its internal affairs in such matters as sanitation and health;
d) refuse the United States bases and coaling stations;
e) allow any other country to have a base;
f) prevent the United States intervening in Cuba for 'the protection of life, liberty and individual property'.

The convention was unwilling to accept the Platt Amendment since it limited Cuban independence. However, the United States refused to end the military occupation until it was accepted as part of any future constitution for Cuba. It was under these terms that a treaty was signed for Cuba's 'independence' in May 1903. The Platt Amendment governed American relations with Cuba until it was withdrawn in 1934.

United States involvement in the Caribbean before 1900

As the nineteenth century progressed, the Caribbean area became of increasing importance to the United States. But apart from Cuba, there were few other areas of active government involvement.

Hispaniola

In 1821 Hispaniola claimed independence from Spain, but was almost immediately taken over by Haiti from 1822 to 1844. In that year, it broke away from Haiti and declared itself the Dominican Republic and asked for annexation by the United States. The Commission of Inquiry sent by the United States recommended annexation, but the Senate refused. The Dominican Republic still felt threatened by Haiti and again asked for annexation in 1870. Another Commission of Inquiry suggested three possibilities for its future:
a) annexation by the United States (as the Commission had recommended);
b) acquisition by another stronger power;
c) independence in a federation with Cuba and Puerto Rico.
The Commission felt that annexation would bring benefits to the island but the Dominican Republic had to wait until the twentieth century for American rule.

Puerto Rico

During the Cuban War of 1895–98, Spain had promised internal self-government in Puerto Rico. She granted a constitution in 1897, but before it could come into effect an American expeditionary force was sent to Puerto Rico in July, 1898. By August the island had been taken. For the most part, the people had welcomed the American soldiers and there had been little resistance because the Puerto Ricans hoped for political rights and economic benefits. By the Treaty of Paris Puerto Rico was ceded to the United States. There was an American military government for two years until Congress passed the Foraker Act which set up a civil government. However, this was controlled by appointees of the United States government and most Puerto Ricans were still denied political rights. As in Cuba, the aim of the administration was the thorough americanisation of the island, culturally and economically.

The Venezuelan border dispute, 1895

The border dispute between British Guiana and Venezuela shows how the United States was interpreting the Monroe Doctrine by the end of the nineteenth century. Venezuela, on the point of a territorial war with British Guiana, appealed to the United States who wanted the dispute referred to arbitration, but Britain refused.

President Cleveland was adamant about arbitration and told Congress that the United States should resist Britain by every means within its power. The United States was prepared to go to war with Britain but Britain backed down and submitted to arbitration which found in Britain's favour.

The results of this partial diplomatic victory for the United States were profound. She gained great confidence which led to a more adventurous attitude to foreign affairs and to imperial questions.

Woodrow Wilson

2
The United States in the Caribbean in the twentieth century

The Panama Canal

Early history

The idea of building a canal across the neck of land between North and South America was originally a Spanish one. Britain and the United States took up the idea; Britain because of her interests in the Caribbean and her worldwide empire, and the United States because she was expanding across the continent to the Pacific and wanted a short sea-link to the West Coast. In 1850 Britain and the United States signed the Clayton-Bulwer Treaty by which both countries agreed to share in the construction and control of an isthmian canal.

Throughout the nineteenth century and into the twentieth, two routes were under consideration for this canal. One was across the Isthmus of Panama, the narrowest point and where the route would be made easier by the Gatun Lake. The other was further north in Nicaragua where natural waterways would leave little cutting to be done. Here the canal route could follow the San Juan River, across Lake Nicaragua and then proceed by a channel cut through the Rivas Peninsula. When gold was discovered in California in 1848, this became the route used by the prospectors to reach the west coast quickly. Both routes had their supporters in the United States.

In the second half of the nineteenth century

Britain became much more interested in a Suez route to her eastern empire, Australia and New Zealand. Meanwhile France showed greater interest in a Central American Canal, and Ferdinand de Lesseps, builder of the Suez Canal, formed a French company to construct a Panama canal. This company obtained rights for a canal, valid until 1904, from the government of Colombia to whom Panama belonged. The French project began in 1881, but was abandoned within a decade due to construction difficulties and the high death rate from malaria and yellow fever. The French company left their assets and treaty rights in Panama outstanding.

The United States reached the Pacific coast with the founding of the state of California in 1850. For commercial reasons, eastern businessmen pressed for a canal which would cut the journey to the west coast to one-third of the time of that round Cape Horn. Later, as a result of the 1898 Spanish-American War, the United States acquired an empire in the Caribbean and the Pacific. The strategic advantages of a canal which would enable warships to pass quickly from the Atlantic to the Pacific became obvious.

Diplomatic moves

The Clayton-Bulwer Treaty prevented the United States building a canal on her own. Britain was reluctant to release her from this agreement without compensation and safeguards about the use of the canal, but the United States was determined to press ahead with or without Britain's co-operation. Britain, facing reality, decided that more was to be gained by co-operation. This resulted in the signing of the Hay-Pauncefote treaty in 1901. The United States was given the sole rights to build and control the canal, provided that it would be open to the commercial and fighting ships of all nations. Britain agreed to the demand of the United States Senate that they be allowed to fortify the canal.

The route had still not been decided on. Meanwhile, another French company, the New Panama Canal Company, had acquired the assets and rights of de Lesseps Company for Panama. They were anxious to sell these assets before 1904 when they would revert to Colombia and the Company would not receive any compensation. The Maritime Canal Company of Nicaragua was also anxious to reach an agreement with the Americans. By June, 1902, the French negotiators had won the great canal debate, but the Nicaraguan route was still left open for the United States to take up in the future. The Bryan-Chamorro Treaty gave her the sole right to build a canal through Nicaragua.

Next the United States had to negotiate with Colombia. The Secretary of State, John Hay, forced Colombia to sign a treaty by threatening to take up the Nicaraguan route if she would not agree. In fact the United States had already agreed to pay the New Panama Canal Company $40,000,000 for its rights on Colombian soil. In March, 1903, Tomás Herrán of Colombia signed a treaty by which Colombia would receive $10,000,000 down payment and $250,000 annually from the United States for ceding a Canal Zone ten kilometres wide across the Isthmus of Panama.

The Panama revolution

Later in 1903 there was a change of government in Colombia. The new government held that the money was inadequate compensation for the territorial loss involved and the threat to Colombian independence. Hay then tried to bully Colombia into accepting the Treaty, with the result that the Colombian Senate unanimously rejected it in August. Some people in the United States felt that Colombia was trying to delay until 1904 when the rights expired, so that it would receive the $40,000,000 payment due to the New Panama Canal Company.

President Theodore Roosevelt and Hay were determined to have the canal. Their thinking was similar to that of the United States newspaper which wrote: 'The simplest plan of coercing Colombia would be inciting a revolution in Panama and supporting the insurrectionary government'. Of course, with $40,000,000 in the balance, the French company were willing to co-operate in such a scheme and stirred up the desired revolution. The United States sent the USS *Nashville* with marines to seize the Panama Railroad and prevent any Colombian force landing within eighty kilometres of Panama. Thus Colombia was powerless to stop the revolution succeeding. The United States quickly recognised the new government and signed a treaty with it on the original terms.

Roosevelt had entered into this ruthless and immoral scheme fully conscious of what he was doing. His attitude was that the end justified the means. With hindsight, Roosevelt's action probably did not speed up the completion of the canal but it did make the United States unpopular throughout the world, especially in Latin America. Later President Woodrow Wilson apologised to Colombia and after Roosevelt's death, $25,000,000 was paid in compensation.

The Canal and the Caribbean

Construction began in 1904 directed by a United States Army engineer, Colonel George Goethals. Much of the manual labour was done by West Indians. The problems of malaria and yellow fever were largely overcome by a United States Army medical officer, Colonel W. C. Gorgas. The canal was completed within ten years and the first ocean-going ship passed through on 15 August, 1914.

The Panama Canal dominated American policy in the Caribbean. Once built it was regarded as a 'lifeline' and the United States felt that she not only had to defend the Canal Zone itself, but also secure the approaches to the canal.

American policy in the Caribbean was controlled by four major needs:
1 To defend the canal zone itself. This was easily done by establishing marine bases there.
2 To increase her naval bases in the Caribbean.

Minneapolis Journal.
Uncle Sam throws his hat in the ring.
(But in the Panama Canal dispute there is really no question of the Monroe Doctrine, simply one of Presidential electioneering intrigue.)

Mucha.]   'Warsaw.
Uncle Sam's long arm stretches through an open canal at Panama, menacing Japan.

Le Cri de Paris.]
Pay, and you may pass through !!
A French view of the attitude of the United States.

Minneapolis Journal.,
Putting His Foot in It.
An American view of the action of the Senate with regard to the Panama Canal dues.

Cartoons on the Panama Canal

The latter was assured by the Platt Amendment in Cuba.
3 To assume a 'police rôle' in Latin America, a policy begun by Roosevelt.
4 To stop independent Caribbean states falling into potentially hostile hands. 'Dollar Diplomacy' was the policy used to prevent this.

The Roosevelt Corollary

In his annual message to Congress in 1904, Roosevelt announced a clear change from the traditional United States' policy of non-intervention in the affairs of other states. He said:

> Chronic wrong-doing may in America, as elsewhere, ultimately require intervention by some civilized nation, and in the Western hemisphere the adherence of the United States to the Monroe Doctrine may force the United States, however reluctantly, in flagrant cases of such wrong-doing or impotence, to the exercise of an international police power.

This statement, which became known as the 'Roosevelt Corollary to the Monroe Doctrine', influenced American policy towards Latin America and the Caribbean until 1930. It was particularly addressed to the Caribbean because of the importance of the Panama Canal.

The Monroe Doctrine had pledged the United States to prevent European intervention or extension of territory in the Americas. The Roosevelt Corollary justified United States intervention in the Americas in order to prevent European intervention. Its reception in Latin America was hostile, but Roosevelt was unconcerned with the feelings of people whom he publicly despised as 'dagoes'.

'Dollar Diplomacy'

At the beginning of the twentieth century most foreign trade and investment in Caribbean territories was in the hands of European countries. After the decision to build the Panama Canal, the United States was conscious of the potential danger of this. She felt that unrest and disturbances in the Caribbean might lead to a takeover of Caribbean states by European powers which the United States did not want in the approaches to the Panama Canal. This danger had been demonstrated in 1902–3 when Venezuela failed to pay its debts to foreign creditors, and Britain, Germany and Italy blockaded the coast to force repayment. Germany actually destroyed a Venezuelan town before the United States persuaded the parties to submit to arbitration.

United States policy aimed at bringing about a transference of the debts of Caribbean states from European to North American creditors. This policy of dollar diplomacy was attributed to William Howard Taft, Secretary of War in 1904. It operated so successfully in the Caribbean between 1905 and 1930 that, by 1924, the United States was actively directing the financial affairs of five Caribbean States, namely Cuba, the Dominican Republic, Haiti, Nicaragua and Honduras. The United States was prepared, if necessary, to turn this into political control by putting financial pressure on the governments concerned and even by military occupation.

In 1913, both President Wilson and Secretary of State Bryan condemned dollar diplomacy but, with the First World War impending, it was not a good time to change a policy which had provided stability for the United States in an important strategic area like the Caribbean. In fact Wilson showed that he was just as prepared to intervene as Roosevelt and Taft had been when United States security was threatened. He ordered intervention in Haiti in 1915, the Dominican Republic in 1916 and in Cuba in 1917.

The Dominican Republic

The first application of the Roosevelt Corollary was in the Dominican Republic in 1905. Ulises Heureaux, a ruthless dictator, had dominated the Republic from 1882 to 1899. He had brought stability and economic growth. On his assassination in 1899, political chaos and instability returned. The United States was the major trading partner of the Dominican Republic by 1905, and private investment by the United States was increasing. When the Dominican Republic failed to pay its foreign debts in 1905, the United States, fearing European intervention in a territory of such strategic importance, acted first.

After a show of force she was 'invited' to administer customs collection in the Dominican Republic. A proportion of customs revenue was set aside to cover foreign debts. This proved very successful and was re-negotiated in 1907. President Taft (1909–1913) hoped that the financial administration in the Dominican Republic would become the model for the extension of dollar diplomacy elsewhere in the Caribbean.

There was further political trouble in 1916. The United States insistence on further control of the government of the Dominican Republic led to a conflict between American officials and President Jiménez. The latter resigned and the United States took complete control of the government. Woodrow Wilson was worried that Germany would intervene in the Dominican Republic while the country was politically impotent. Thus he felt compelled to break his earlier promises on non-intervention.

United States occupation lasted from 1916 to 1924. It was unpopular although it led to the building of new roads and schools, the extension of communications and the improvement of sanitation and health services. In 1924 the United States decided to hand back the country to an elected civilian government. The marines supervised the elections in which Horacio Vásquez was elected President. Then they withdrew from the Dominican Republic.

An important and unintentional result of military occupation in the Dominican Republic and elsewhere was the creation and training by the marines of a unified military constabulary. This was later used by the dictator Trujillo to seize and keep control of the country.

Haiti

In the 1890s the United States had tried to gain military and commercial privileges in Haiti, and by 1905 they had taken control of Haiti's customs revenues to secure repayment of debts. From then until 1914 American business interests gained a firm hold over Haiti's economy.

In 1915 the President of Haiti was overthrown and put in prison where he was brutally murdered. The United States claimed the right to apply the Roosevelt Corollary on humanitarian grounds as Haiti offered a case of 'chronic wrongdoing'. Haitians, on the other hand, had no doubt that the United States had intervened to safeguard her own investments. Another strong reason for intervention was that Haiti was of even greater strategic importance to the United States than the Dominican Republic. Haiti commanded

A Haitian village

the Windward Passage through which American ships passed from New York to Panama. The United States was looking for another naval base to protect the approaches to the Panama Canal.

Haiti signed a treaty with the United States for a ten-year occupation of the country. The marines occupied Haiti in 1915, but did not leave until 1934, the ten-year limit apparently forgotten. It was an extremely unpopular occupation because the marines showed little regard for the interests of Haiti's predominantly black peasant population. They allowed the mulattoes, about five per cent of the population, to take control of those government offices which were not in American hands, thus re-creating the old mulatto élite. In 1916 they re-enacted an old law of Henri Christophe which permitted forced labour on the roads. The aim was to reduce unemployment, but the peasants saw it as slavery and revolted against it. The 'revolt of the cacos' brought the death of about 2,000 peasants before it was suppressed in 1920. In 1918 the marines passed a law which allowed foreigners to own land in Haiti. In a land of peasant smallholdings with a density of population of 175 persons per square kilometre, the people saw this as a cruel and unjust measure. Moreover, the benefits of occupation – roads, schools, health clinics – were far fewer than in the Dominican Republic and failed to satisfy the Haitians.

With increasing external and internal pressure against the United States occupation, the marines allowed a National Assembly to be elected in 1930. It was dominated by nationalists who elected Sténcio Joseph Vincent as their President. In 1932 the marines began to withdraw and their occupation ended in 1934. The United States retained official control of the country's finances until 1941, and unofficial control until 1947.

Nicaragua

The most blatant example of dollar imperialism occurred in Nicaragua in 1911. After a revolution American bankers took charge of the country's finances. Then in 1912 President Adolfo Diaz invited the United States to control the administration because of continuing political disorder, and a small force of United States marines entered Nicaragua. Revolution followed their withdrawal in 1925 and the marines resumed control on the orders of President Coolidge.

The occupation was very unpopular and a special envoy was sent in 1927 to restore a civilian, national government. Both rebels and government were satisfied with the result of the American-supervised election of 1928. However, one group led by General Sandino refused to accept the result and guerilla attacks delayed the withdrawal of the marines until 1933.

Honduras, Nicaragua's neighbour, was also the object of United States business imperialism from 1908 to 1923, but on a smaller scale. When there was a revolution there in 1923, marines landed to protect American interests.

The Danish Virgin Islands

In 1867 the King of Denmark tried to sell the Danish Virgin Islands – St Thomas, St John and St Croix – to the United States. He told his subjects in these islands that they would be better off under the United States. To his surprise the United States Senate refused to ratify the purchase and the islands remained under Denmark.

In 1902 the position was reversed. This time the offer came from the United States, but the Danish government refused to sell. Finally, in 1917, a very generous offer of $25,000,000 from the United States was accepted. The islands became 'The United States Virgin Islands'. This happened during the First World War and the United States was particularly interested in establishing a naval base on St Thomas to defend the approaches to the Panama Canal.

Factors influencing United States policy

1 In modern times there can be no defence for a policy which leads to intervention in the internal and external affairs of other countries, but American intervention and occupation took place at a time when imperialism was universal. The United States was a new and very minor imperial power.
2 The Americans had become so obsessed with the importance of the Panama Canal that they saw any disturbance in the Caribbean, even if it was not anti-American, as a danger to their national security.
3 The completion of the Panama Canal coincided with the rising international tension that had led to the First World War. This heightened

American concern over the strategic importance of the Caribbean states and explains why an anti-imperialist like Wilson ordered the occupation of Haiti, the Dominican Republic and Cuba, and the purchase of the Danish Virgin Islands.

4 Occupation brought material advantages to the countries concerned, although it was generally unpopular. Law and order was restored and finances were put on a firm footing. Trade with the United States flourished, *per capita* incomes rose and unemployment decreased. Public works were undertaken and health and education services expanded and improved. However, the nationalists felt that nothing compensated for the loss of independence, and the United States was unpopular throughout Latin America.

'Good Neighbour Policies'

Even within the United States, intervention in other countries was not popular. Towards the end of the 1920s there was a desire to change this policy. This coincided with bold attacks by Latin-American countries on American imperialism. At the Inter-American Conference in Havana in 1928, some Latin-American delegates were bold enough to denounce the United States' interventions publicly.

The Americans were sensitive about this issue and did not want to make more enemies in Latin America at such a critical time in world affairs. At the end of 1928, a conference was called in Washington at which the United States signed Treaties of Conciliation and Arbitration with the Latin-American countries. In the same year Herbert Hoover, the President-elect, made a goodwill tour of Latin America and in his inaugural address he said: 'We have no desire for territorial expansion, for economic, or other domination of other peoples'.

The United States did not intervene in Mexico in 1929, nor in Brazil in 1930, although both these were occasions when past policy would have dictated intervention. In 1932, El Salvador defaulted on repayment of interest on a bond issue, a classic case for United States intervention in the past, but again there was none. Finally the withdrawal of marines from Haiti in 1932 made it clear that American policy had changed.

Franklin D. Roosevelt announced his 'Good Neighbour Policy' in 1933. This policy dominated United States foreign relations in the 1930s. At a conference of American States in Montevideo in 1933, the United States signed the following agreement: 'No state has the right to intervene in the internal or external affairs of another.' Once again the United States followed the statement with positive proof. There was a major political upheaval in Cuba in 1933–4, but the United States did not intervene and even released Cuba from the Platt Amendment in 1934. The good neighbour policy was maintained throughout the 1930s, and in 1939 the United States gave up its treaty rights in Panama and increased its annual rent payments for the Canal Zone almost voluntarily.

Trade and cultural relations between the United States and Latin America were also extended. The old distrust could never be fully overcome, but by the outbreak of the Second World War the United States had no actual enemies on the American continent.

Franklin D. Roosevelt

The United States and Cuba, 1902 to 1959

The United States left Cuba in 1902 with a pro-American President, Estrada Palma, who actually wanted Cuba to be annexed by the

United States. The nationalist group had been forced to accept the Platt Amendment and the administration was not popular with the liberals. In 1905 Estrada Palma tried to prolong his term of office, but there was a liberal revolt and the administration resigned.

Once again the United States intervened and, this time, administered Cuba directly through Charles Magoon as Governor, and an Advisory Law Commission. Magoon kept the United States' presence 'low profile' and allowed the Cuban flag to fly over public buildings. Apart from the personnel at the top, he followed the old Cuban constitution. He withdrew after revising the electoral law and supervising the elections.

José Miguel Gomez, a liberal President, took over in January, 1909. He set the pattern for corruption and social injustice which continued in Cuba until 1959. Afro-Cubans were discriminated against in jobs and politics. In 1912 Evaristo Estenoz and Pedro Ivonet tried to have a law passed removing racial discrimination in politics and employment. This turned into a bloody revolution when the marines were called in to protect American lives and property. Over three thousand Afro-Cubans were killed, but social injustice continued.

The administration of Menocal was also unpopular, but the United States insisted on political stability during the First World War, even sending marines to crush opposition to him in 1917. Economic, rather than political, developments were foremost at this time. Cuba became a one-crop economy dependent on the United States. During the war there was a sugar boom in Cuba and the United States took nearly all the Cuban crop. The boom lasted for two years after the war. When the 1919–20 crop was put on the open market (the United States had taken all the previous season's crop) there was a rush to buy sugar which Cuban journalists called 'The Dance of the Millions' – the price of sugar was over $400 per tonne and Cuba had put over 4,000,000 tonnes on the market! The result was inflated offers for estates and mills which most Cubans could not resist. So sugar production passed into the hands of American owners.

After the boom came the crash. The production of European beet sugar had recovered and by the end of 1920 the price of sugar had fallen by half. On top of this the United States placed a huge duty on foreign sugar early in 1921, and the

Havana in the 1920's

Fidel Castro

economy of Cuba collapsed. There was unemployment, widespread bankruptcy and more selling of estates, this time for rock-bottom prices. More and more Cuban property passed into American hands.

In this period Cuba was becoming an American 'playground'. From 1919 to 1933 there was Prohibition in the United States. Hundreds of thousands of Americans came to Cuba for liquor, mainly to Havana. Gambling and vice flourished and this attracted still more tourists. After Prohibition ended, Cuba still attracted Americans because the hotel facilities were very good and the night clubs and casinos were renowned. Cuba remained an American playground until 1960. The popularity of Cuba impeded the development of the tourist industry in other parts of the Caribbean.

President Menocal handed over the government to his own candidate, President Zayas. The opposition claimed, probably justifiably, that the election had been rigged. This brought about the last direct American intervention in Cuba. General Crowder was sent to restore economic and political stability. He forced Zayas to conduct the government without corruption and secured loans from the United States. However, Crowder's intervention in Cuba was unpopular with the nationalists who gained strength from Cuba's entry into the First World War. The sugar fluctuations had also demonstrated to the Cubans how dependent they were on the United States. After Crowder left there was a nationalist reaction, but there were no widespread anti-American demonstrations because Cuba enjoyed a period of relative prosperity later in the 1920s. The United States became sensitive to Cuban nationalism and resolved not to interfere in Cuban affairs again.

This allowed the establishment of a brutal dictatorship under Geraldo Machado, one of the worst the world has ever known. He terrorised the people with armed thugs. Opponents were killed or tortured and freedom of expression was stifled. Eventually Fulgencio Batista, a sergeant in the army, led the 'Sergeants' Revolt' in 1933-4 which overthrew Machado. For a year Cuba had a provisional government led by Carlos Manuel de Cespedes.

Coinciding with Batista's coup, but not because of it, the United States withdrew the Platt Amendment in 1934. She gave up all right to intervene in Cuba. The administrations which Batista installed from 1933 to 1940 were recognised by the United States, and received increasing moral and material support as the years passed. In 1944 a left-wing communist-supported government came to power on Batista's retirement, but even then the United States did not intervene to overthrow a government which she hated.

Batista voluntarily stayed out of power for eight years. He returned to Cuba in 1952 and stood for the Presidency. He did not win the election, but afterwards staged a coup with the help of the army. His dictatorship lasted for seven years. This was another period of brutality and oppression for the Cubans, but Cuba did not suffer economically because American support for Batista was obvious. Fidel Castro appealed to the United States not to send arms to Cuba in 1957, but to no avail. However, the United States could not maintain Batista in power because, although he controlled the army, he had lost all support from the people and civil administration. Fidel Castro with a force of only about 1,000 was able to hold out in the Sierra Maestra until Batista was forced to flee into exile at the end of 1958.

The United States and the British Caribbean after 1939

Naval bases

In 1940, there was the possibility that Germany would occupy the Caribbean territories of France and the Netherlands. The United States was at that stage a neutral power but she did not want German acquisitions in the Caribbean. The German navy was operating against British and Allied shipping in the Caribbean. American ships were free from danger, but the United States resented the interference with trade and shipping in the western hemisphere.

In September, 1940, Franklin D. Roosevelt compromised the neutrality of the United States by making an agreement with Britain to exchange fifty obsolete but usable destroyers for the right to establish naval bases on British islands. Britain needed the destroyers to counter the German submarine threat and the United States wanted more bases to guard her shipping lanes. The bases were on a ninety-nine year lease and rent-free.

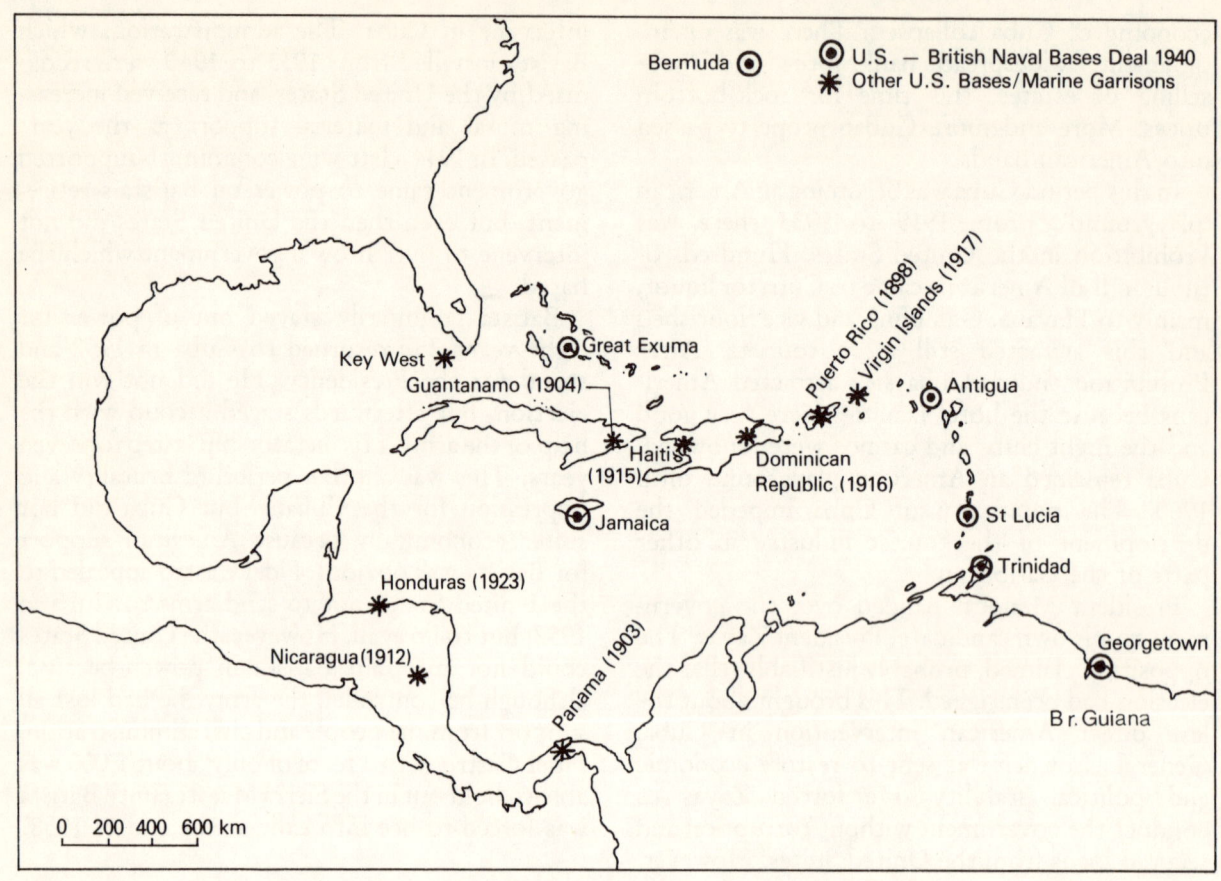

Map 3   United States bases in the Caribbean in the twentieth century

The bases were in Newfoundland and Bermuda in the Atlantic, in Antigua, the Bahamas, Jamaica, St Lucia and Trinidad in the Caribbean, and in British Guiana. The United States did not have to build bases under the agreement; but they could exercise their right to do so if they wished.

In general, the Caribbean people accepted this agreement. The need for bases was clearly demonstrated in 1942 when German submarines sank several ships in the Caribbean, including one outside the harbour in Barbados and another in the harbour in Castries. However, there was concern about American racial attitudes to the local black populations because of the behaviour of the marines in Cuba and Haiti. In some islands there was anger about the area of land taken for the base, for example, in Trinidad the Chaguaramas area in the north-west was selected. Hundreds were made homeless, and Port of Spain lost some of its most popular bathing areas. The people did not understand the need for so much land surrounding the actual base. Later Dr Eric Williams said that the base restricted the development of Port of Spain. On the other hand, in the case of Bermuda, the Americans actually increased the size of the island from about fifty square kilometres to about fifty-three square kilometres by dredging up land from the sea during the construction of the base.

Usually there were good relations between the islands and the bases. There was a patronising attitude on the part of some United States personnel, but there were also cases of firm friendships being made, and even marriages. The islands benefited from the employment of thousands of local labourers in construction work. The local economies were boosted by the influx of U.S. dollars.

After the war the government of the West Indies Federation claimed that it was entitled to negotiate a new agreement with the United States about the bases. Trinidad negotiated alone because it wanted the United States to give up Chaguaramas on the grounds that it was the best site for the Federal capital. The federal government did not approve of this unilateral initiative by Trinidad. Elsewhere, by 1960, some of the bases had already been given up and United States personnel withdrawn. In 1961 the federal government reached an agreement with the United States under which some bases should continue as United States defence areas, but that most of the land should be given up.

Other American interests

Geography made it inevitable that, as British influence in the Caribbean declined, American influence would increase. Of course, this was especially true with the coming of independence. For example, the United States took over from Britain as Jamaica's biggest trading partner. By 1970 she was taking fifty-three per cent of Jamaica's exports, and contributing forty-three per cent of her imports. Soon after independence Sir Alexander Bustamante signed a defence agreement with the United States

> to make available to the Government of Jamaica such defence articles and defence services as the Government of the United States may authorise.

Jamaica naturally moved into the United States' orbit economically and politically, although this implied a restriction of freedom of action politically which Jamaica began to resent later. Jamaica's experience was typical of the other ex-British islands.

In 1948 the Organisation of American States was founded. One of the motives of the United States in promoting this body was to 'continentalise' the Monroe Doctrine. The O.A.S. became collectively responsible for the defence and internal security of the Americas, although the United States did not withdraw her right to unilateral action if she saw her interests threatened. Only independent countries could join the O.A.S. The ex-British islands felt that their interests would best be served by joining, although historically and culturally they were divided from the Latin-American group of countries forming the bulk of the O.A.S. membership. In 1967 Barbados and Trinidad joined; in 1968 Jamaica and, more recently, Guyana. Membership of the O.A.S. implies anti-communist policies, although this is understood rather than stated. In 1962 Cuba was expelled from the O.A.S. for her communist sympathies and since then the other members have curtailed their trade with Cuba.

Tourism has turned the British Caribbean into an American playground, since the break between Cuba and the United States in 1960. Jamaica, Barbados, Antigua and the Bahamas have been the chief islands to benefit from the dollar-earning capacity of tourism. Tourism has become a major industry and is expanding in most of the islands. It is resented by some nationalists who feel it brings a loss of pride when local people have to cater and defer to foreign tourists for the sake of the dollars they bring. It brings dissatisfaction also to the waiter who sees the tourist spending more on one meal than he earns in a week.

The United States has considerable cultural influence on the British Caribbean. This is natural because the language is the same. American movies, television programmes, film stars and television personalities are very popular. On the other hand, calypso, reggae or cricket easily outweigh the cultural influence of the United States. One cannot see baseball gaining much ground in Barbados!

3
Trade unions in the British Caribbean

Sir Alexander Bustamante

Introduction to trade unionism

Workers form unions in order to protect their interests and improve their working conditions. Usually this means fighting for such things as higher pay, shorter hours, compensation for injury or sickness and pensions on retirement. Unions give workers more power in negotiations with their employers because their collective voice is more likely to be heard than that of an individual. Moreover, if it is not, the workers have a final weapon: they can go on strike.

The more members there are in a union, the stronger it is. For example, if all the members of a factory are members of a union and that union declares a strike, production stops completely. The employer has nothing to sell, so he makes no profit. In such a case, the union has enormous bargaining power. The very threat of a strike is often enough to make the employer concede its demands. If a union contains all the workers in an industry, its power is even greater. If that industry is one of the mainstays of the economy, the union has considerable power over the government of the country. On this scale it is easy to see how, long ago, unions were considered treasonable.

The interests of employers are often opposed to those of the unions, and this was especially true in the past. They wanted to keep wages down, to impose long working hours and to avoid paying compensation for injury, sickness benefit and retirement pensions. Today, the employers bargain with the unions and, if all goes well, a compromise is reached by which both sides are satisfied. If not, there may be a strike. Strikes are like industrial 'wars' between unions and employers, and sometimes become violent. For example, striking workers often try to stop others working. This is called 'peaceful' picketing, but often force is used. Sometimes the feelings of the strikers against their employers can be so strong that they damage the employers' property – land, buildings or machines. When a strike reaches this stage, it is really a riot and the police or army are called in, which often results in more violence.

The first unions had to fight for legal recognition. In the British West Indies, the unions were lucky in that this struggle had been won by British trade unions in the nineteenth century. Some of the privileges they gained were inherited by the West Indian unions. The initial attitude to unions in Britain was that they were associations of workers to restrain trade and that they were harmful to both employers and fellow workers and therefore should be made illegal. It was felt that, on a large scale, a union was a conspiracy to damage industry; on a very large scale, it was treason against the country. However, in 1824, the British government recognised the right of workers to combine to try to better their position.

The next problem was to decide whether the unions should have the legal right to strike. A law of 1825 stated that unions were acting illegally if they combined to hurt their employers or fellow workers. In practice this made the strike illegal because it was left to the courts to decide whether the workers were hurting their employers by striking. The attitude of the courts, however, gradually became more sympathetic towards workers, and in 1875 the Conspiracy and Protection of Property Act was passed. Unions striking in a trade dispute were not considered to be hurting their employers, and it even allowed peaceful picketing of non-striking workers. The final point at issue was whether a union was responsible for claims for damages done by strikers. The Trade Disputes Act of 1906 said that the unions were not liable. Thus unions in Britain had considerable protection under law by the beginning of the twentieth century.

Unions in the British West Indies before 1938

At the beginning of the twentieth century, trade unions had no legal recognition in the British West Indies. Unions existed and were tolerated because the British West Indies followed the practices and attitudes of Britain. However, they were liable to be brought to court on charges of conspiracy and even treason.

Trade union laws were passed in Jamaica in 1919, in British Guiana in 1921, in Trinidad in 1932, in St Vincent in 1933, but not in Barbados until 1939. The main aim of these laws was to avert civil unrest in times of hardship by encouraging the formation of unions. Registration of unions was compulsory and there was legal recognition and protection of funds, but in other respects the powers of British West Indian trade unions were very limited and about fifty years behind their British counterparts. Unions were unwilling to register because they could still be liable for claims for damages done by their members in a trade dispute. Moreover, the law did not permit even peaceful picketing. Lacking these essential powers and safeguards, very few unions registered before 1938.

British West Indian assemblies were still anti-union because they were dominated by the employers. It was the governors who wanted to encourage unions. For example, Sir Leslie Probyn, Governor of Jamaica, passed the Jamaica Trade Union Law in 1919, because there had been civil disturbances since 1917. In 1929 the Secretary of State urged the island governments to pass trade union laws but they were unresponsive, and the expansion of trade unionism grew out of the riots and strikes of 1935 to 1938.

The early unions

In Britain after the Industrial Revolution there were large factories and great manufacturing industries. Workers lived in large cities and it was easy for workers to organise themselves into trade unions. In the British West Indies the situation was entirely different. Workers lived on scattered estates, industries were small and undeveloped and town populations were small.

In the British West Indies the attitude of the employers to their workers was almost feudal. This was natural in the sugar islands where employment was on estates. The employers were planters and the workers were former slaves who were usually resident on the estate because they lived in tied cottages. The employers had not become accustomed to an industrial labour force dependent entirely on wages. They still thought of their labourers as servants and tenants on the estate.

The first unions in the British West Indies were formed in the 1890s. They were small in membership, about sixty to eighty workers, and usually composed of skilled workers in one particular trade. They should properly be called 'craft unions'. By 1896 the fall in the price of sugar had led to very depressed conditions throughout the islands and much attendant suffering. Some workers with the ability to organise formed the earliest unions to protect themselves against reductions in wages. In Jamaica the Artisans' Union was formed in 1899.

The number of unions grew in the early years of the twentieth century. The craft unions in Jamaica, such as the Printers' and Tobacco Workers' Unions of 1907 and 1908, were typical. In 1907 the Printers' Union struck for higher wages. (In British Guiana Hubert Critchlow had led the dockers in a strike in 1906, but this was not an official strike by a union, just a spontaneous walk-out.) In 1908 the Jamaica Trades and Labour Union was formed by groups of skilled workers. One of the first unskilled labour unions in the British West Indies was the British Guiana Labour Union. It was formed by Critchlow in 1919, largely from the dockers of Georgetown.

However, hardly any of these early unions survived the 1920s. They were not suppressed by the government or the courts, but they failed for the following reasons:

1 In the period 1890–1920 it was difficult to maintain membership because of the widespread emigration out of the West Indies and migration between islands. This was heightened by the large number of West Indians who went to serve in the First World War.
2 Fluctuations in the economy resulted in great variation in workers' conditions, from great hardship for the unskilled to relative ease for skilled workers. For the latter there did not seem to be an urgent need to be in a union.
3 Most workers in the British West Indies were agricultural workers and it was very difficult to form them into unions.
4 Employers and workers were sharply divided by class, and often by race also. Employers discouraged unions and gave little thought to the hardships and sufferings of the workers. As late as 1937 the employers in the Trinidad Oilfields, giving evidence to the Royal Commission, claimed that they did not even know that their workers were suffering and discontented.
5 West Indian Unions were unsure of their legal position. They did not want to risk prosecutions in the courts and so when trouble arose they just disbanded.
6 Without legal recognition and legal powers, workers felt that there was little point in forming unions. They would be too weak to be effective.
7 Membership was very small and organisation weak. For example, the 1907 Printers' Union in Jamaica collapsed because the treasurer ran off with the strike funds. Very often it was the internal weakness of the unions that caused them to disband.

The new unionism that arose after 1938 changed the situation considerably.

Working class difficulties

In the British West Indies in the 1920s and 1930s wages were very low and working conditions were deplorable. There was widespread unemployment, running at about twenty per cent in Barbados in 1925. Workers received no compensation for sickness and injury, and no pension in old age. Many workers lived in shanty towns and slums with almost no health or education facilities. The middle classes tended to thank God for their good fortune and gave little thought to the suffering masses. There were some exceptions; Arthur Cipriani in Trinidad, Charles Duncan O'Neal in Barbados and Alfred Thorne in British Guiana protested against the hardships of the working class, but most people expected the workers to help themselves.

Governments realised the plight of the working classes, but they could do little to help because they too were poor. They did not have money for unemployment relief or for government projects to create employment. In those days better conditions for the working classes could only come about if private industries flourished, thus creating more jobs, paying higher wages and offering other benefits. The workers could achieve these improvements more quickly if they formed unions. This did not happen, however, until the British West Indies suffered even greater hardship in the 1930s. Depression led to riots and strikes between 1935 and 1938 and, from these troubles, influential unions arose.

Riots and strikes, 1935–1938

The economic difficulties in the British West Indies were caused by the decline of the sugar industry and the failure of most of the alternative crops to provide a satisfactory substitute by 1925. In this year the 'safety-valve' of emigration was shut off. The United States closed its doors to all but a few selected immigrants. By 1921 the Panama Canal Zone was no longer a source of jobs. Worse still, especially for Jamaica, Cuba began to deport thousands of sugar labourers who had emigrated from the British islands during Cuba's sugar boom. Unemployment was already high, so the ending of emigration was a catastrophe.

The position became worse in the 1930s because of the effects of the Great Depression. This had begun in 1929 in the United States and developed into a world-wide recession in trade. Manufacturing countries like Britain cut back production when they could not sell their goods and therefore had less money to spend on imports from primary-producing countries like the West Indies. This led to a cutback in production in the British West Indies, resulting in lower pay and more unemployment. By 1935 the working classes were desperate enough to seek their own remedies in a series of riots and strikes.

Timetable of disturbances

Year	Territory	Nature of disturbances and results
1935 (Jan)	St Kitts	Sugar estate workers struck for higher wages. Suppressed by police. Warship summoned.
	St Vincent	Government raised customs duties. Working class protest resulted in disturbances. State of emergency declared after violence and damage. Press censored. Warship summoned. Treason charges against rioters failed to be upheld. Working Men's Association pressed for free land and a new constitution.
	St Lucia	Strikes at the coaling station in Castries. Suppressed by soldiers and appearance of a warship.
	British Guiana	Disputes and strikes on sugar estates lasted three months. Demands for higher wages. Manpower Citizen's Association formed.
1937 (June)	Trinidad	Oilfield workers protested about low pay. Uriah Butler addressed worker's meeting at Fyzabad which developed into riot when police tried to arrest him. Two fires in the Apex oilfield. Cruisers *Ajax* and *Exeter* landed troops to help Trinidad Light Horse Volunteers suppress strikes. Butler called to give evidence to Royal Commission. Workers' demands heard. Unity of Trinidadian working classes demonstrated. Butler became labour leader.
	Barbados	Clement Payne urged Barbadian workers to form unions and strike. Stirred up population in Bridgetown. Deportation of Payne on grounds of false declaration of citizenship. Grantley Adams won appeal against deportation which still went ahead. People rioted in protest. Police brutally suppressed riots; 14 killed, 59 wounded. Grantley Adams emerged as labour leader. Barbados Progressive League formed. Trade Union Law passed. First unions.

Year	Territory	Nature of disturbances and results
1937 (June)	British Guiana	Further strikes and riots on sugar estates. Protests about mechanisation in sugar industry. Unions aware of their power.
	Jamaica	Widespread unrest on sugar estates. Cane cutters receiving under 1/- per ton; struck for 2/-. 1400 workers at Serge Island, St Thomas, refused 1/-. Bustamante petitioned King. Police broke up meetings and arrested speakers. Killed 4 rioters at Frome.
1938	Jamaica	Strikes and riots on Tate and Lyle estates at Frome. Much destruction. Dockers' strike in Kingston. Mobs wrecked city transport system. Bustamante addressed crowds. Bustamante replaced Coombes as labour leader. Arrested for holding meeting during strike. Brutal police action failed to stop riots. *Ajax* arrived. Manley offered his services to Jamaica unions. Eight killed, 170 wounded, 700 arrested.
	British Guiana	Strikes on sugar estates. Unions decided to call Labour Conference.

New unions, new powers

These disturbances gave great impetus to the formation of new trade unions throughout the British West Indies because they showed the power of unified labour. Very few of these unions were survivors of the earlier ones and even if they had links with an early union, they emerged with a new name. The main unions formed between 1938 and 1940 were: the Bustamante Industrial Trade Union in Jamaica; the Oilworkers' Trade Union in Trinidad; the Manpower and Citizens' Association in British Guiana; the Antigua Trades and Labour Union. The Barbados Progressive League registered 23,000 in 1939; the Antigua Trades and Labour Union, 12,000 in 1940; the Bustamante Industrial Trade Union, 6,000 in 1939; the Manpower and Citizens' Association, 4,000 in 1939. All these figures are approximate.

The larger the union, the stronger its power in collective bargaining, the bigger its threat in strike action and the larger its funds to maintain a strike. However, most of the trade unions in the British West Indies were small, under 1,000 members. Individually their bargaining power was small, but in federations they became strong. This was another development in unionism after 1938. The best example was the Trade Union Advisory Council formed by Norman Manley in Jamaica in 1939 to combat the power of the Bustamante Industrial Trade Union. The T.U.A.C. never registered as a trade union itself, but represented registered trade unions. A Trades Union Council was formed in British Guiana in 1941; by 1943 it represented fourteen unions.

The number of registered unions in the British West Indies multiplied rapidly after 1938. Between 1938 and 1943 fifty-eight new unions were registered with a total membership of 65,000. Another seven were registered in 1944. This was not only a result of the riots of the late 1930s, but was also due to the influence of the Moyne Commission which had been sent out in 1938 to investigate the causes of the unrest in the British West Indies. The Commission interviewed trade union representatives and recommended the encouragement of trade unions and their compulsory registration. In this new unionism British Guiana led the field. By 1939 it had twelve registered trade unions. By 1943 this had increased to twenty-four.

The governments had been forced by the strikes and riots to realise the new strength of trade unions. New legislation was therefore introduced to placate the unions so that the workers would be less likely to riot. Barbados, which had had no trade union legislation, passed the Barbados Trade Union Act of 1939, although this gave only the weak powers of the former acts in the other islands. However, in 1942, it was amended to permit peaceful picketing and give unions immunity from claims for damages during industrial disputes. In 1938 the Jamaica Trade Union Law of 1919 was amended in the same way. By such amendments throughout the British

West Indies, local trade union laws were brought into line with those of Britain. Labour Departments with responsibility for the overall employment situation were also established. They could help to control labour disputes and intervene in negotiations and disputes between employers and workers, if invited. For example, Barbados passed a Labour Department Act in 1942 to deal with all labour matters and in the same year the British Guiana Labour Department was established.

Therefore, by the end of the Second World War, the British West Indies had a great number of unions with a total membership of about 100,000. These unions had much greater powers as a result of the experiences of the late 1930s and the new trade union laws.

The 1938 Labour Congress

When the labour leaders in the British West Indies realised that unrest was widespread throughout the islands, they decided to meet together to unify their aims and demands. In order to do this the British Guiana and West Indies Labour Congress was convened in Georgetown in 1938.

An outstanding feature of the labour movement was the close link between unionism and politics. At the Congress the representatives expressed the aims of union leaders and nationalist politicians. Their demands were not confined to rates of pay, hours of work, conditions of work, social security benefits, health services and education. They extended to politics as well, with demands for universal adult suffrage, internal self-government and federation. At Georgetown, labour and political demands were tabled together. This was not really surprising because many of the delegates, like Arthur Cipriani and Grantley Adams, were both labour leaders and nationalist politicians. The labour demands were:
1 immunity for trade unions from claims for damages resulting from strikes;
2 immunity from charges of conspiracy;
3 the right to picket peacefully;
4 minimum wage legislation;
5 the forty-four hour week;
6 old age pensions;
7 national health insurance and sickness benefits.
The political demands were:
1 British West Indian Federation;
2 universal adult suffrage for a legislative assembly;
3 powers of the governors to be limited;
4 free, compulsory elementary education;
5 a limit of twenty hectares for a privately owned sugar estate;
6 nationalisation of the sugar industry;
7 state ownership of public utilities;
8 co-operative marketing of produce.
After the Congress, many of the delegates went home and began to write these demands into their political programmes.

Four outstanding labour leaders

Hubert Critchlow

Critchlow was employed as a waterfront worker in Georgetown by Booker Brothers, the largest commercial company in British Guiana. He became the unofficial dockers' leader and led them in the strike of 1906. Thereafter he became their spokesman and was influential in stopping the dockers becoming violent in their wage demands during the First World War. In January 1917, he led a thirteen-day strike of waterfront workers which spread to other industries. As a result of this, Critchlow won a nine-hour day and higher wages for the dockers. Employers in other industries followed with similar concessions. Prices continued to rise and at the end of the same year Critchlow negotiated another wage rise without resorting to strike action.

In 1918 he was sacked by Booker Brothers and the following year founded the British Guiana Labour Union, which was the most powerful union in the British West Indies at that time. It became the first registered trade union in any British colony throughout the world when the British Guiana Trade Union Ordinance was passed in 1921. The British Guiana Labour Union was a 'blanket' union. This means that it was not confined to the workers of any one industry, but was open to workers in a wide range of industries, skilled and unskilled. In practice the majority of its members were blacks from the waterfront because very few of the East Indians on the estates were unionised at that time.

By the 1920s Critchlow was the most experienced trade union leader in the British territories.

He was still the champion of the dockers and was involved in the dock strike of 1924 which became widespread because of the blanket union. Unlike some other labour leaders, Critchlow was first and foremost a trade unionist. He advocated universal adult suffrage because he saw that it would give his members political power to advance the union cause.

In the 1930s Critchlow lost some of his dynamism, and in 1937 the B.G.L.U. fell behind the Manpower Citizens' Association which was composed mainly of sugar estate workers. However, Critchlow was still greatly respected as the 'father' of trade unionism in British Guiana and was made Secretary of the British Guiana Trades Union Council in 1941. This enabled him to maintain a dominant role in the trade union movement because the Council controlled seventy per cent of the trade unionists in British Guiana.

Arthur Andrew Cipriani

Cipriani was a white middle-class Trinidadian who was educated at St Mary's School in Trinidad. In the First World War he joined the British West India Regiment and rose to the rank of captain. When he returned from the war he became one of the few middle-class figures in the British islands to take up the cause of the working classes. His popularity as a leader of men in war was transferred to his leadership of the workers in peacetime Trinidad.

He became President of the Trinidad Working Men's Association. He wanted to legalise trade unions in Trinidad, but it took over ten years before the Trinidad Trade Union Ordinance was passed in 1932. Cipriani was a socialist and in 1932 he founded the Trinidad Labour Party. He wanted nationalisation, not just of industry but also of jobs, by excluding foreigners and promoting Trinidadians to the highest posts. He especially disliked the employment in Trinidad of white South Africans and Americans whom he suspected of racialism.

In 1925 Cipriani won a seat in the Legislative Council, but he was frustrated by what he called the 'toryism' (anti-socialism) of its members. His policies had no chance of success because he was the only practising socialist there. He pursued his socialism more effectively through the Port of Spain City Council of which he was a member from 1926 to 1941. He was also mayor of the city eight times. His outstanding socialist success was the nationalisation of the tramways and electric lighting in Port of Spain, hitherto the monopoly of the Electric Light and Power company.

In 1935 the Trinidad Labour Party published its own newspaper, *The Socialist*. By writing in this paper, Cipriani was able to tell the working classes what he was doing for them and what was being said in the two councils on which he sat. Year after year he advocated old age pensions, minimum wages and a completely elected assembly. However, by 1938 Cipriani had lost his place as the workers' leader to Uriah Butler who had a much more emotive appeal to the workers and had split with Cipriani in 1935. Another political leader, A. G. Rienzi, an Indian lawyer, was also supporting the cause of the workers.

Cipriani died in 1945 and has become a Trinidadian hero. He had no racialism; he was for Trinidadians of any background and for Trinidad for Trinidadians. Poor Trinidadians were closest to his heart because he felt they needed his sympathy and help the most. He was anti-colonial and anti-ruling class, striving to give the masses their birthright – the land and wealth of

A. A. Cipriani

Trinidad. He has been honoured by a statue in Independence Square, Port of Spain.

Uriah 'Buzz' Butler

Uriah Butler was born in Grenada in 1891. He served in the First World War, but on his return to Grenada he found it hard to obtain a satisfactory job so he migrated to Trinidad in 1921 to work in the oilfields. Later he received an injury at work which left him permanently lame.

Butler joined the Trinidad Labour Party shortly after it was formed. In 1935 he led a hundred and twenty men on a hunger march into Port of Spain in protest against rising prices. Cipriani quarrelled with Butler over the march. As a result Butler was expelled from the Labour Party and the rift between the two was never healed. Butler then formed his own party, 'The British Empire Workers' and Citizens' Home Rule Party' which claimed a membership of one thousand, mostly blacks working on the oilfields.

At this stage Cipriani was still leader of the working classes, but then events played into Butler's hands. The employers in the oilfields claimed that there had been no demands for higher wages, but clearly there had been, and the hardships of the workers were obvious for all to see. Inflation was running at seventeen per cent. The workers were underpaid and overworked. Butler had great appeal for these workers. He appealed to their emotions, calling them martyrs and heroes who were standing up against the might of the British Empire. He also told them that they were downtrodden because they were black. By playing on their feelings he was able to become their leader.

In June 1937 he threatened to stage a sit-down strike on the oilfields. The centre of the unrest was the village of Fyzabad. While addressing a meeting there he was approached by police with a warrant for his arrest. Butler quickly turned this to his own advantage by appealing to the crowd to save him. The crowd charged the police and Butler escaped. Two of the police were killed. A reward of $500 was offered for Butler's arrest, but no one would betray him. He came out of hiding to give evidence before the Royal Commission investigating the troubles.

Butler was imprisoned during the Second World War because he was considered a danger to the war effort. He remained a hero to the black working classes, but was not able to organise his union or to form a political party. In the first elections after the war, held on a basis of universal adult suffrage, he stood as one of the Port of Spain candidates but was not elected. His appeal was more to the black workers of the oilfields than to the cosmopolitan citizens of Port of Spain. His party won the 1950 elections, but was unable to form a government because it did not have an absolute majority. A coalition of the opposition and nominated members could muster more seats. His emotional style was not suited to the Legislative Council and eventually he lost his seat in 1961.

Sir Alexander Bustamante

He was born in Jamaica of mixed race in 1884 with the name 'Alexander Clarke'. He left Jamaica in 1899 and spent over thirty years in the Spanish-speaking countries of Central America and the Caribbean. When he returned to Jamaica in 1932 he changed his name from 'Clarke' to 'Bustamante'. (This was believed to be the name of a sea captain who had adopted him in his youth.)

Bustamante was ambitious, but instead of following the white man's ways and ideals as most aspiring brown politicians did, he adopted the black man's culture. Blacks usually regarded browns as just as much their oppressors as the whites in the labour field. Bustamante decided that a brown man throwing in his lot with the blacks would have a special appeal. His speeches were emotional, likening labour disputes to class wars and playing on racial tensions. Most startling of all, he appeared in public wearing six guns which gave a melodramatic air to even an orderly meeting.

On his return to Jamaica he allied with A. G. S. Coombes, the workers' leader, and in 1935 they formed the Jamaica Workers' and Tradesmen's Union. They tried to bring agricultural workers into a blanket union with the craft workers under the leadership of Coombes. Bustamante was treasurer of this union, but soon he dominated Coombes, stirring up public opinion against the poor conditions of the workers. In 1937 he petitioned George VI about the poverty of the Jamaican people. This recalled the appeal to Queen Victoria by the peasants of St Ann's in 1865. The historical allusion was a cleverly calculated appeal.

At the end of 1937 and the beginning of 1938, unrest came to the surface in Jamaica. In May, 1938, Bustamante was imprisoned for holding a public meeting during a strike. Imprisonment helped his cause because it made him a martyr. Norman Manley offered his services as a lawyer and secured his release. Once out of prison, Bustamante formed the Bustamante Industrial Trade Union and was made Life President. It was a blanket union of dockers, agricultural workers, clerks and factory workers and had a membership of 6,000. The immediate aims were to win minimum wage legislation and achieve industrial peace.

Manley obviously wanted an alliance between the B.I.T.U. and the People's National Party, but Bustamante kept his union out. He decided to be a union leader first and a politician later if he had to be. In February, 1939, as a show of power, he called for a general strike in Jamaica, but the Governor, Sir Arthur Richards, announced a state of emergency and the strikers returned to work after four days.

Bustamante made the split with Manley more open in October, 1939, when he withdrew his union from the newly-formed Trades Union Council. Bustamante was then interned without trial for seventeen months at the beginning of the war under the Defence Regulations. Manley and the People's National Party agitated for his release and took over the administration of the B.I.T.U. However, on his release in 1942 he resumed the leadership of the union and refused a political alliance with Manley. It became clear to Bustamante that the B.I.T.U. must have its own political party to contest Jamaica's first election under universal adult suffrage, so he formed the Jamaica Labour Party. His union controlled eighty-eight per cent of the organised labour in Jamaica and consequently easily won the 1944 election. He and Manley were now opponents in politics and in the labour field. As Manley built up his own union support, the rival unions clashed frequently, often with considerable violence. In 1946 nineteen people were killed.

After his defeat in the election of 1955, Bustamante was given a knighthood by the Queen, but he was not yet ready to retire from public life. When the wider issue of the federation came, Bustamante was suspicious about British motives in encouraging it. He asked for a guarantee of self-government for Jamaica inside or outside the federation. The British agreed. He was also worried about the interests of his workers who were relatively well off compared with those of the Eastern Caribbean. Bustamante accepted the federation, but was not as enthusiastic about it as Manley. When Manley agreed to put the federation issue to a referendum in 1961, Bustamante saw his chance to make political capital out of the unpopularity of federation with the workers. He convinced them that they would be supporting the less productive Eastern Caribbean. Federation was rejected, and on the same platform Bustamante won the 1962 election. Thus he became the first Prime Minister of an independent Jamaica.

By 1967 Bustamante had retired from politics and went to live on his estate. His popularity was still great and he did not refrain from using his influence in politics, especially through the unions.

Trade unions and politics

How union-political party links arose

An interesting feature of twentieth-century politics in the British West Indies has been the close association of trade unions and political parties. This link occurred in four differing circumstances:
1 Where the union came first. This happened in Antigua, where the Antigua Trades and Labour Union set up a political committee in 1940 to contest seats for the Legislative Council. In the same year, union leaders in St Kitts created the Workers' League which won the elections there. In Jamaica the Bustamante Industrial Trade Union decided to form a political party to enter the 1944 election, and thus the Jamaica Labour Party was formed.
2 Where the political party came first and created its own union support. In Jamaica the People's National Party instigated the Trade Union Advisory Council which was the forerunner of the Trade Union Council and then the Trade Union Congress. All these federations failed to give the People's National Party the support it wanted. Thus Manley created the National Workers' Union in 1952.
3 Where the union and political party already existed and came together for their mutual

advantage. In British Guiana the Guiana Industrial Workers' Union was founded in 1946. Dr Jagan founded the People's Progressive Party in 1950. He sought union support and as a result the union and party came together for the 1953 election.

4 Where the union and the political party were one and the same. This occurred in the early stages of nationalist politics in the British West Indies. In Barbados the Progressive League, registered as a trade union, entered politics without even forming a separate political wing. It won five seats in the 1940 elections. In 1943 the Barbados Progressive League divided into the Barbados Workers' Union and the Barbados Labour Party. However, the link between them remained very strong. In British Guiana the Manpower Citizens' Association, a trade union, put up candidates from among its members in the 1947 election.

Most of these union-political party links have been long-lasting, providing solid support for the party. However, there was a notable split in the traditional alliance in Barbados in 1954 when the Workers' Union broke away from the Labour Party.

The reasons for these links can be traced to the circumstances of the late 1930s and the beginnings of nationalist politics.

1 Unions were impatient with the government's failure to pass satisfactory labour laws.

2 The British Guiana and West Indies Labour Congress of 1938 demanded universal adult suffrage. The unions stood to gain from this as most of their members did not have the vote. However, it meant that they had to have their own representatives to vote for, so they formed political wings or separate parties.

3 The approach of self-government led unions to enter politics, fearing that if they did not do so, they would be making a free gift of political power to the middle classes.

4 Socialism linked trade unions and political parties. Politicians thought it wise to incorporate socialist policies into their party manifestos to attract union support. For example, Grantley Adams put the nationalisation of the sugar industry into the manifesto of the Barbados Progressive League.

Trade unions and political parties cannot be completely parallel in everything. Trade unions exist to protect the interests and improve the conditions of the workers. Political parties need a much wider range of interests and responsibilities; for example, foreign affairs which would normally come outside the scope of trade union interests. Therefore West Indian political parties cannot merely be the servants of trade unions, they must appeal to and serve other interests, not just one section of the community. This explains why trade union-political party links have become weaker than they were in the early days of nationalist politics.

In Barbados

Grantley Adams, a lawyer, achieved recognition and popularity with the workers when he defended Clement Payne and won his appeal against deportation. In April, 1938, Adams, H. G. Cummins and W. A. Crawford drew up the programme for the Progressive League. At this stage the League was registered as a political party. It attempted to appeal to all interests – socialists who wanted nationalisation of the sugar industry and government ownership of all factories; nationalists who wanted universal suffrage and self-government; unionists who wanted workers' compensation, wage boards and factory supervision; and small firms who wanted co-operative schemes in agriculture and marketing.

The Progressive League won five seats in the 1940 election. This number was small because the property qualification was still high. The party managed to steer some of its policies through the Legislature, notably the Workmen's Compensation Act in 1942. Grantley Adams, President of the Progressive League, realised that with self-government in prospect, union and party interests would have to be distinguished. Therefore, in 1943, the Barbados Workers' Union and the Barbados Labour party were formed.

The turning point came in 1950 when Barbados was granted universal adult suffrage. The Barbados Labour Party won the election of 1951 and was able to carry through legislation on behalf of the workers, such as the creation of the Wages Board to arbitrate on rates of pay, the introduction of holidays with pay, and new Trade Union and Factory Acts.

The importance of union support in Barbadian politics was demonstrated by the break between union and party in 1954. It started as a personal rift between Frank Walcott, General Secretary to the Barbados Workers' Union, and Adams, but by 1958 there was a complete severance between union and party. The Barbados Workers' Union went over to the opposition, the Democratic Labour Party, in that year. Inevitably the Barbados Labour Party and Adams were defeated at the election. They were unpopular with the union for not creating job opportunities in a period of high unemployment. The swing to the Democratic Labour Party was substantial. They won fourteen seats and Adams' party won only five. The transfer of union support had been critical.

In Jamaica

Perhaps Jamaica provides the best examples of the links between unions and parties. In 1938 Bustamante formed the Bustamante Industrial Trade Union. He did not like some of the People's National Party's policies so he withheld his union's support. While Bustamante was in prison, Manley tried to establish links with the B.I.T.U., but again Bustamante renounced any alliance with the P.N.P. in 1942.

The Jamaica Labour Party, founded by Bustamante, won twenty-three out of thirty-two seats in the 1944 elections because it commanded about 30,000 working-class votes. The P.N.P. won only four seats because it lacked major union support.

There were twenty-eight unions in Jamaica at this time, but most of them were small so that the B.I.T.U. carried the most weight in politics. Manley desperately sought the union support that Bustamante had cut off in 1942. In 1945 he turned the Trades Union Council into the Trades Union Congress and tried to make it a blanket union to support the P.N.P. Between 1945 and 1948, when there were bitter clashes between the rival union groups, the B.I.T.U./J.L.P. alliance was solid and Bustamante held power.

Manley realised that the T.U.C.'s support was neither sufficient nor reliable enough to bring the P.N.P. to power. In 1952 he created a new union, the National Workers' Union, to give the P.N.P. the sort of support it needed. This time his tactics worked. The N.W.U. was a blanket union whose membership was approaching that of the B.I.T.U. It carried Manley and the P.N.P. to power in the 1955 election by eighteen seats to the J.L.P.'s fourteen.

From 1955 to Independence, Jamaican politics were dominated by two parties and the two unions supporting them. The P.N.P./N.W.U. alliance was emerging as the stronger of the two alliances between union and party, until the federation issue upset the usual pattern of union politics. By opposing federation in 1962 Bustamante was able to win working-class votes from the P.N.P. and he came to power in the Independence elections of 1962.

Trade unions in the 1960s

Achievements

By 1958 the trade union movement in the British Caribbean no longer needed help from the British Trades Union Congress. West Indian trade unionists were no longer sent to England for instruction but were taught at home. In the early 1960s the Trade Union Education Institute opened in Jamaica. The achievements of West Indian trade unions are even more remarkable when the relative poverty of the area is taken into account. In the West Indies where there was no comprehensive welfare state, no state pension, no unemployment pay and high unemployment, union demands had to be for the basic minimum standards in working conditions first, and for some welfare services which developed countries took for granted.

By the mid-1960s trade unions in most West Indian territories had achieved some or all of the following benefits and conditions:
1 *Minimum wage law* This is an admission by the unions that they have been unable to negotiate satisfactory wage levels in all fields. Therefore they press the government to pass a law guaranteeing basic pay for workers who are not unionised or whose unions are ineffective.
2 *Minimum age* The youngest age at which a person can be engaged in full-time employment in the British Caribbean is usually fifteen years.
3 *Workmen's compensation* A worker injured at work, except through his own negligence, must be paid compensation. If he is killed at work, his relatives are compensated.
4 *Sick leave* A worker can be paid while absent from work for sickness. Conditions vary, but usually for absence up to three days a certificate is not needed.

5 *Holidays with pay* Most major industries in the British Caribbean give a minimum of two weeks holiday with pay.
6 *Factory inspection* Company or government inspectors check periodically that machinery is well-maintained and that moving parts are guarded. Safety procedures must be displayed and workers instructed in them. Minimum standards of sanitation are also inspected, such as washing facilities, drinking water and first-aid equipment. For health reasons minimum rest periods must be observed.
7 *Pension schemes* These can be operated by companies or by a state insurance scheme. This is a limited benefit because contributory pension schemes are by no means universal.
8 *Redundancy pay* If a worker loses his job through no fault of his own, he must be paid compensation.

Procedure in disputes

Before about 1952 British West Indian trade unions had followed British procedures in collective bargaining and disputes. However, when the North American Bauxite companies came into the British Caribbean, they wanted to follow an American pattern. In North America company unions are illegal and unions tend to be industry-based and nationwide. Consequently there are nationwide rules for procedure in collective bargaining and disputes. This has had some influence on trade union procedures in the British Caribbean.

However, local Caribbean influences remain strong.
1 The West Indies are developing countries. Thus disputes and strikes are regarded as more dangerous to economic progress than they are in developed countries. There is a tendency to avoid strikes at all costs. In fact some industries are designated 'essential services' and strikes in them are illegal; for example, the power industries like electricity and gas.
2 Socialist ideals are strong in many of the islands and government intervention in disputes between unions and employers is expected.

The usual procedure in collective bargaining and disputes is as follows:
1 Unions and employers bargain to fix conditions of employment within the framework of labour legislation.
2 Outstanding grievances can be put before the employers by the unions and a settlement negotiated.
3 If this fails, there is a legitimate dispute, and unions and employers meet again in full session to re-negotiate conditions.
4 Any extension of the dispute calls forth government intervention. Meanwhile, in most West Indian territories, the Minister of Labour has the power to order the workers back to work while the settlement is pending.
5 If the government's *conciliation* attempts fail, the dispute goes before a government-appointed Arbitration Tribunal or Council for *arbitration*.
6 The decision of the Arbitration Tribunal is called the *award* and must be accepted by both sides.

Queen Victoria

4
Constitutional developments in the British Caribbean, 1866 to 1944

Breakdown of the representative system of government

The representative system

This was adopted in British colonial government in the North American colonies and the West Indies, but it was not applied to British colonies in the East and Africa until very modern times. It developed in the Americas because many of the colonies started off as proprietary colonies. In their original charters, the King gave the proprietor the right to summon the freemen of the colony to meet in an assembly. Early colonies in the Americas also differed from later British colonies in that they had a large proportion of free English settlers. They wanted representation in the government of their colony, just as the landed classes had representation in the Commons in England.

Apart from Barbados, which had its Assembly in 1639, most of the West Indian assemblies developed in the Civil War period and the Commonwealth, 1642 to 1653, when the English Parliament was asserting itself successfully. On the restoration of Charles II these assemblies were given formal recognition. The St Kitts' Assembly is first mentioned in 1650. Probably Antigua's Assembly dates from the same time. By 1663 there were six colonial assemblies and this remained the number until the eighteenth century. After the Seven Years War, George III granted constitutions to the conquered islands which authorised the calling of local assemblies. The Assemblies of Grenada and St Vincent date from 1766 and Dominica's from 1775. Conditions had changed in that black slaves made up the majority of the population in each island, but the representative principle was an established part of West Indian government.

The first assemblies were summoned from amongst the freemen of the island. Indentured servants and slaves had no political rights. The sugar revolution led to a great decline in the number of freemen and an increase in the number of slaves which made the assemblies even more unrepresentative than they had been before. Even among the free whites, membership of the assemblies was exclusive and the franchise was qualitative, depending on property or education. The Legislative Council was even more exclusive. Colonies were governed by oligarchies – a few relatively prosperous free white landowners.

Probably when an assembly was first summoned, all the freemen attended, but as the population grew this became impossible. The freemen then chose some of their number to represent them. This is how the 'representative' idea arose. Choosing was probably by acclamation at first, then by a show of hands. The secret ballot came very late in the British West Indies, as late as 1946 in one part of the Bahamas. Choosing representatives in public made it more likely that the most prominent citizens would become members of the assemblies. The richest planters would probably be nominated by the Governor to the Legislative Council. The less wealthy, but still relatively prosperous, would be elected to the Assembly. So the government would be an oligarchy of wealth as well as number. When a merchant class arose, they were represented in the Assembly, but not in the Legislative Council where for a long time the possession of land seemed to be an unwritten qualification.

Assembly Buildings in Nassau

After emancipation it was ridiculous to apply the term 'representative' to the assemblies. They represented under one per cent of the total population in most colonies. Out of a total population of about 20,000 in St Kitts in 1850, only 160 were qualified to vote. This was an average of about eighteen voters per parish. At the same time the members of the Antigua Assembly were representing on average only seventeen voters each. Jamaica was even worse, for under half of one per cent of the population could vote. When the assemblies had become so obviously unrepresentative they were serving no useful purpose for the colony as a whole. They were just serving the selfish interests of a few privileged white and brown people in some places. The British government saw how unfair and out-of-date the assemblies were, but they did not want to extend representation to masses of illiterate blacks. They thought that British governors and officials could represent the majority of the people within the Crown Colony system.

Non co-operative assemblies

Lack of co-operation from the assemblies and their frequent conflicts with the governors encouraged the British government to abolish them. In the eighteenth and nineteenth centuries the tendency towards conflict with the metropolitan government grew. The governor always had the ultimate authority, but if he could work with the co-operation of the assembly, it appeared that he was ruling according to the wishes of the people. The assemblies, on the other hand, wanted to control the administration themselves and make the governor a figurehead. The metropolitan government would not let this happen and the governor frequently had to insist on very unpopular legislation such as the Navigation Acts. This caused conflict in the seventeenth century.

The assemblies wanted control over taxation and expenditure. Because an island's revenue came from taxes on the freemen, it was felt that their representatives should control it. This principle had been established in the first parliament in England in the thirteenth century, *Quod omnes tangit, ab omnibus approbetur* (That which concerns everyone ought to be approved by everyone).

In wartime, colonial assemblies voted money readily, but in peacetime this was not so. The governor was dependent on the assembly for money to carry on his administration. By threatening to withhold money, or by actually withholding it, the assemblies could force the governors to do what they wanted.

The conflict between the Assembly and the Governor in Jamaica was long and bitter. In 1791 the Assembly had used its 'power of the purse' to force the Governor to send a force to St Domingue to assist the Royalists. Further conflict arose over the abolition of the slave trade which caused great bitterness in the Assembly. In 1811 there were rumours of a party in the Jamaican Assembly which wanted political separation from Britain. The conflict grew deeper over amelioration. In 1823 the House of Assembly protested against 'interference in their internal legislation'. Therefore, by the 1820s, the British government was considering ending the representative system in Jamaica.

The Jamaican Assembly became increasingly unco-operative in voting money. It was clear that it would do nothing to help the freed slaves. The West Indian Prisons Act of 1838 brought into the open all the bitterness which the Jamaican Assembly had been nurturing against the British government over abolition and emancipation. By this Act colonial governors were empowered to take control of the regulation and management of prisons. The Jamaican Assembly refused to pass the Act on the grounds that it was an interference in its internal affairs. The Governor dissolved the Assembly and wanted to suspend the Jamaican constitution. In 1839 he introduced a bill to put all legislative power in the hands of the Governor and Council for five years. However, the new Governor, Sir Charles Metcalfe, made a compromise with the Assembly which saved it for the time being. This was short-lived, because the Sugar Duties Equalisation Act renewed the conflict. The Assembly wanted the British government to repeal the measure, but the latter refused. From 1849 to 1853 the Jamaican Assembly refused to renew the Revenue Acts or to vote other monies.

Sir Henry Barkly, who had found a solution to a similar problem in British Guiana, was sent to Jamaica. He saved the Jamaican Assembly for another ten years by persuading it to agree to an amendment to the constitution in 1856. An

Executive Committee consisting of three members of the Assembly and one member of the Legislative Council would carry out the administration with the Governor. The Executive Committee was a device to bypass the Assembly in the control of finance, leaving it with only the control of local government, social services and the militia. Barkly was able to 'persuade' the Assembly to accept this reform by offering a loan of £500,000 to tide Jamaica over the difficulties caused by the equalisation of sugar duties. Executive Committees were established in other islands but were soon abandoned. It was obvious that a more radical constitutional change was necessary to counteract the obstructiveness of the assemblies.

The irresponsible attitude of the assemblies did not help their cause. By the mid-nineteenth century the majority of the population were freed slaves. There could be no progress until they were allowed to participate in economic and political development. The assemblies still wanted to suppress the blacks. Sir Lionel Smith, the Governor of Jamaica, wrote to the Secretary of State in 1838 as follows:

> It is impossible for anyone to answer for the conduct of the House of Assembly. Many are there in the island who would be delighted to get up an insurrection for the pleasure of destroying the negroes and missionaries. They are, in fact, mad.

The irresponsibility of the few towards the many prevented progress. The Lieutenant-Governor of St Kitts pointed out that the failure of the assemblies was due to their own selfishness.

There seems little doubt that the assemblies would have been abolished by the British government because they were totally unrepresentative, irresponsible and at loggerheads with the metropolitan government. However this was not necessary because the Morant Bay Rebellion persuaded the assemblies to abolish themselves.

The judiciary

In the British islands the judiciary was the most neglected part of the constitution. For the majority of the population, the slaves, justice was administered on the plantation by the overseer. The public courts dealt with only the free and in some islands, like the Leewards, this meant that only just over 1,000 in Nevis or 3,500 in Antigua came under their jurisdiction.

The keynote of the judicial system was amateurism. Very few magistrates and judges were trained in the law. At the lowest level the British West Indies copied the English amateur magistracy of justices of the peace, though they were usually referred to as 'magistrates'. They were invariably members of the rich planter class because they were not paid for their services. Even at the level of judge, non-professional men were chosen; a good social and financial standing was the usual qualification governors looked for in appointing judges. For example, in Barbados in 1700 there were thirty-nine judges, a ridiculously high number considering that there were only about 18,000 people under their jurisdiction. Not one of these judges was trained in the law. The white community in Barbados was divided into cliques and the administration of justice was far from impartial. The poor whites had little hope of favourable decisions. Even the Chief Justice was often untrained.

A report from Jamaica in 1774 said that probably only two barristers had ever held the post of Chief Justice. Social standing and wealth seemed more important qualifications for the post. Christopher Codrington lamented this

Court House in Montego Bay

situation in Barbados in 1701 and asked for an Attorney General to be appointed to help the Governor deal with appeals, but the Colonial Office seemed to dislike professionalism as much as the islands.

In the eighteenth century every parish usually had a court. In the larger islands there were precinct courts as well. These minor courts could deal with cases up to £20 if they were under a judge, and up to £2 under a justice of the peace. In Jamaica all the magistrates in a parish came under the chairmanship of a 'Custos' who acted as the 'guardian' of the law in that parish. The larger islands, like Jamaica, had their own Supreme Courts, but the smaller islands, like the Leewards, shared a Supreme Court. Within an island, appeal could be made from a minor court to a higher court, and from the Supreme Court to the Governor who then sat with his Council as a court of appeal. Outside an island, appeal went to the Privy Council in England but the case had to be serious, like a murder in a criminal case, or a sum of over £500 in a civil case. It is not surprising that many appeals from the West Indies were successful in view of the amateur state of their judiciaries.

Local government

The system of local government in the West Indies was even older than that of the assemblies. In 1629 Sir William Tufton, Governor of Barbados, divided the island into parishes. Each parish came under the local vestry, a church body originally, but adapted to carry out local government. On the vestry was the vicar or minister, and prominent citizens of the parish who by the eighteenth century were elected. The justices of the peace sat on the vestry *ex officio*.

The functions of the vestry were to maintain the courts and the prisons, register births, deaths and marriages, look after the poor and orphans, and sometimes provide sanitary and health services.

Status of British Guiana, St Lucia and Trinidad

The three territories acquired in the Napoleonic Wars were not given the same status as the other islands. Where their government institutions were well established, as in the case of Trinidad and British Guiana, they were allowed to keep them. Trinidad, conquered in 1797 and formally handed over by Spain in 1802, became a Crown Colony. By an Order-in-Council of 1815 the Crown retained the right to legislate for Trinidad. The British residents in Trinidad wanted an assembly but in 1815 they were very much in a minority. If they had been given an assembly they would have taken control of the island because the Spanish and French, both more numerous, would have been excluded from the government as foreigners. The British government refused to allow such unfairness. Another important consideration in adopting Crown Colony government was that the Spanish system had been by direct rule of the Crown. However, perhaps the most important was the fact that the British government had some unpopular legislation to pass, namely abolition and emancipation. It would be easy to enforce these measures in Trinidad by Order-in-Council but difficult if an assembly existed.

As few constitutional changes as possible were made. The policy was to let the changes come about gradually when the island was ready. The Spanish language and laws continued and the English language was not used in the courts until 1814, seventeen years after the conquest. English civil laws only gradually took over from Spanish laws. Major constitutional change did not take place in central government for over one hundred years.

France formally ceded St Lucia to Britain in 1815. It was not given an assembly, but was ruled as a Crown Colony until 1838 when it was placed under the authority of the Governor of Barbados. From 1838 to 1885 St Lucia shared the administration of the Windward Islands.

Britain took over Berbice, Demerara and Essequibo from the Dutch in 1814. In 1831 they united to form British Guiana. It was not given a representative assembly because it already had two representative bodies, the Court of Policy and the Combined Court which consisted of the Court of Policy and six Financial Representatives. The Combined Court was the equivalent of an assembly in the old islands except for the method of election. The two Guiana courts were indirectly elected. In a primary election the planters chose an electoral college, the Kiezers. In the secondary election the Kiezers chose the members of the Court of Policy and the Combined Court.

The town of Morant Bay

Under the terms of the capitulation in 1803, the British promised to keep this rather complicated constitution. As with Trinidad, the British wanted the transfer of power to be as smooth as possible and to let changes come about gradually.

In the first half of the nineteenth century the Combined Court proved just as unco-operative as the assemblies. It used the power of the purse to try to make the government pass the laws it wanted. For example, in 1840 it would not vote supply unless an immigration act was passed because the planters wanted East Indian indentured labour at the government's expense. In 1848 the Combined Court wanted the Sugar Duties Equalisation Act repealed and insisted on a twenty-five per cent cut in officials' salaries. They said that they would not vote supply unless the Governor accepted these measures. Sir Henry Barkly persuaded the Combined Court to give way without reducing the salaries on the Civil List by offering a loan which was spent on immigrant labour schemes.

Therefore, by 1865 all British territories except Trinidad had their own assemblies, or participated in a 'federal' assembly as in the case of the Windwards. British Guiana had a sort of assembly in the Combined Court. Ten years later most of these colonial assemblies had disappeared. Their survival was doubtful anyway, but it was the influence of the Morant Bay Rebellion which brought most of them to an end between 1866 and 1875.

The Morant Bay Rebellion

The hardships of the 1850s and 1860s

In the mid-nineteenth century, conditions in the British West Indies were mostly bad, especially in Jamaica. The sugar industry was in decline due to high costs and out-of-date methods. These economic problems were made worse by the Sugar Duties Equalisation Act 1846 which reduced the price of sugar by up to ten shillings per cwt. Planters were giving up, thus throwing thousands of labourers out of work. Those who were still employed had been forced to accept a reduction in wages and were being paid between 9d and 1/- per day by 1860. Most people were dependent on cash income for food, but the price of food was rising due to the American Civil War, 1861–65. Supplies of the popular, traditional foods were cut.

On top of these man-made difficulties came a succession of calamities. In 1850 to 1854 a cholera epidemic swept through the Caribbean. It struck Jamaica in 1851 and 40,000 deaths were recorded. In the next year a smallpox epidemic killed thousands more. Thousands were left destitute when the money-earners in the family died. The British government thought it was the concern of the Jamaican Assembly to provide relief, but the latter did little to help. On top of all these troubles came three years of extraordinary drought up to 1865, reducing the peasants to a state of desperation.

Two key personalities

The Governor, as the representative of the Crown, should have shown concern for the welfare of people in Jamaica, but just when the people needed help and sympathy, an aloof and pitiless Governor was appointed, Edward John Eyre. In 1862 he was made Lieutenant-Governor while C. H. Darling was on leave. Eyre was chosen because of his past colonial experience. He had been in Australia from 1833 to 1846, and in 1836 had been made Resident Magistrate and Protector of the Aborigines. He had shown sympathy in his dealings with the Aborigines. He was made Lieutenant-Governor of New Zealand during the first Maori War in 1846 and he had helped set up the system of reserved lands for the Maoris after the war. Thereafter he had had West Indian experience as Governor of St Vincent in 1854 and as acting Governor of the Leewards from 1860 to 1861.

Eyre became unpopular with the Assembly very quickly. He was not an approachable Governor for any except the leading planters who made up the Government House set. In 1863 the Assembly asked the Secretary of State to remove him, but instead he was appointed Governor in 1864 when Darling was transferred to Australia. The Assembly was so furious that it tried to bypass the Governor and deal directly with the Secretary of State, but without success.

Eyre either failed to appreciate the desperation of the poor blacks, or he deliberately overlooked it. When the distress was brought to his notice he said that the reports were exaggerated. Eyre was backed by those planters who regarded compassion as a sign of weakness and thought the way to deal with the blacks was with firmness and repression.

Eyre came into conflict with the most important personality on the black side, George William Gordon. Gordon himself was coloured. His father had been an attorney on a sugar estate and his mother a slave. By hard work and an aptitude for mathematics he was able to buy his own, and his mother's, manumission. Thereafter he did so well that he is reputed to have amassed £2,000 by the age of eighteen, an almost unbelievable achievement. He helped his father out of financial difficulties even though his father had refused to acknowledge him earlier. Later he helped his father's white family even though they would not accept him as their brother. However, Gordon's greatest sympathy was shown towards the poor. He seems to have been a naturally humanitarian man. He rejected the imitative white culture which most coloureds adopted and championed the cause of the blacks. He used his money to buy abandoned estates and sub-divided them for sale to the poor. He founded the Jamaica Mutual Life Assurance Company which helped to relieve the distress caused by the losses of the 1850s.

Gordon came into conflict with the authorities in Church and State. He was nominally a Baptist, but, in fact, rejected any particular denomination. He was particularly against the Church of England which had a long record of indifference and neglect towards the blacks. He criticised all the members of the Church of England, but one in particular, the Reverend Cooke, Rector of St Thomas. Gordon charged him with neglect of duty towards the welfare of those in his parish, especially those in prison. Cooke was furious. At the time Gordon was a member of the St Thomas vestry. When Cooke found out that Gordon was an ordained Baptist, he persuaded the Custos, Baron von Ketelhodt, to have Gordon forcibly removed from a vestry meeting on the grounds that only Anglicans could be members. Both Cooke and von Ketelhodt were on Eyre's side. At the time Eyre said of Gordon:

> A most mischievous person, and one likely to do a great deal of harm amongst uneducated and excitable persons, such as are the lower classes of this country.

Gordon had entered politics about 1850 with his election to the Assembly for St Thomas-in-the-East. He was also a member of the Kingston Common Council. In the Assembly he belonged to the Town Party led by Edward Jordon. His fellow party members were mostly middle class, prosperous coloureds who were in politics for the advancement of their own class. Gordon decided to use his efforts to help the poor blacks. Once again his outspokenness resulted in a clash with authority. He criticised the state of education, the prisons, the Kingston Public Hospital and the condition of Indian immigrants. When Gordon saw that Eyre was unlikely to do anything about the distress of the poor, but would probably make their position worse, he denounced him strongly in these words (1863): 'I have never seen an animal more voracious for cruelty and power than the present Governor of Jamaica'.

Gordon's attacks on the Governor, Assembly, poor administration and social services reached a wide audience because they were reported in newspapers, especially the *Watchman* which he owned at one time. His words were reported because they were popular even with the members of the Assembly who hated Eyre and wanted to see him brought down. Also Gordon's language in the Assembly was free from restraint and consequently even stronger than the words he used outside. However, as he was later blamed and executed for stirring up trouble and rebellion, it is important to establish if he openly advocated the use of violence. The nearest he came to it was probably in these words: 'If we are to be governed by such a Governor much longer, the people will have to fly to arms and become self-governing'.

Events leading to the rebellion

1 *Underhill Meetings* In April, 1863, Dr Edward Underhill, secretary of the Baptist Mission Council in England, visited Jamaica and stayed until January, 1865. During this period he kept a notebook about life and conditions in Jamaica, noting especially the hardships caused by the drought and the rising prices resulting from the American Civil War. At the end of his visit he wrote to the Secretary of State about the distress of the peasants. The Secretary of State asked Eyre for his comments. Eyre said that the report was an exaggeration. The Established Church and government officials agreed with Eyre.

Throughout Jamaica meetings were held by the poor to complain about their conditions and to ask for relief. These meetings were early signs that the poor were preparing to act themselves because there was no help forthcoming from the government. Gordon addressed one particular

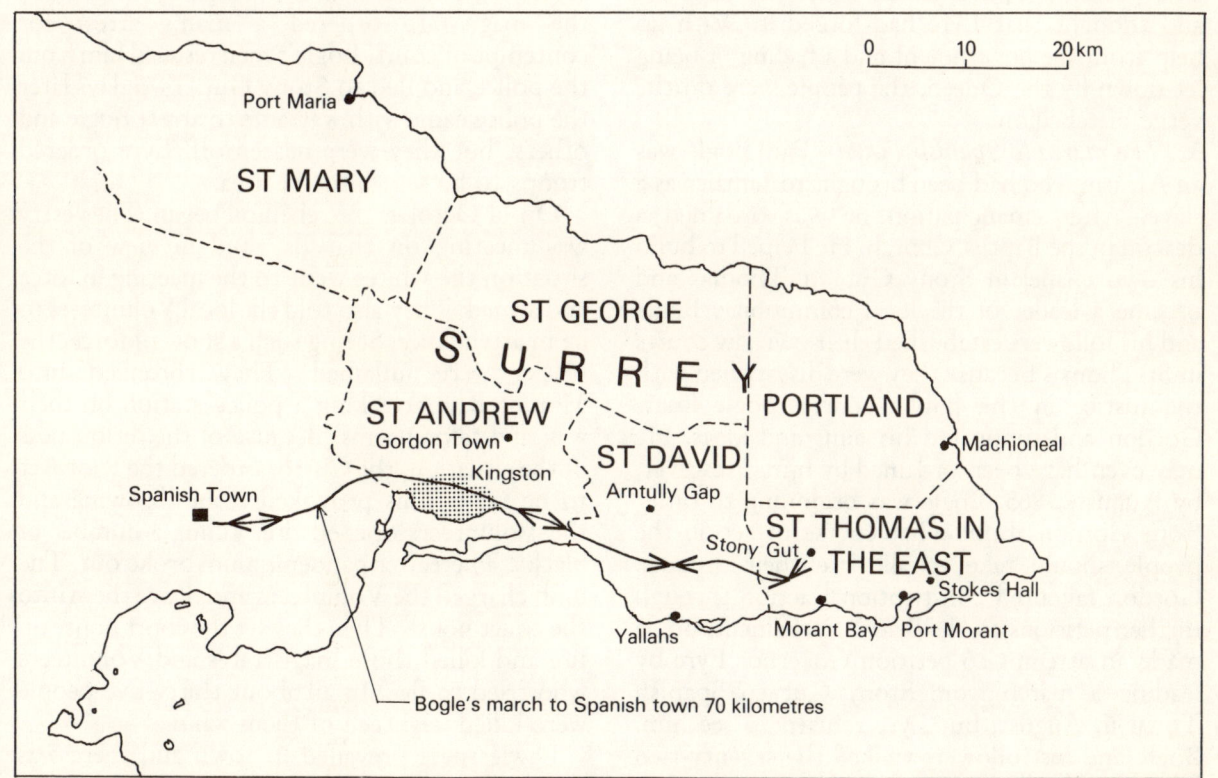

Map 4   Eastern Jamaica at the time of the Morant Bay rebellion

stormy, crowded meeting in Kingston in May, 1865 which was later used as evidence that he was stirring up the people to rebel.

2 *The Queen's Advice* Early in 1865, some people from St Ann sent a petition to Queen Victoria giving details of their poverty, requesting help and asking, in particular, to be allowed to cultivate Crown land. They had faith in Queen Victoria because they believed that she had been responsible for their emancipation. Perhaps because of Eyre's response to the Underhill report, the Secretary of State drafted an unsympathetic reply on behalf of the Queen which was sent to Jamaica in June, 1865. It stated that the peasants could find their own remedy by

> working for wages, not uncertainly or capriciously, but steadily and continuously at the times when their labour is wanted, and for so long as it is wanted ... from their own industry and prudence and not from any such schemes as have been suggested to them, that they must look for an improvement in their conditions.

Governor Eyre had 50,000 copies of the reply published and displayed throughout the island. The peasants were shocked at its heartlessness and thought that Eyre had forged it. With no help from the government and a feeling of being let down by the Queen, the people were on the verge of rebellion.

3 *The march to Spanish Town* Paul Bogle was an African who had been brought to Jamaica as a slave. After emancipation he was ordained a deacon in the Baptist Church. He helped to build his own chapel in Stony Gut, St Thomas and became a leader of the local community. Bogle and his followers established their own law courts in St Thomas because they were dissatisfied with the justice in the public courts. Bogle knew Gordon and supported his aims and ideas. He may even have been ordained by him. However, by August, 1865, Bogle was beginning to differ from Gordon about what course of action the people should take to alleviate their distress. Gordon favoured constitutional action through further petitions to the British Parliament. Bogle made an attempt to petition Governor Eyre by leading a march from Stony Gut to Spanish Town in August, but Eyre refused to see him. Bogle and his followers walked the seventy-two kilometres back to Stony Gut planning what they would do next. Then Bogle seems to have decided

Paul Bogle and George William Gordon

that violence was the only way. He started to hold secret meetings in Stony Gut, and began to train and arm his followers.

The Morant Bay Rebellion

On 7 October 1865, Paul Bogle led two hundred armed men to Morant Bay Court House. When the magistrate ordered a man's arrest for contempt of court, Bogle's men rescued him from the police and fled to Stony Gut. Two days later the police came with warrants to arrest Bogle and others, but they were beaten off. Eyre ordered troops to be sent into the area.

On 11 October the rebellion began. The vestry was meeting on that day and in view of the situation the whites went to the meeting in force and armed. They also told the local Volunteers to be in attendance. Seeing such a show of force, the blacks were inflamed. They thronged into Morant Bay, attacking a police station on their way and taking arms. Because of the seriousness of the situation, the Custos ordered the Riot Act to be read. This provoked stone-throwing and the Volunteers opened fire, killing a number of blacks. Thereafter pandemonium broke out. The mob charged the Volunteers and drove them into the court house. Then they set the court house on fire and killed those magistrates and Volunteers who tried to flee. In all about thirty-five people were killed, eighteen of them white.

Lawlessness prevailed in town and there was violence and looting. Bogle returned to Stony Gut to prepare for the coming of the troops.

Some irresponsible people took advantage of the breakdown of law and order to raid the plantations in the countryside. From 11 to 15 October more whites were murdered and their property damaged. The troops which Eyre had ordered on 9 October arrived on 12 October. First they went into Morant Bay and buried the dead. By this time Morant Bay was quiet, but the rebellion was widespread in St Thomas. Governor Eyre ordered more troops to this area and arranged for others to be stationed in the west of the island to stop the revolt spreading. He also called up two warships. At this stage the key to the success or failure of the rebellion depended on the attitude of the Maroons. Bogle thought that they would join their black brothers, but they did not. They joined the government side and were in fact just as brutal as the local militia in suppressing the rebellion.

Eyre proclaimed martial law throughout Surrey. From 15 to 23 October the troops swept the countryside, putting an end to all resistance. However, even after the capture of Paul Bogle by the Maroons in Stony Gut on 23 October, martial law continued. It was ended on 13 November, much later than was necessary.

The repression

The horror of the Indian Mutiny of 1857 is often put forward as the excuse for Eyre's acquiesence in the brutality that accompanied the suppressing of the rebellion. In the Indian Mutiny native Indian troops sadistically murdered white men, women, children and even babies. The retaliation by the British was equally atrocious. Governor Eyre acted as if the Morant Bay Rebellion was a miniature Indian Mutiny.

The worst acts were committed by the West India Regiment and the Maroons. The troops and sailors landed from the *Onyx* and *Wolverine*, the two warships which Eyre had ordered, behaved responsibly. The West India Regiment killed about fifty rebels without trial, and the Maroons, twenty-five. Any person suspected of having been in the rebellion was shot. About one thousand houses of the poor were burnt with deliberate and unnecessary cruelty. Many people were executed by sentence of the courts-martial. The presiding officers were inexperienced and uninstructed on how to proceed. They accepted any kind of evidence in capital charges and hanged 354 people. Others were flogged on no evidence at all. The total casualty list for the Morant Bay Rebellion was 608 killed in the fighting or by execution, about 600 flogged and 1,000 homes destroyed.

When the Morant Bay Rebellion occurred, George William Gordon was in Kingston which was outside the martial law area. Gordon gave himself up as he knew Eyre would blame him for the rebellion. This was on 17 October. He was taken to Port Morant so that he could be tried by court-martial. He faced the court on 21 October and was found guilty of high treason. He was hanged on 23 October on gallows erected on the site of the Morant Bay Court House. Later the same day Bogle, too, was hanged there. The Court House was later rebuilt and there is now a statue of Paul Bogle by Edna Manley in front of it.

Judgement on Eyre

The opinion of whites and coloureds, as expressed in the Assembly and the newspapers, was that Eyre had acted legally and correctly in his repression of the rebellion. They felt that he had stopped a racial war in Jamaica by his firm action. Eyre had acted legally because there was martial

Edward John Eyre

law at the time. However, there is a vast difference between the letter of the law and a reasonable and humane application of it. In the case of Gordon there are grounds for saying that Eyre acted illegally.

There is no doubt that Eyre over-reacted to the dangers at Morant Bay. Modern opinion considers that it was just a local revolt and would not have led to a racial war in Jamaica. The proclamation of martial law was necessary, but Eyre allowed it to go on for too long. He also allowed the troops and the courts-martial to behave in an unnecessarily harsh way.

About Gordon, Eyre said a year later:

> I can only repeat my conviction that however defective it may have been in a strictly legal point of view, Mr Gordon was the proximate occasion of the insurrection, and of the cruel massacre of particular individuals whom he regarded as his personal enemies, and that, therefore, he suffered justly.

However, Gordon denied that he had stirred up the violence. After his sentence he wrote to his wife:

> All I ever did was to recommend the people who complained to seek redress in a legitimate way. I did not expect that, not being a rebel, I should have been tried and disposed of in this way.

Paul Bogle told his accusers in his court-martial that Gordon had never told him to use violence. It is very doubtful that Gordon wanted anything like Morant Bay to happen.

Eyre acted illegally in bringing Gordon from Kingston into a martial law area in order to secure his conviction. There is absolutely no evidence that Gordon told the mob to murder one of his personal enemies, (perhaps Eyre was referring to the death of the Custos).

People in the West Indies and in England were uneasy about Eyre's conduct and did not want him to escape justice. A Royal Commission under Sir Henry Stokes, his successor, investigated the complaints while Eyre was still on the island. It praised Eyre for his prompt action in suppressing the rebellion and justified his proclamation of martial law. It considered that there was a danger of rebellion spreading throughout the island and even further afield into other islands. It did not comment on Eyre's treatment of Gordon. However, it remarked unfavourably on the excessive number of death sentences, the brutality of the floggings and the wanton destruction of houses.

The British Parliament took almost the same view. However, the Secretary of State was harder on Eyre and accused him of lack of 'sound judgement'. Therefore Eyre was suspended from office and retired to England. He maintained silence about the Morant Bay Rebellion for the rest of his life and died in 1901 at the age of eighty-six.

The change to Crown Colony government

The Morant Bay Rebellion brought a swift end to the representative system of government in Jamaica and thereafter in nearly all the other colonies. The British government did not have to order the change; the colonial assemblies abolished themselves. Four considerations influenced their actions:

1 Governor Eyre had convinced the white ruling classes in Jamaica that the Morant Bay rebellion was just a forerunner of a racial war. He argued that strong government was necessary so that decisions could be made quickly and carried out with all the power of the metropolitan government. The Crown Colony system would mean direct rule by Britain without the delays and conflicts caused by an assembly.

2 The Assembly also feared that as more people acquired the vote the blacks would swamp the whites in the Assembly. The whites, mistakenly, thought that Crown Colony government would protect their privileged position.

3 There would be the relief from the constant conflicts over taxation and expenditure. The Assembly had frequently tried to deny the government the money it needed for administration. The Morant Bay Rebellion had demonstrated what resources the government commanded, the extra troops and warships which could be summoned so promptly. There would still be taxation under Crown Colony government but its necessity would no longer be questioned.

4 Promptness of action was achieved at Morant Bay because the Governor had proclaimed martial law and could legislate by decree. Crown Colony government would allow the Governor to operate with a free hand and no delays.

How Crown Colony government was established

There were two methods by which the representative system was brought to an end and replaced by the Crown Colony system.

1 *Jamaica and the Windward Islands* The local Assembly handed over all responsibility for making a new constitution to the British government which then issued an Order-in-Council setting up the Crown Colony. Thereafter the British government always had the right to legislate by Order-in-Council for these islands in constitutional and other matters.

In December, 1865 the Jamaican Assembly passed an act dissolving itself. Then they proposed a single Legislative Chamber in which there would be twelve nominated and twelve elected members. However, the Secretary of State would not accept the elective principle because it would perpetuate all the faults of the old representative system. He insisted on a single, completely nominated chamber.

Therefore the Jamaican Legislative Council passed a second act which said:

> In place of the Legislative abolished by the first section of the recent Act, it shall be lawful for Her Majesty the Queen to create and constitute a government for this island, in such form, and with such powers as to Her Majesty may seem best fitting, and from time to time to alter or amend such government.

This shows clearly how all constitution-making power was handed over to Britain. Following this, in June 1866, by Order of the Queen in Council, a Legislative Council consisting of six officials and any number of nominated members (six in practice) was called for October, 1866.

At first the Windward Islands, St Vincent in 1867, Tobago in 1874 and Grenada in 1875, made their own constitutional changes by vote of their own legislature. They allowed for an equal number or, in the case of Tobago, a majority of elected members. Then in 1876 they copied Jamaica and authorised the British government to make their constitutions for them. By an Imperial Act the three islands were all given completely nominated chambers in 1877.

2 *The Leeward Islands and British Honduras* The constitutions were changed by local acts of the legislatures and the British government was not given the power to legislate for these colonies by Order-in-Council. In 1866 St Kitts, Nevis and Antigua voted for single chamber legislatures with a majority of nominated members. In 1878 St Kitts and Nevis amended their constitutions to completely nominated chambers, and in 1898 Antigua and Dominica did the same. They were bringing their constitutions into line with Jamaica and the Windwards and there is no doubt that they did this to please the British government. British Honduras adopted the single chamber in 1870 and in 1892 voted that there must not be less than five nominated members in the legislature.

According to the usual process of constitutional development, Crown Colony government was a backward step. West Indian nationalists had accepted Crown Colony government between 1866 and 1875 in the aftermath of the Morant Bay Rebellion. However, by about 1880, some nationalists were lamenting their loss of independence. They wanted the return of the elective principle and a majority of elected members in the legislature.

The British government pointed out that the local assemblies had voted the changes voluntarily. Once a colony had decided to accept Crown Colony government there was no point in half measures such as allowing some elected members in the Legislative Council. The Crown could only legislate effectively if the Governor was supported by the Legislative Council. Three classes could always be relied upon for support; the *ex-officio* members like the Attorney General, the Colonial (Chief) Secretary and the Financial Secretary; the nominated officials such as the Secretary for Health or the Secretary for Agriculture – any civil servants whom the Governor chose; and the nominated unofficials, those from the island society whom the Governor trusted for their loyal support. Colonies which started off with elected members in their single chamber legislatures went over to completely nominated chambers so that the Crown would have no opposition in government.

Bahamas, Bermuda and Barbados

These islands retained their old constitutions without change in this period. Therefore their assemblies survived.

Barbados, for example, felt that there was no

reason to give up its old constitution. There was little racial tension so that they had no fear of the Morant Bay Rebellion influencing the blacks in Barbados. The planter class was almost completely white but the island was so small and so much a one-crop economy that this mattered less than in other islands. Barbadians had a very strong attachment to their Assembly. It was the oldest in the British West Indies and had served the island well. The coloureds were as proud of the Assembly as the whites. In 1843 Samuel Prescod, a coloured, had become a member of the Assembly and he saw it as the way to reform what was wrong in the island. He hoped that more people would be given the vote so that coloureds and blacks could win greater representation in the Assembly.

In 1876 Barbados nearly lost its Assembly because of the conflict between the Governor, Pope-Hennessy, and the Assembly over the Windward Islands Federation. Barbados did not want to join, partly because the Federation was under Crown Colony government. Pope-Hennessy wanted the Assembly abolished because of its opposition, but Conrad Reeves and others fought to save it. After serious riots in Barbados, Pope-Hennessy was withdrawn and posted to Hong Kong. The Barbados Assembly survived.

In 1881 the Assembly amended the constitution and set up an Executive Committee with financial control. This was to stop possible conflicts between Governor and Assembly over money matters. It was known that the British government favoured executive committees although they had not been successful in other colonies.

Crown Colony government at work

Contrary to white expectations, Sir Henry Taylor of the Colonial Office intended Crown Colony government to work in the interests of the community as a whole. He felt that the Crown had a mandate to look after the needs of the majority of the people which had been long neglected under the representative system. If the government was serving the interests of a minority and neglecting those of the majority, machinery existed to put things right under the Crown Colony system. Any maladministration could be reported to the British Parliament. The Secretary of State was responsible to Parliament and would communicate any complaints to the Governor.

The planter-dominated governments of the British West Indies had neglected public works and social services which would have benefited the people as a whole. Crown Colony government made such reforms a priority in order to fulfil its mandate of representing the people. For example, in Jamaica Sir John Peter Grant, Governor from 1866 to 1874, did his utmost to repair the neglect of the past governments. First he put the island's finances in order. Then he tackled long overdue reforms to benefit the common people. He set up new district courts throughout Jamaica and established a police force to take the place of the local volunteers. He created a Public Works Department which constructed many new roads serving peasant communities. He began a Health Service. Near the capital, the Rio Cobre irrigation scheme was undertaken on the Governor's own initiative. This opened up new lands for the common people. In education, payment by results was introduced. The schools which proved their efficiency by this test were given higher grants. The money for education came from the funds released by the disestablishment of the Church of England, which Grant realised was not the church of the people.

Under Crown Colony government similar public works and social services were begun in other territories.

Modifications to Crown Colony government, 1884 to 1944

Crown Colony government survived until the mid-twentieth century, with only minor changes. The Governor ruled with the advice of a single chamber of which the members were officials and nominated non-officials.

Towards the end of the nineteenth century West Indian nationalists were pressing for the elective principle to be re-introduced into the Legislature. In Jamaica in 1884 an equal number of elected members were introduced into the Legislative Council. The Council was then composed of four *ex-officio* and five nominated members, and nine elected members. Six elected members could carry the vote on financial bills. In 1895 the number of official members was

Parliament Buildings in Port of Spain

increased to fifteen, and elected members to fourteen. Then nine elected members could carry the vote on financial matters. These modifications did not affect the Governor's overall control. He was always assured of a majority in the Legislative Council.

Trinidad had to wait until the twentieth century for even small modifications. Middle-class nationalists like Cipriani wanted local representation in the Legislative Council. In many islands Representative Associations had been formed. Their demands were investigated by Major Wood of the Colonial Office on his tour of the West Indian colonies in 1921. The Secretary of State agreed to the election of some of the members of the Legislative Council provided that some form of qualitative franchise was retained. (A typical West Indian voting qualification at that time was to own £5 worth of freehold property or to earn an income of £50 per year.)

In Trinidad the Legislative Reform Committee and the Working Men's Association secured a constitutional change in 1924 after over one hundred and twenty years of Crown Colony government. Seven elected members entered the Legislative Council. This gave the unofficials a majority over the officials of thirteen to twelve. However, the government was unlikely to be outvoted because the nominated unofficials would support it.

In 1925 the elective principle was adopted in the Legislative Councils of Dominica, Grenada and St Vincent. These islands were allowed three elected members each. In 1936 the number was increased. In the same year elected members were introduced into Antigua, St Kitts-Nevis, Montserrat, St Lucia and British Honduras.

The elected members still had no real power in the government. The governor had reserve powers which he could use to overrule any opposition by vetoing legislation or carrying through his own legislation. While the governor had such powers there was still Crown Colony government.

The troubles of 1935 to 1938 exposed the weaknesses of Crown Colony government, especially its lack of contact with the masses. This time, unlike 1865 and the Morant Bay Rebellion, the speed and efficiency of the governor's absolute power was to no avail. The troubles showed that the nationalists and working classes had to be given what they wanted – greater representation and more responsible government. However, the Second World War came so quickly that constitutional changes were delayed. The British government had been prepared to make constitutional changes in the late 1930s but it was not until 1944 that the changes began which resulted in the end of Crown Colony government in the British West Indies.

5

Movements towards independence I

The unfurling of Jamaica's new flag 1962

Self-governing British Territories

Decolonisation

The handing over of independence by Britain to her West Indian colonies was part of a world-wide movement of decolonisation by the imperial powers. Some countries, for example Cuba, fought wars for their independence; others achieved it by more peaceful means. Independence came peacefully in most of the British colonies. The nationalists in the colonies wanted independence and Britain made no attempt to withhold it. On the contrary, much of the initiative came from Britain herself.

Attitude to empire

The British empire had been acquired in a piecemeal fashion, apart from the twenty years from 1880 to 1900 when Britain had made a systematic effort to acquire colonies. Commerce had been the strongest motive in building the empire and the usual pattern was for the 'flag to follow trade'. It also proved to be the strongest motive in retaining colonies in the second half of the nineteenth century with British investment reaching about £2,500,000,000 by the end of the century.

However, during the twentieth century, attitudes to empire changed in Britain. Investments had to be withdrawn to finance two world wars and people were no longer looking to the colonies for their steady five per cent interest. The direction of colonial trade was changing also. For example, the British West Indies were expanding their markets in the United States and Canada. Thus the links with the mother country were becoming weaker as commercial interest in the empire declined. By the outbreak of the Second World War there was less opposition to the idea of decolonisation. Both parties in Britain, and especially the Labour Party, were prepared to give independence to the colonies.

External pressures for self-government

1 *The Atlantic Charter* At the beginning of the Second World War Britain was particularly anxious to make an alliance with the United States. The latter felt that if the war was being fought to defend the free world, pressure must be put on Britain to free her own colonial peoples. In August, 1941, on a warship in the Atlantic, Winston Churchill and Franklin D. Roosevelt signed a joint declaration outlining the common aims of their two respective countries. In Clause 3 they said they 'respected every people's right to choose its own form of government and wanted sovereign rights and self-government restored to those forcibly deprived of them'. If these were not to be meaningless words, Britain would have to do something about her colonies.

2 *The independence of India* Soon after the end of the Second World War in 1947 the largest and one of the poorest colonies in the world was given its independence. The significance of this to the colonies of Africa, the West Indies, the East and the Pacific, was immense. Previously Britain had only given self-government to the well-developed, white-ruled dominions of Canada, Australia, New Zealand and South Africa. In giving India independence, she was showing the black, brown and yellow colonial peoples that their independence, also, was a possibility. This led to increased agitation for independence by nationalists in the black colonies.

3 *The United Nations* The greatest pressure on Britain to decolonise came from the United Nations. Article 73 of the United Nations Charter, drawn up in 1945, said that members of the United Nations responsible for administering non-self-governing territories agreed to ensure the people of such territories 'just treatment, protection against abuses, and advancement toward self-government'. Later a Special Committee of the General Assembly of the United Nations tried to obtain political information about progress towards self-government in colonial territories, but the colonial powers generally resisted its attempts. Britain did not deny that she still held colonies, but felt that the United Nations was moving too quickly towards independence. She had planned a slow, orderly progress to independence but this did not satisfy the United Nations. The latter exerted considerable pressure on Britain and she was forced to bring forward the date of independence in practically every case. For example, Ghana, Britain's most advanced black colony in Africa which Britain wanted to be her model for decolonisation, was given independence in 1957, whereas Britain had planned it for the early 1970s.

The movement towards independence accelerated in the late 1950s and 1960s. As more colonies gained their independence, international pressure mounted in the United Nations. The

Sir Winston Churchill

newly-independent countries joined the United Nations and added their voice to the anti-imperialist bloc calling on Britain, France and Portugal to decolonise. Any reasons these countries might have for withholding independence were swept aside by the champions of decolonisation.

The climax of the anti-colonial movement in the United Nations came in 1960 when the General Assembly adopted a resolution sponsored by forty-three Afro-Asian states, entitled: 'The Declaration on the Granting of Independence to Colonial Countries and Peoples'. This resolution strongly condemned the colonial powers for retaining their colonies and said:

> Immediate steps shall be taken to transfer all powers to the peoples in the colonies without any conditions or reservations in accordance with their freely expressed will and desire in order to enable them to enjoy complete independence and freedom.

This was adopted by eighty-nine votes to nil with nine abstentions. In 1961 a Special United Nations Committee on Colonisation was established. The pressure which came from this movement led to a wave of decolonisation in the early 1960s which included independence for Jamaica and Trinidad in 1962.

By 1965 the few colonies that existed were retained because it was felt that they were too small, too poor or too isolated to stand on their own feet politically. However, the decolonisation movement in the United Nations took no notice of these considerations and pressed for the complete ending of colonisation everywhere. The Gambia, given independence in 1965, proved that smallness was no obstacle. Botswana, given independence in 1966, proved that poverty was no obstacle. About half its people were being fed by international famine relief and there were only twenty-one kilometres of tarmac road in the whole country at the time of independence. Smallness and isolation were inhibiting factors in some of the West Indian islands, but since territories such as the Tuvalu Islands with a population of 8,000 were given independence in 1978, there can be no reservations about more decolonisation in the West Indies.

The nationalist movements in the British West

Signing of the United Nations Charter

Indies found that Britain was anxious to co-operate over independence. The fact that there were no wars or revolutions in the British West Indies does not mean that nationalist movements there were less strong than in other parts of the world. At a time when world opinion was in favour of decolonisation, there was no need for violent struggle to achieve independence.

Internal pressures for self-government

Internal pressures for independence began to build up in the British West Indies in the 1920s and 1930s, but before the Second World War there were still very few West Indians who actually saw a separation from Britain as possible or desirable.

1 *Education* One of the arguments used by colonial governors to deny representation in the government for the common people was that there were too few educated people to make any worthwhile contribution of opinion. In the small islands it was true that it would have been hard to find local members for the legislature who were well educated in the nineteenth century. However, by the second and third decades of the twentieth century there were plenty of Cambridge Certificate holders who resented the fact that they had no political rights. Their pressure led to the widespread introduction of the elective principle in 1924–25.

Those who had taken Island Scholarships rarely took part in nationalist movements. The obvious reason for this was that many of them did not return to the West Indies. Initially, the nationalists were drawn from the clerks and teachers. The higher professional classes such as doctors and lawyers made their big impact on the nationalist movement in the late 1930s when lawyers like Grantley Adams and Norman Manley entered nationalist politics.

2 *Economic development* Before the second half of the twentieth century, it was felt that a colony that was economically poor and dependent on the mother country could not be given independence. In the first thirty years of the twentieth century West Indian colonies had made great efforts to diversify their economies. They had also developed new markets which reduced their dependence on Britain. They were still colonial economies in that they could not generate their own investment for development in agriculture and industry, but relied on overseas investment chiefly from the mother country. Trinidad had the best prospects because of her mineral resources, but these were in the hands of foreigners.

However, the fact that they were colonial economies was not a drawback to attaining self-government. The important consideration was whether the colony was 'viable', that is, able to feed itself, able to pay for its imports with its exports and maintain an adequate standard of living for its people. The large colonies in the British West Indies were considered to be in this position and independence could not be withheld for economic reasons.

3 *Representative associations* In many islands the place of political parties was taken by representative government associations whose aim was to put pressure on the Colonial Office for a greater share in government. These associations were active in the 1920s. For example, in 1921 the Grenada Association demanded 'such a measure of representative government as will enable them to have an effective voice in their own government'. They wanted more people to be given the vote, elected members in the legislature, and later a majority of elected members over officials and nominated members.

Trinidad had perhaps the greatest claim for representation because the people had been denied it for well over a hundred years. There the demands came from the Legislative Reform Committee and the Trinidad Working Men's Association. In 1924 they were granted seven elected members.

4 *The Wood Report* In 1921 Major E.F.L. Wood, an under-secretary in the Colonial Office, was sent to the West Indies to report on social conditions, poverty, health and education after the recent distress. He also listened to the demands of the representative associations. He noted that education was becoming more widespread and creating a black and coloured class who were politically conscious. He recommended giving them some representation to prevent them adopting a more revolutionary attitude. The Wood Report and the demands of the representative associations were responsible for the constitutional changes before the Second World War.

5 *Working class unrest* The strikes and riots of 1935 to 1938 in the British West Indies probably

Marcus Garvey

made the greatest impact for constitutional change, although the impact was a negative one. The strikes and riots demonstrated the failure of Crown Colony government to achieve any contact with the common people and its inability to relieve distress or prevent disorder. The strikers were not demanding the right to vote for elected members, but were only making economic and social demands, like higher pay and more education. After the riots Crown Colony government had to give way to a more representative government. West Indians knew this and the British government had to accept that changes were necessary.

6 *Marcus Garvey* It is hard to assess the influence of Marcus Garvey and his United Negro Improvement Association as a force in bringing about constitutional change. His appeal was to the black masses who had no voting rights in the 1920s and were not at the time interested in their own political advancement. They hoped for improvement in their economic and social status first, and Garvey encouraged them to overcome the barriers which lay in the path of their rise in society. However, by giving the blacks a pride in their colour and hope for the future, he was laying the foundations for their future demands for political power.

The vast majority of the working classes were black. They had political 'muscle' through the trade union movement, but not through representation. The middle class nationalists were gaining representation. However, there was no alliance between these two classes. If there had been, the West Indian nationalist movements would have been much stronger and probably the advance towards self-government would have been much swifter. Unfortunately, just as the alliance between workers and nationalists was beginning in 1938 and 1939, the Second World War broke out and constitutional development was halted for five years.

7 *The Moyne Commission* The Royal Commission which visited the West Indies under Lord Moyne in 1938 to look into the causes of the recent unrest and make recommendations for the

Constitutional progress to independence

Comparative constitutional progress in the British West Indies

Territory	Elective principle	Majority elected in Leg. co.
Barbados		
British Guiana	1891 (Direct election)	1943
Jamaica	1884	1944
Trinidad	1924	1941

future, made its biggest contribution towards self-government in a roundabout way. It did not propose any definite constitutional reforms, but by setting up the Colonial Development and Welfare Organisation it helped the colonies to achieve economic viability and improved educational services. This created the foundation on which constitutional development could be made. As the Commission said, social reforms must come before constitutional development.

The Moyne Commission did not recommend self-government, but said that the people should have a greater share in their own government. However, it was referring to sectional representation, that is, business, industry and agriculture, rather than universal adult suffrage. The West Indian nationalists wanted universal adult suffrage because all sections would be represented if everyone had a vote. The Commission was probably trying to secure safeguards for minorities, in particular, for white interests which the nationalists did not want. The vagueness of the report on constitutional matters was one of its major weaknesses. The publication of the report was delayed until after the Second World War and by that time Jamaica had already achieved universal adult suffrage.

As a result of the Moyne Commission, the British government passed the Colonial Development and Welfare Act in 1940 by which a Welfare Fund was established. The money available to the British West Indies far exceeded the £1,000,000 per year recommended by the Moyne Commission. Between 1940 and 1964 an average of nearly £3,000,000 per year was drawn by the British West Indies. (Actually the average was lower in the early years, rising by the end of the period). While drawing on the fund the British West Indies were not, strictly speaking, economically viable, but as the capital drawn was used to establish industries and develop agriculture, viability was assured for the future. In the 1960s, the West Indies were more viable than many African countries which were given independence. The average per capita income was considerably higher.

Party system	Universal adult suffrage	Ministerial system	Prime Minister or Premier	Cabinet government	Full internal self-government	Independence
1946	1950	1954	1954	1958	1961	1966 (Nov)
1947	1953	1957	1953 Chief Minister 1961 Premier	1961	1961	1966 (May)
1944	1944	1953	1953 Chief Minister	1957 Council of Ministers 1958 Cabinet	1959	1962 (Aug)
1946	1945	1950	1956 Chief Minister 1959 Premier	1959	1961	1962 (Aug)

Explanation of terms

Elective principle Some members of the legislature are elected by the people. Initially, only a small proportion of the members are elected, rising to equal numbers with the officials, then to a majority over officials and nominated members. Eventually all the members of the legislature are elected.

Qualitative franchise The right to vote is based on a condition. Either the voter has to own a certain amount of property, earn a certain income, or be literate, or have a combination of these qualifications. There were qualifications for voting in the British West Indies until 1944.

Universal adult suffrage Everybody has a right to vote. At first, adult meant twenty-one years and over, but later it was lowered to eighteen.

The Executive This is the branch of the government which carries out the laws, usually the civil service. In colonial times the Governor was, and, sometimes still is, the head of the executive. In colonial times, members of the executive sitting in the legislature were known as 'officials'. They were career civil servants and were paid by the Crown.

Ministerial system The head of a government department (ministry) is chosen from the elected members of the legislature. Therefore some (or all) of the executive are elected by the people. They are not career civil servants, but their office depends upon election.

Responsible government The executive is responsible to the legislature because the ministers are chosen from the legislature and are answerable to it for their actions. They can be removed from office if their administration is not satisfactory.

At another stage in responsible government, the legislature is responsible to the electorate. Members of the legislature who, individually or collectively, do not satisfy the electors, will lose their seats.

Cabinet government The government is directed by a body of ministers (the cabinet) chosen by the Prime Minister. It is collectively responsible for the policy of the government and for its administration. One stage in constitutional development is when the Executive Council becomes a Cabinet.

Internal self-government The Prime Minister and his Cabinet from the majority party in the legislature control the government of the country in all domestic matters except, perhaps, security. Internal self-government may be partial when the governor retains his reserve powers of veto, or the right of proclaiming a state of emergency. Full internal self-government is when the governor no longer has reserve powers.

The difference between internal self-government and independence lies usually in the control of foreign affairs, defence and internal security. When responsibility for these is handed over from the colonial power to the national government, then the country is independent.

Typical stages to independence

The movement towards independence was by evolution, not by revolution, in the case of the British West Indian colonies. The moment of independence is a proud and dramatic one in a nation's history. But it is the final act in a process which has been taking place for months, if not years.

The movement towards independence is a constitutional one. Changes are made in the laws by which a country is governed, giving local people an ever-increasing share in their own government. It begins when people elect representatives to the legislature. For example, the people of Dominica were allowed to elect three members in 1925 – a small number, but it initiated a process which eventually led to independence in 1979.

The next step is an increase in the number of elected members. This usually coincided with an increase in the official and nominated members in the legislature. The balance is changed when the elected members become a majority. This enables them to carry through their own legislation or defeat the government's proposed legislation. This stage is not as radical as it appears because the elected members are not a united force, like a political party, and the Governor still has overriding powers to carry through government legislation and to veto other legislation.

In the British West Indies, Crown Colony government came to an end initially in Jamaica in 1944. One house of the legislature was completely elected by universal adult suffrage, enabling the elected members to make the laws. The other house could block these laws or the Governor could veto them, but that would have been against the spirit of the constitutional changes which aimed at handing over the legislative power to the representatives of the people. It was this stage that West Indian nationalists regarded as the turning point between remaining a colony or proceeding to independence. It was accompanied by a gradual reduction in the number of officials in the Upper House (Legislative Council) until it became a Senate of West Indians, nominated by party leaders and formally approved and appointed by the Governor.

The Executive Council in a colony consisted originally of leading colonial civil servants, plus one or two others nominated by the Governor. The Council was solely responsible to the Crown and the legislature had no control over it. The evolution from Executive Council to Cabinet began when an elected member from the legislature was nominated to the executive. At first this made little difference because the elected member was not given responsibility for a government department. Once he was given this responsibility, it marked the beginning of the ministerial system. When there were several such ministers, the executive could be called a Council of Ministers, although there were still *ex-officio* members, such as the Attorney-General, the Financial Secretary and the Chief Secretary. When these officials were dropped from the Council, the executive became a Cabinet. This is fully responsible government and very close to independence.

Once there was a totally elected house in the legislature, parties were formed to control a majority of votes in the elected chamber. When elected members were promoted to the executive, they had to be chosen from the majority party if responsible government was to be achieved. Earlier ministers had been chosen with a view to keeping a balance between the parties. When all ministers were chosen from the majority party, the leader of that party became the 'Prime Minister' or 'Premier'.

Before independence there were usually two houses, one completely elected, the other with a majority nominated by the Prime Minister and a minority nominated by the Leader of the Opposition. The Prime Minister selected a Cabinet from the elected members. They decided government policy and were individually responsible for a government department. They were collectively and individually responsible to the elected chamber and therefore responsible to the people who elected it. The only remaining official in the government was the Governor. He stood between colonial status and independence, although his powers had gradually been reduced. At the last stage, he held responsibility for foreign affairs, defence, and, sometimes, internal security. When he handed these over, there was independence.

Independence in the British West Indies was part of a peaceful process of constitutional development. Rebellion or unrest merely delayed the process, as happened in British Guiana which achieved independence four years after Jamaica and Trinidad, although it had been running almost parallel in constitutional development ten years earlier.

The other side to the independence movement was the political one in which the passions of the nationalists played their part. They did not quarrel about the goal and often not even about the timetable, but about who was to control the power when independence was achieved and what policies were to be followed.

Independence in the 1960s

Jamaica

After the troubles of 1938, Norman Manley formed the People's National Party and demanded universal adult suffrage. This was a direct appeal to the workers who responded with a seventy-two per cent turn-out at the 1944 elections, a very high percentage for a developing country. The 1944 Constitution made the House of Representatives fully elective. The Legislative Council was nominated. Five elected members joined five officials and the Governor on the Executive Council, but the elected members did not have responsibility for individual government departments.

The Jamaica Labour Party won the 1944 election, gaining twenty-five of the thirty-two seats, and it also won the 1949 elections, although with a reduced majority. The firm support of the Bustamante Industrial Trade Union made these victories possible.

The Constitution of 1953 was initiated by the progressive Governor, Sir Hugh Foot, in consultation with Bustamante and Manley. It brought in the ministerial system with a Chief Minister and seven ministers who held a majority in the Executive Council. All these seven were elected members of the House of Representatives. It resulted in some degree of responsible government, although a colonial-appointed Attorney-General was still the government's legal officer and a Colonial Secretary controlled internal security, the police and the Civil Service. Bustamante was the first Chief Minister and the Jamaica Labour Party was the first partially responsible government.

The support of the National Workers' Union enabled Manley and the People's National Party to win the 1955 election by eighteen seats to fourteen from the Jamaica Labour Party. The Chief Minister was given more power to govern by the 1957 Constitution which set up a Council of Ministers of eleven, of whom eight or nine were to be appointed from the Legislative Council on the advice of the Chief Minister. This was still only partial internal self-government, since the Attorney-General remained *ex-officio* in the executive. However, an elected Minister of Home Affairs replaced the Colonial Secretary and a Minister of Finance replaced the Financial Secretary.

The Constitution of 1958 brought about full internal self-government because the Attorney-General was removed from the executive, which then became a Cabinet. Internal affairs were controlled by an elected government, although the Governor retained control of foreign affairs and defence. However, he could use his reserve powers, for example to suspend the Constitution and declare a state of emergency, only on the advice of the Prime Minister.

Manley was a firm believer in federation; Bustamante supported it with reservations. When the Federation did not live up to expectations, Bustamante declared it to be against the interests of Jamaican workers. Manley agreed to a referendum on federation and in September, 1961, the Jamaican people rejected both it and Manley. It was a triumph for Bustamante.

Jamaica withdrew from the Federation and asked the British government for separate independence. Before the end of 1961 an Independence Constitution had been drawn up by Special Committees of both Houses.

There was to be a House of Representatives of forty-five members, and a Senate of twenty-one members, thirteen nominated by the Prime Minister and eight by the Leader of the Opposition. The latter was a safeguard against any constitutional change which might lead to a one-party state. The executive was to be under the control of a Cabinet responsible to both Houses. A Governor-General was to represent the Queen. Jamaica was to be a Dominion within the British Commonwealth.

The date set for Independence was 6 August, 1962. In the pre-Independence election the Jamaica Labour Party won twenty-six seats, the People's National Party, nineteen. Therefore Sir Alexander Bustamante became the first Prime Minister of an independent Jamaica.

Trinidad and Tobago

Trinidad was the last of the four major colonies to have elected members in its legislature (1924). There were no further changes until 1941 when a majority of elected members over nominated members in the Legislative Council and an unofficial majority in the executive was granted. Universal adult suffrage was introduced in 1945 and in the 1946 election there were two main parties, the British Empire Workers' and Citizen's Home Rule Party led by Uriah Butler, and the West Indian National Party led by Dr Patrick Solomon. Both parties were unsatisfactory contenders for political power. Butler failed to win a seat for himself, and the West Indian National Party was very disunited.

Butler won a seat in the 1950 election, but was not called upon to form a government because he could not command a majority. The Governor preferred to call upon a coalition of nominated and official members together with other elected members under Albert Gomes.

The first truly united national party in Trinidad and Tobago was formed in 1956 by Dr Eric Williams. It was called the People's National Movement and was pledged to carry the nation to early self-government and independence. The People's National Movement won the 1956 election by a bare majority and increased its majority in the 1961 election. The increased majority was the result of a vigorous programme

Independence parade in Trinidad

of public works and social services in the party's five year plan. The party was fortunate in that this programme coincided with a period of extraordinarily high economic growth between 1955 and 1961. Many of the projects were financed from internal sources which gave proof of Trinidad's economic viability.

The People's National Movement took Trinidad and Tobago into the Federation in 1958, but had second thoughts later when the issue of freedom of movement between member countries arose. With such a buoyant economy Trinidad felt that she would be swamped by immigrant workers from the other islands. After Jamaica's withdrawal, Trinidad too withdrew, although Williams and the People's Party still felt committed to some larger association, such as a Caribbean Economic Community.

Eric Williams decided to press for independence outside the Federation. Trinidad had proved that it could support itself and had avoided the racial conflict that plagued British Guiana, although its racial composition was similar. Williams had been careful to emphasise that the People's National Movement was a multi-racial party, although it attracted more African than Indian support. The Democratic Labour Party under Dr Rudranath Capildeo became the predominantly Indian party.

An Independence Constitution was drafted by members of both parties. Capildeo was most concerned about safeguards for minorities and for the parliamentary opposition. In May, 1962, both parties and the British government met at a Constitutional Conference in London, and the date set for independence was August, 1962. It was agreed to hold elections before independence to decide who should form the first national government. Dr Eric Williams and the People's National Movement had a clear victory. On 31 August, 1962, Trinidad became an independent state within the British Commonwealth.

British Guiana

British Guiana had institutions which were further advanced constitutionally than most other territories in the British West Indies. In the Combined Court the elected members had had control over finance for a long time. However, due to its overspending, the Combined Court was abolished in 1928 and a Legislative Council was set up. The Court of Policy still appeared, but it was given an entirely new function. In 1943 the elected members became a majority in the Legislative Council.

Political parties first appeared in the 1947 election. They were the Political Affairs Committee of Dr Cheddi Jagan, the British Guiana Labour Party of Dr J. B. Singh and the Manpower Citizens' Association, a group of candidates put up by a trade union. In 1950, the Political Affairs Committee and the British Guiana Labour Party merged to form the People's Progressive Party which had the support of the masses or those of the masses entitled to vote. Jagan was its leader and Linden Forbes Sampson Burnham, who had recently returned to British Guiana, was its chairman.

A new Constitution in 1953 brought in universal adult suffrage, a House of Assembly of twenty-four elected and three *ex-officio* members, and a State Council of nine, of whom six were nominated by the Governor, two by the leader of the majority party and one by the leader of the opposition. Six of the ministers in the Court of Policy were selected from the elected members of the House of Assembly to be responsible individually for a government department. However, they were not to be responsible to the legislature, but to the Governor. Officials made up the rest of the Court of Policy.

In the 1953 election the People's Progressive Party won eighteen of the twenty-four elected seats. Jagan campaigned on a programme of rapid self-government. His speeches were anti-British and anti-Imperialist and the British government suspended the Constitution in October, accusing Jagan of communist subversion. This was a big set-back for the constitutional progress of British Guiana because for four years, from 1953 to 1957, there was a caretaker government nominated entirely by the Governor.

Jagan and Burnham parted company in 1955, a move with lasting repercussions for British Guiana. Jagan was open about his anti-British feeling. He was not prepared to work with the Governor and officials, was impatient for independence and boasted of his links with the communists. Burnham was more pragmatic, realising that Jagan's tactics had hindered the cause of self-government. However, the greatest repercussion was on race relations. Jagan was Indian by race, and Burnham, African. Party politics was henceforth divided on racial lines and Jagan appeared to encourage the division. For example he introduced the slogan *apanjaht* into politics. This meant 'supporting one's race'. After the split Jagan remained leader of the People's Progressive Party and Burnham formed the People's National Congress.

The People's Progressive Party won the 1957 election and the 1961 election, but with a reduced majority. Another new party, the United Force, led by Mr Peter Stanislaus d' Aguiar, entered the election. It was a right-wing party attempting to counter-balance Jagan's left-wing party. However, the United Force and the People's National Party could only control fourteen seats together, while the People's Progressive Party had twenty.

By 1961, there was an elected Assembly and a Cabinet. The majority party was responsible for government and really only the Governor stood between British Guiana and self-government. The 1960 Constitutional Conference had considered setting a date for independence in 1962. However, once again Jagan's bold policies led to trouble and independence was delayed for four years. His austerity budget in late 1961 caused more trouble. It brought in exchange control, placed prohibitive duties on imported luxuries, high duties on imported foods and very high taxation on the wealthy. Trouble broke out early in 1962. The Trades Union Council called a general strike. In Georgetown all the shops closed and, in the riots which followed, they were looted and homes set on fire. Inter-racial violence increased, reaching a climax in 1964. The Governor declared a state of emergency and the chances of early independence receded.

Nevertheless, there was a Constitutional Conference in London in October, 1962, to plan an Independence Constitution. The party differences were brought into the open and were irreconcilable. The People's National Congress allied with the United Force to demand elections before independence. They wanted the voting age to be twenty-one and, most important of all, proportional representation to lessen the influence of voting on racial lines. The People's Progressive Party wanted no elections before independence, the voting age to be eighteen years, and a single-member constituency system. In 1963 the three party leaders asked Duncan Sandys, the Secretary of State, to resolve their differences. He adopted the People's National Congress/United Force proposals in their entirety. Jagan reacted by calling a Citizen's Freedom Rally and a strike by the Guiana Agricultural Worker's Union. Neither action led to the show of support he had hoped for. The racial clashes were becoming worse. Africans resented Jagan's pro-Indian measures, in particular the control of schools; the Labour Relations Bill which gave official recognition to the Guiana Agricultural Workers' Union, composed mainly of Indian estate workers, and gave them thirty per cent control on the Trades Union Council; increased acreage for rice cultivators; subsidies for small farmers; and incentives for Indians in business. By 1964 British Guiana was so sharply divided on racial lines that 176 people were killed, over 900 injured and 1,400 homes destroyed.

In spite of this the British government wanted British Guiana's independence. Party antagonism became more acute when Jagan won the 1964 election with twenty-four seats, but this was not an overall majority. Burnham formed a coalition with the United Force which gave him twenty-nine seats and the Governor asked him to form a government. Jagan was furious at losing power for the first time since 1947 and boycotted the 1965 Independence Conference. There were no further elections before independence and Forbes Burnham became the first Premier of the independent state of Guyana in May, 1966.

Barbados

Barbados had never been a Crown Colony. Her Assembly had been in existence for over three hundred years. In spite of this, she was the last of the four major colonies to achieve independence. Delays were caused by minority governments, internal party strife and, finally, federation.

Rioters in Georgetown

After a further extension of the franchise in 1944 the electorate was only one step away from universal adult suffrage. Political parties were contesting twenty-four seats in the 1946 election, which was important not only because of the large number of electors, but also because of the Bushe Constitution. This was an experiment in responsible Government whereby the leader of the majority party was to head a group of four elected members in the Executive Committee. However, the election was inconclusive; no party had an overall majority. Grantley Adams' party, the Barbados Labour Party, had to form a coalition with the West Indian National Congress. Together they controlled sixteen seats, but Adams could not take all the places on the Executive Council for his party, which made responsible government impossible.

Adams again failed to obtain a satisfactory majority in the 1948 election. In fact, after nominating a Speaker for the Assembly from his party, he was leading a minority government. He felt frustrated by both his political and his constitutional difficulties. His party was supported by the Barbados Workers's Union and he was pledged to carry out a policy of nationalisation of public utilities and some government ownership in the sugar industry. The Legislative Council, composed entirely of whites, blocked his reforms because they supported private ownership. A conflict between the Assembly and Council developed. In 1949 the Council threw out a bill for holidays with pay, another essential part of Adam's labour legislation.

The introduction of universal adult suffrage strengthened Adams' position because, as labour leader, he could rely on the working-class vote. Adams felt that it was time to press for further constitutional changes towards self-government in 1950. He proposed a ministerial system consisting of five ministers who would be individually responsible for their ministries and collectively responsible for the government's policy which the Governor would have to accept. The Barbados Labour Party won the 1951 election with an overall majority as expected. Unfortunately, party strife began to bedevil Barbadian politics and it soon slowed down the pace of constitutional advance. Adams abandoned his old policies of nationalisation, and the leadership of the left wing of the party passed to the newly-elected Errol Barrow. Thus a split in the party occurred just when Adams had achieved a working majority. Eventually Barrow formed a new party, the Democratic Labour Party, which later took over the support of the Workers' Union.

Initially, the split did not seem important. The Barbados Labour Party won fifteen seats in the 1956 election, an overall majority. Barrow lost his seat. Adams was at the peak of his power in 1958 when the Cabinet system was introduced in Barbados. He was the Premier and his government seemed firmly in control. Later in the year he became Premier of the British West Indies Federation. However, Frank Walcott broke the traditional alliance between the Barbados Workers' Union and the Barbados Labour Party and transferred his support to the opposition. Barrow created a 'shadow' cabinet and was able to convince Iain McLeod, the Secretary of State, that there was a responsible opposition. While Adams was involved in the Federation, Barrow and his party were gaining popularity and joining in the attacks on Adams' premiership of the Federation.

Errol Barrow

The Barbados Labour Party played into the hands of the opposition by the Deep Water Harbour Scheme. This was necessary for the economic development of the island, but one of its immediate results was the loss of two thousand jobs. The Democratic Labour Party attacked the government over this and criticised it for failing to create employment. The result was that the Democratic Labour Party had a sweeping victory in the 1961 election, winning most of the working-class vote because of the past government's unemployment record. In the run-up to the election, the Barbados Labour Party missed Adams' leadership and did not conduct such a vigorous campaign as the opposition.

Barrow felt that it was essential for his government to do something about job creation because he had attacked the Barbados Labour Party on this issue. He initiated many public works and improvements in social services, building roads and dams, cutting canals, clearing land and planting forests, improving sanitation and cleaning the streets. All these projects created jobs and convinced the voters that they had elected a man of action who kept his word.

At this stage Barbados had a strong government which was in full control of the internal affairs of the country, just one step away from independence. However, Barbados was a member of the Federation and even when Jamaica and Trinidad left in 1962, Barbados did not do so. She remained associated with the 'Little Eight'. It was not loyalty to the smaller islands which kept Barbados in this association, but a genuine belief that she had to be part of a larger economic unit and a fear that she could not support herself so well in the future.

Politically Barrow's position was secure apart from one setback in 1964 known as the 'Windfall Crisis'. Adams backed the sugar workers in their demand for a share-out of the industry's unexpected profits, whereas the Barbados Workers' Union Executive wanted to put the profits into a fund. The Union Executive was forced to give way and Barrow lost some support because he put off holding the election promised for 1964. Otherwise his record in office was very good and in 1965 he decided to ask for the separate independence for which Barbados had been ready four years earlier.

Barbados withdrew from the 'Little Eight' and a Constitutional Conference was held at Lancaster House to draw up an Independence Constitution. The date for independence was set for November, 1966, and Barrow agreed to an election to see who should form the first government. In spite of his impressive record Barrow did not win this election as easily as he had anticipated. The Democratic Labour Party won fourteen seats, the Barbados Labour Party eight, and the Barbados National Party two. The relative narrowness of this result was because Adams campaigned on a slogan of 'democracy v dictatorship' and there was a rumour that Barrow was seeking to establish a one-party state.

On 30 November, 1966, Barbados became an independent state within the Commonwealth, with the Queen as Head of State, represented by a Governor-General and with a Prime Minister as head of government. The latter governs with a Cabinet which is responsible to an elected House of Assembly and a nominated Senate. This Constitution can only be amended by a two-thirds majority of both Houses or by a referendum of the people.

The non-self-governing British Territories

Constitutional development

The territories considered here are Antigua-Barbuda-Redonda, British Honduras (Belize), Cayman Islands, Dominica, Grenada, Montserrat, St Lucia, St Kitts-Nevis-Anguilla, St Vincent, Turks and Caicos Islands and the British Virgin Islands.

Between 1951 and 1954 they were granted universal adult suffrage. They had single-chamber legislatures in which the majority of members were elected. In the mid-1950s, ministerial systems were introduced. Finally, by the early 1960s they were self-governing colonies, with their legislatures almost entirely elected, although usually up to three nominated officials remained. Their Executive Councils consisted of locally-elected ministers responsible for minor departments such as health, education, agriculture, tourism and natural resources, with the key ministries like finance, internal affairs and justice in the hands of colonial officials.

In most colonies except the very small ones there were active political parties. The leaders of the majority parties were known as Chief Ministers from 1960–61. For colonies to run smoothly under such constitutions required considerable co-operation between Chief Ministers and Governors. The Crown always retained control of foreign affairs and defence and, in some colonies, internal security, including all aspects of law and order.

Associated statehood

Most of the smaller territories joined the Federation of the West Indies in 1958 as separate units. These were Antigua, Montserrat, St Kitts-Nevis-Anguilla from the Leeward Islands, and from the Windward Islands, Grenada, St Vincent, St Lucia and Dominica.

When Barbados withdrew in 1965 from the East Caribbean Territories, known as the 'Little Eight', the remaining colonies became separate units again. In 1966 each became an 'Associated State'. Under the Associated State Agreement, 1967, Antigua-Barbuda-Redonda, St Kitts-Nevis-Anguilla, Dominica, Grenada, St Lucia and St Vincent entered into a free and voluntary association with Britain. Either the British government or an individual state can terminate this Agreement unilaterally.

The constitution for each island was as follows:
1   A Governor representing the Queen as Head of State;
2   A two-chamber legislature consisting of a Senate and a House of Representatives, the latter elected by universal adult suffrage;
3   The government to be controlled by a Premier and a Cabinet drawn from the majority party;
4   The seven states to share one Supreme Court.

This constitution could only be amended by negotiation with Britain or by a referendum of the people. Any proposal by an island for independence would require either a two-thirds majority of both Houses or a two-thirds majority in a referendum. Each state had full internal self-government with the Crown retaining control over foreign affairs and defence.

Apart from their general agreement with Britain, the states were linked to each other under the West Indies (Associated States) Council of Ministers which met periodically to discuss common problems. In 1968 they formed an economic federation known as the East Caribbean Common Market (E.C.C.M.). Individually they participate in the Caribbean Free Trade Area (CARIFTA) and the Caribbean Development Bank.

Remaining colonies

The Cayman Islands, Montserrat, Turks and Caicos and the Virgin Islands chose to keep Crown Colony status with partial self-government. For example, the Attorney-General, Financial Secretary and Chief Secretary usually remained colonial officials. The Crown has retained control of more departments like police and immigration, and influences others like health and education.

Independence in the 1970s

Grenada   Grenada was the first territory to end its associated statehood with Britain. Eric Gairy, leader of the Grenada United Labour Party and Chief Minister in the early 1960s, had always favoured an independent course from the other East Caribbean islands. He kept Grenada outside the 'Little Eight' and stopped trying to associate Grenada with Trinidad and Tobago when he realised that she would probably become merely a ward of Trinidad. In 1966 Grenada accepted associated statehood, but when Gairy was re-elected as Chief Minister in 1972 he announced his intention of seeking independence for Grenada. This was achieved in February, 1974. Unfortunately many Grenadians felt that Gairy had sought independence as a political manoeuvre rather than from genuine conviction and because of this there were riots and strikes.

Dominica   Dominica became independent in November, 1978. As with Grenada, it was accompanied by much controversy because Patrick R. John, leading the Dominica Labour Party, did not submit to an election first or call for a referendum.

St Lucia   St Lucia attended a constitutional conference on independence in 1978 and John Compton, the Prime Minister, announced December, 1978 as the date for independence. Because of opposition, however, independence was not finally achieved until February 22, 1979.

St Vincent   Milton Cato proposed to take St

Vincent to independence in 1979, but this was postponed.

Antigua Antigua, under Vere Bird as Prime Minister and leader of the Labour Party, did not consider independence until recently. The opposition have insisted on a general election before the matter is carried further.

St Kitts-Nevis-Anguilla Soon after this group entered associated statehood, Anguilla seceded with much bitterness on both sides. This was caused by Anguilla's dislike for Robert Bradshaw, the Prime Minister of St Kitts. St Kitts wanted Anguilla to be brought back into the group and negotiations went on for two years. In 1969 Ronald Webster declared himself 'President' of an independent Anguilla. The British sent in paratroops and were accused of 'bullying' and, more seriously, of operating double standards because they had not taken the same action when white-ruled Rhodesia declared independence in 1965. On the other hand, Anguilla's unilateral declaration of independence was not popular amongst other Caribbean territories. Anguilla was forced to accept a special constitutional agreement with Britain with separate self-government, but not independence, in 1976.

Belize (British Honduras) The constitutional advance of Belize almost matched that of the larger territories which gained independence in the 1960s. The chief obstacle to independence is the claim that her neighbour, Guatemala, is making on her territory. While this continues, Belize remains under the protection of Britain for defence and foreign affairs, but has full internal self-government.

Premier George Price, leading the People's United Party, has raised the question of independence many times. In 1977 and 1978 Britain discussed the ceding of some territory to Guatemala to appease her claim, and then giving independence to Belize. However, Belize would not agree to any loss of territory nor was she convinced that Guatemala's claim would be appeased by this. In 1978 there were discussions between Belize, Britain and Guatemala in New York and Guatemala was less pressing. Britain is attempting a solution, and if this is achieved Belize will move immediately to independence.

British paratroopers in Anguilla

Post-independence problems

Political problems

1 *'Westminster pattern' or one-party state* Most British West Indian states have had three hundred years of colonial rule. In this period they inherited the British system of government known as the 'Westminster pattern' of government. Although suited to a developed country like Britain, it has been criticised and attacked in the post-independence, developing world, and has been abandoned by some countries, for example, Tanzania. As yet no ex-British Caribbean state has officially abandoned it, although this is a possibility in St Lucia and Grenada after two recent coups.

The argument against the Westminster pattern is that in the developing world the keynote must be development. Developing countries cannot afford the luxury of the two-party system or opposition. Thus many of them have become one-party states.

However, the long traditions of the Westminster pattern have bred a suspicion of any alternative and a real fear of the one-party system. British Caribbean countries sought safeguards against one-party government and dictatorship in their Independence Constitutions. To amend the constitution in many states requires a two-thirds majority in both Houses. In the Senate sometimes one-third of the seats are nominated by the Leader of the Opposition. This effectively stops constitutional change and the adoption of the one-party system. In some states the constitution can be amended by referendum. This means that a very popular leader could secure a constitutional change and bring in a one-party state.

Advocates of the one-party system for developing countries argue that it is not a denial of democracy. Opposition can exist but it is contained within one party.

2 *Political independence and economic dependence* It is argued that a state cannot be politically independent if it is economically dependent on foreigners. British Caribbean states, on achieving independence, still had the legacy of colonial economies which had permitted foreign ownership of their resources, industries and agriculture. Development is dependent on foreign investment and yet politicians in newly independent countries are in a dilemma. They want to be completely independent, but to break away from economic dependence would hurt national development and bring hardship to their people. Politicians realise that, if they value democracy, they are dependent on the votes of the people to keep them in office. They either have to persuade the people that some suffering is necessary to maintain independence or they have to accept the passive role of puppets of foreign powers. The other possibility open to them is to abandon democracy and set themselves up as dictators to force through unpopular measures.

3 *Non-alignment* Newly-independent countries are very proud of their status and resent any threat to their independence. Each country wants to keep apart from others and is wary of any political associations. Isolationism is a problem, because even the whole of the British Caribbean is small in a world context and individual countries of the Caribbean are smaller still. It is difficult for them to pursue independent foreign policies, especially as the super-powers, the United States and Russia (through Cuba), will not allow them to be isolationist.

The British Caribbean suffers the threat of domination by the United States because of its geographical position and because the latter has taken over the role of economic partner and military protector. The United States favours capitalist democracies and vigorously opposes socialist and communist governments throughout the world, but especially in the Americas.

Independent Caribbean states resent this kind of American pressure which seeks to destroy their independence even in internal policies. Some feel powerless to resist it because of their smallness. Others do not want to resist because they admire the United States and support her policies. Those who want to end United States domination have turned to Cuba.

Cuba herself successfully challenged United States domination in 1959. To many, Cuba under Castro has become the 'success story' of the Caribbean; a demonstration of how the small can successfully resist the big. Yet Cuba has passed from United States to Russian domination. Castro has established Moscow-style communism in the Caribbean and has admitted that Cuba will be heavily dependent on Russia for the next twenty years.

If ex-British Caribbean states seek Cuba's help to break away from United States domination, they are not making themselves independent but merely substituting one foreign influence for another. Castro is definitely trying to spread Cuban-style communism throughout the western hemisphere. It seems from the 1979 Summit of Non-Aligned Nations in Havana that he is succeeding.

Earlier in 1979, he was encouraged by the successful left-wing Sandinista revolt against a United States-backed regime in Nicaragua. Also in 1979, Sir Eric Gairy's government was overthrown by a left-wing coup which Castro praised. Since then he has sent Cuban aid to Grenada. Three other areas in the British Caribbean where Cuba has been extending her influence are Jamaica, St Lucia and Guyana. In Jamaica, Michael Manley has been accepting Cuban aid for the past five years and adopting socialist policies for even longer. At the 1979 Havana Summit, Forbes Burnham gave support to Castro's foreign policies and, like Manley, he claims that to follow Cuba does not mean to put oneself in the Russian camp.

The United States has urged Britain to use her influence to resist Cuba's new role in the Caribbean. British Caribbean states are facing the same problems as the rest of the Third World in the question of non-alignment. Can a small, developing country be non-aligned? Tanzania claims that it is possible. However, in the bi-polarised world it seems that to throw off one of the super-powers is to fall under the influence of the other.

Economic problems

A newly-independent country must aim at a high level of economic growth to satisfy the expectations of its people. Economic growth creates political stability which encourages investment and promotes further growth. Thus a circle of growth is produced:

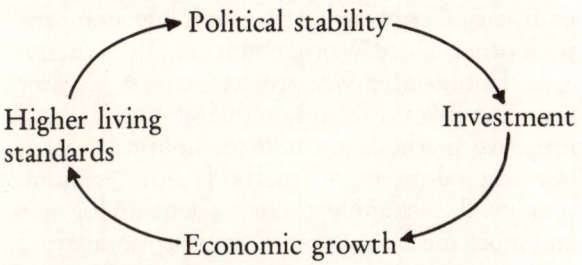

A growth rate of five per cent is considered good, but if this falls to one per cent the government is usually blamed even though the fall may be due to forces beyond its control.

In the British West Indies the Colonial Development and Welfare Act in 1940 resulted in a high level of development in the immediate pre-independence era, but this has since been difficult to maintain.

1 *The colonial economy* The problem of the colonial economy is a basic one in all ex-British Caribbean countries. Their resources, industries and businesses were owned by foreigners; sugar estates throughout the islands, oil in Trinidad, bauxite in Guyana and Jamaica, banks and insurance companies everywhere, even a relatively new industry like tourism, were foreign-owned. This economic dependence was intolerable for a newly-independent government.

Development could only continue while foreign investors maintained confidence in the country and while their investments were profitable. Confidence depended on political stability, and investors could be frightened off by socialist policies, especially nationalisation, and by closer links with Cuba in foreign policy.

Nationalisation is a means of breaking the colonial economy because the state takes over the assets of foreign-owned companies. However, it brings other problems. Nationalisation without compensation inevitably brings retaliation, such as the cutting off of loans, or even intervention. Nationalisation with compensation means that the government has to find large sums of money to buy the assets, or work out terms by which the money can be paid over a longer period. Frequently developing countries work out an arrangement whereby the state takes over sixty per cent of the stock and the foreign company retains forty per cent. Even a 51–49 per cent division of stock is common in developing countries. Foreign companies usually accept these arrangements to cut their losses. In the ex-British Caribbean the most famous example of nationalisation has been the takeover of the Demerara Bauxite Company by the Guyana government in 1970. Nationalisation ends private foreign investment unless the government gives special guarantees, but some governments consider that it is worthwhile. They may be intending to rely on loans from foreign governments and international bodies like the World Bank.

Developing countries often set up their own Development Corporations. These bodies have to work closely with politicians and advise them as to what projects are feasible. Development Corporations give confidence to foreign governments willing to lend money, because they have assessed the viability of the project beforehand. They are common in the ex-British Caribbean states, for example, the Barbados Development Board of 1955 which became the Barbados Industrial Development Corporation in 1969, and the Guyana Development Corporation, founded in 1963. Often these Development Corporations have a monopoly of industrial development so that the government can co-ordinate its development programme. Thus a private individual wanting to build a hotel or factory must apply to the Development Corporation for approval.

The ideal way to break the colonial economy is for the developing country to generate its own investment. However, most countries are unable to do this. If they could, they would not be 'developing'. In the ex-British Caribbean, Trinidad is best placed to do so. At the time of independence, many of the ex-British territories founded their own development banks. These are not commercial banks, most of which are still foreign-owned, but investment banks; for example, Jamaica has the Development Finance Corporation and the Bank of Jamaica (1960), which is the government bank. Such financial institutions help to provide money from internal sources for investment and have been very useful in helping to break the colonial economy. For the ex-British Caribbean as a whole, there is the Caribbean Development Bank with its headquarters in Bridgetown. This provides loans from internal funds for high-priority projects throughout the region.

On the approach of independence and the prospect of the ending of the colonial economy, money is often withdrawn from a country. To prevent this, governments introduce exchange controls, but with reluctance because they inhibit any money being brought into the country. Thereafter, to attract foreign money, governments have to give guarantees that interest on investments or profits can be taken out in foreign currency. The imposition of exchange controls is a sign of loss of confidence in a developing country and, while they exist, it is hard to restore that confidence even by special guarantees.

2 *Unemployment* By comparison with other developing countries, the level of unemployment in the ex-British Caribbean is not high. In a book entitled *The Economics of Underdeveloped Countries* by Bauer and Yamey, published in the early 1960s, the definition of 'under-developed' was when eighty per cent of the population were subsistence livers with no cash income. Definitions have changed, but even to-day most developing countries have over fifty per cent of their population who are not dependent on wage income. In the ex-British Caribbean the level of unemployment varies, but it is well below fifty per cent in the four major territories. It fluctuates from between twelve to fifteen per cent and often depends on which politician is making the assessment.

Although this is low compared with the rest of the Third World, it signifies considerable hardship as there is not much subsistence living in the ex-British Caribbean, especially in an island like Barbados. Moreover it is a comparatively high level of unemployment for the Americas. The proximity of the United States and the fact that the dollar bloc is such a fast-growing area, makes a twenty per cent unemployment level seem unacceptable.

In the ex-British Caribbean, unemployment will remain high while the birth-rate is high. The population growth in most territories is about three per cent. Barbados has been most successful in reducing population growth to about one per cent through family planning, but the other territories have not done so well. The birth-rate outstrips the rate at which new jobs are created and there is increasing unemployment. It is significant that, where the overall unemployment rate is perhaps twenty per cent, in the sixteen to twenty-five year-old group it is over thirty per cent.

Another reason for the high level of unemployment is that the average *per capita* income in the ex-British Caribbean territories is high compared with other Third World countries. This discourages labour-intensive projects, since investors want the greatest return on their money. Labour-intensive methods are best for political reasons, but capital-intensive methods for economic reasons. For example, there is a demand for more and more mechanisation in the sugar industry. It is resisted because the industry is such a large employer that greater mechanisation would cause intolerable unemployment.

3 *High per capita income* Paradoxically, a high *per capita* income causes problems when it accompanies high unemployment. In 1977, the *per capita* income in Barbados was $2,700 (local dollars). Contrast this with an average *per capita* income of $200 in the poorest Third World countries. The contrast between relatively rich income-earners and the extremely poor unemployed with no state welfare assistance creates social problems which result in a high level of crime and social and political unrest, for example, the frequent troubles of all kinds in West Kingston.

What seems a high *per capita* income by Third World standards is very low by United States standards, and this also causes dissatisfaction. The proximity of the United States to the Caribbean makes awareness of the different standards of living unavoidable. Economic influences from the United States pervade the Caribbean. In a Dominica hotel a United States tourist may spend more on an evening meal than the waiter earns in a week.

4 *Diversification* In colonial times, one of the greatest economic problems was monoculture, or the one-crop economy. From 1900 to 1925 there were attempts at diversification in agriculture, but most of these failed with the exception of the banana industry. This dependence on agriculture is a handicap to economic development in most of the territories. Only Trinidad with asphalt and oil, and Guyana and Jamaica with bauxite and alumina, have significant mineral resources to help their development.

Since independence, Jamaica has diversified considerably. Exports were dominated by sugar until fruit took over in the 1950s. Sugar came back in the 1960s, but bauxite and alumina were rising in value and by 1969 minerals accounted for half the value of Jamaica's exports.

Barbados still relies heavily on sugar, but tourism has rescued the country from the dangers of the one-crop economy. The tourist boom started as long ago as 1960, but the really tremendous surge came in 1969 when Barbados recorded its lowest sugar output for twenty years. The effects of the world recession of 1974–5 were felt in 1976 when tourism declined. In 1977 it recovered again, but these fluctuations show that it is not safe to rely on tourism which is subject to forces beyond the control of the island governments.

Tourism has also rescued Antigua whose economy had been heavily dependent on sugar and sea-island cotton. The airport has been enlarged, the harbour deepened and new hotels constructed. In a small island like Antigua, tourism supports many secondary industries like crafts and also provides long-term work in the construction industry. Thus the whole economy expands and the *per capita* income rises.

Tourism is a possible means of economic growth for most of the islands. However, its success depends on internal political stability. In 1979, unrest in Dominica, Grenada and St Lucia put their tourist industries at risk.

6
Movements towards independence II

Luis Muñoz Marin

The French Caribbean

The present-day French Caribbean consists of the islands of Guadeloupe and Martinique in the Lesser Antilles, and French Guiana or Guyane in South America. Guadeloupe itself has many dependent islands; the neighbouring ones of Marie Galante, La Désirade and Les Îles des Saintes and the far-flung ones of Saint Barthélemy and Saint-Martin in the Leewards. With the exception of St Barthélemy, bought from Sweden in 1877, these territories were French possessions by 1814–15.

After 1815 the constitutional position of the French empire reflected the constitutional changes which took place in France. Basically, when there was a monarchy there was absolute rule with strong centralised government, and when there was a republic there was popular representation and more local autonomy. In 1815 Louis XVIII was restored to the French throne. French possessions in the Caribbean became part of the royal domain, in other words, Crown Colonies. Slavery, which had been re-established by Napoleon in 1802, continued as a legal institution but, with the creation of the Second Republic in 1848 it was abolished. Immediately the freed slaves were given full political rights and universal adult male suffrage was introduced. However, when Napoleon III made himself Emperor by a coup in 1852, universal suffrage was abolished. This Second Empire lasted from 1852 to 1870. Governors with immense power ruled in the colonies and social and political life was dominated by the *grands blancs*.

In 1871, the Third Republic resulted in many constitutional changes. French Caribbean colonies were given representation in the French Assembly in Paris and this was the beginning of the policy of 'assimilation' which dominated French imperialist policy until the decolonisation struggles in Indo-China and Algeria in the 1950s. It continued in the French Caribbean in spite of the turmoil elsewhere in the French empire. The inherent belief of the French government in *assimilation* was based on its conviction of the superiority of French civilisation and culture. They felt that the different races, cultures and political systems in the French empire should be absorbed into the dominant system of the Mother Country, France. Citizens of the overseas territories should have equal rights with Frenchmen from metropolitan France. Socially it meant that all people in the empire should be Frenchmen, whether black, brown or yellow. They should all speak the French language and adopt French manners and customs. If assimilation was successful, they would lose their separate cultural identity.

At the beginning of the Second World War, France was overrun by Nazi Germany. In July, 1940, a puppet French government, the Vichy Government, was set up. French Caribbean possessions gave allegiance to the Vichy Government until 1943 when they transferred to the Free French cause of General Charles de Gaulle.

Changes in 1946

The final step in political assimilation was taken in March, 1946, when Guadeloupe, Martinique and French Guiana became overseas departments of France. The General Councils in all three territories voted unanimously for this change. The overseas departments were in the same constitutional position as the metropolitan departments with a few exceptions. By Article 76 of the Constitution of the Fifth Republic, the representative of the French government in the French Caribbean became the Prefect instead of the old Governor. The prefects and officials became the executive branch of the government in the departments. Guadeloupe and Martinique were represented by three members in the National Assembly in Paris, two in the Senate and one each in the Economic and Social Council. French Guiana was given one representative in the National Assembly and one in the Senate.

Each department was granted a General Council elected by universal adult suffrage. The members sat for six years, and half were re-elected every three years. Guadeloupe and Martinique had thirty-six members. French Guiana had sixteen members. At first the General Councils were only advisory and administrative. They could not determine policy, which was held to be the business of the French Parliament and the reason for the departments' representation in Paris. This caused resentment in the French Caribbean which resulted in a storm of protest at the end of the 1950s, especially in Martinique. This led to the constitutional reform known as the 'Decentralisation Decrees' of April, 1960. Generally the Caribbean departments were given greater local autonomy. Prefects had their powers increased and General Councils could engage in political debates.

A French department is a large administrative territory which is sub-divided into *arrondissements* which are further sub-divided into *communes*. Guadeloupe is divided into three *arrondissements*, and French Guiana into two *arrondissements*. In all three departments the *communes* are administered by elected municipal councils headed by mayors. In all three, the electoral districts are called *cantons*. There are thirty-six each in Guadeloupe and Martinique and sixteen in French Guiana.

The French system of justice operates in the French Caribbean and the structure of the judiciary is broadly the same in all three departments. The highest court is the *Cour d'Appel* (Court of Appeal). There is one at Basse-Terre in Guadeloupe and another at Fort-de-France which serves both Martinique and French Guiana. There are two *Tribunaux de Grande Instance* (Judicial Tribunals) in both Guadeloupe and Martinique, and one in French Guiana. They consist of a single judge and a jury, and deal with the more serious offences. Under them come *Tribunaux d'Instance* (County Courts), five in Martinique and four in Guadeloupe, presided over by permanent magistrates. At the lowest level of the judiciary are justices of the peace in all the *cantons* of the three departments. In addition to these criminal courts there are *Tribunaux*

Mixtes de Commerce (Commercial Courts), two in Guadeloupe and one in Martinique.

One notable difference between an overseas department in the Caribbean and a department in metropolitan France is that in the former the Prefect has control over the armed forces and can declare martial law without instruction from France. This is necessary because of the distance from France. Otherwise there is strong, centralised control from Paris over the Prefects.

The overseas departments benefit from direct budget support from France in their public expenditure, e.g., on hospitals, schools and roads. Their citizens enjoy the protection of the French army and police, and the full enforcement of all French laws. They also receive the benefits of the French social security system in health, education, unemployment and pensions. As France is a member of the European Economic Community, the French Caribbean enjoys the benefits of this market. To sum up, Guadeloupe, Martinique and French Guiana are constitutionally parts of metropolitan France.

This presented a dilemma to the United Nations' decolonisation movement in the 1960s. When the United Nations committees questioned France about what she was doing about decolonisation in the French Caribbean, she refused to comment on the grounds that Guadeloupe, Martinique and French Guiana were not colonies, but part of France! However, in the eyes of the rest of the world, the constitutional position of the French Caribbean is ambiguous; foreigners do not accept the French argument, and regard Guadeloupe, Martinique and French Guiana as colonies in practice, if not in theory.

Political movements in the French Caribbean

In the French Caribbean there is the basic division in politics between conservatives who want to remain part of France and those who want complete independence. However, in both movements there are many shades of political opinion.

At one extreme are those who want complete assimilation, both political and cultural. Then there are *bekes*, the former *grands blancs*, who are absolutely in favour of being Frenchmen culturally, but who resent the loss of political power under the highly centralised system. They want more local autonomy, as in the advisory councils of the eighteenth and nineteenth centuries.

On the other hand, some of the blacks want to be constitutionally and politically part of France because of the benefits which its brings but, culturally, they want their separate identity. They contribute to the movement known as *négritude* in its cultural aspects only. They are not followers of Aimé Césaire, the poet-politician champion of *négritude* in the French Caribbean because they do not support his politics. The *bekes* on one hand, and those who want to keep an Antillean culture on the other, exhibit the differences between political and social assimilation.

Among those who want self-government or independence are the moderates, who want association with France constitutionally with a high degree of local autonomy. For example, the *Parti Progressiste*, led by Aimé Césaire, wanted Martinique's constitutional attachment to France, but Césaire considered that some French institutions were not suited to Caribbean conditions. He disliked French officials dictating to local politicians, and he wanted Martiniquans to have more control over their own affairs. At the other extreme are the communists who gained strength in the French Caribbean in the 1970s, particularly in Guadeloupe. They favour complete self-government in domestic affairs, and some even want to break completely with France.

However, a majority in the French Caribbean want to preserve the *status quo*. In a referendum in the French Caribbean in 1962, sixteen years after departmental status had been given, the majority voted for no change. In the 1967 elections in Martinique the departmentalists were in a majority. In 1979 the majority still wanted no constitutional change in spite of the economic changes initiated by France. Over the thirty-three years of the departmental system, more and more people in the French Caribbean have been moving towards greater autonomy. The latest proposals for an economic revolution will probably accelerate this move; already the trade unions have begun to swing over to autonomy from their former conservatism.

The future

There is an impending crisis in the French Caribbean. Guadeloupe, Martinique and French

Guiana all spend far more than they earn from their exports. The difference is made up by direct budgetary aid from France. In some years this runs as high as four times the domestic income. For example, in 1977 France put about £500,000,000 into the French Caribbean, which was almost four times the local national income. Considerable financial aid comes from FIDOM (Investment Fund for the Economic and Social Development of the Overseas Departments) because the Caribbean territories cannot finance their own investment needs. In simple terms, the French Caribbean consumes far more than it produces.

The French government is proposing an economic revolution in the French Caribbean by which direct French financial support would decrease and the Caribbean economies would become more self-sufficient. It hopes to achieve this by improving the sugar industry, increasing tourism and diversifying agriculture. Local politicians feel that the economic revolution would lead to the running down of aid without any corresponding increase in revenue from local industry resulting in economic hardship. This is the chief reason why trade unions are abandoning their former pro-French position.

Due to centralisation in administration and immense direct French aid, the public sector dominates the economies of the three territories. It is chiefly responsible for the overseas departments consuming more than they produce, because they are spenders rather than revenue earners as, for example, the health departments. The gap between expenditure and revenue is narrowed by such industries as tourism, but in spite of all efforts to increase tourism, it can never close the gap completely. A decrease in direct French aid would be felt chiefly in the public sector. Increased unemployment, lower *per capita* incomes and falling living standards would be apparent very quickly.

The French Caribbean has a rapidly increasing population. For example, Martinique had a population of about 350,000 at the end of the 1970s. With a density of population of about 300 per square kilometre, it ranks third in the Caribbean behind Barbados and Puerto Rico. There is already considerable unemployment. The public sector is by far the largest employer, with about one-third of the working population, and a decrease in aid would directly create more unemployment. People from the French Caribbean can emigrate freely to metropolitan France because of the departmental status, but emigration cannot solve the unemployment problem. Therefore it looks as if the proposed economic revolution will have to be delayed if the French Caribbean is to avoid a very serious crisis.

Puerto Rico

From its conquest by Ponce de Leon in 1509 until its cession to the United States in 1898, Puerto Rico belonged to Spain. At first it was never completely conquered and parts, particularly in the south-west, remained undeveloped until modern times. In spite of a little gold and the introduction of tobacco and sugar, Puerto Rico remained unimportant economically to Spain. However, when foreigners arrived in the Caribbean in the seventeenth century, Spain quickly realised the strategic value of Puerto Rico. It became a heavily fortified island because it was the outer bastion of the Spanish empire in the Caribbean and Central America, and guarded the approaches to the treasure ports. It was to the windward of the Greater Antilles and the Central American colonies and was, therefore, an important base. Finally, it was the Spanish possession closest to the Leewards where the British and the French began their settlements. In fact, this did not help Spain much because it was to the leeward of the British and French islands, but it enhanced Puerto Rico's value in the eyes of the Spaniards.

Puerto Rico grew slowly and by 1800 the population was just over 150,000. A turning-point came in the Revolutionary and Napoleonic War period when trade with the United States expanded. After 1815 Spanish Loyalists, fleeing from Latin American revolutions, were allowed to settle in Puerto Rico and trade there. This helped the expansion of trade, which had begun twenty years earlier, to continue throughout the first half of the nineteenth century. The Spanish authorities were anxious to attract European settlers from any country to open up plantations so long as the Spaniards retained control of government. The tobacco, sugar and coffee plantations provided Spain with much needed revenue.

At the time of the Ten Year War in Cuba, Puerto Rican liberals agitated for the suppression of the slave trade and political rights for all. There was a short-lived independence revolt in 1868, but Ramón Emeterio Betances and his followers in Cuba were unsuccessful. At the end of the century a moderate reformer, Ramón Baldorioty de Castro, won a charter for self-government for Puerto Rico from the Spanish in 1897 by peaceful persuasion. Unfortunately this important constitutional advance was ignored by the United States, who were victors in the 1898 war, and by the native Puerto Ricans who were more attracted by the expected benefits of association with the United States.

The Spanish-American War and its results

In 1898 there was hardly any resistance to the United States invasion because most people thought they would be better off materially and politically under the United States. The Treaty of Paris gave Puerto Rico to the United States and Congress was made responsible for its constitution. Disillusionment came quickly for the Puerto Ricans. The Foraker Act of 1900 made Puerto Rico a territory of the United States, but it did not help Puerto Ricans gain their political rights. This was the beginning of Puerto Rico's unique and ambiguous position as a territory of the United States. By the Foraker Act, goods entering the United States from Puerto Rico were subject to duty for two years but opponents of the Act said that if Puerto Rico was a territory of the United States, goods should pass freely between the two. In 1901, the United States Supreme Court decided that the Constitution of the United States did not apply to Puerto Rico even though the United States was claiming it by conquest. By the Foraker Act, political rights were withheld from Puerto Rico and the island was adminstered by a United States Governor and officials. After the reform achieved by de Castro in 1897, this was a step backwards constitutionally and it caused much resentment.

The Americans themselves felt uneasy about the treatment of Puerto Rico. They were, traditionally, anti-imperialist, pro-democracy and champions of self-determination on the American continent, yet they found themselves ruling a conquered territory. The early governors pushed ahead with Americanisation as if intending to absorb Puerto Rico into the United States. The sugar industry expanded but it was largely Americans who benefited from this. In spite of the 200 hectare limit set by the Foraker Act, they controlled large estates. Puerto Rico was becoming a one-crop economy, and by 1920 seventy-five per cent of its population was dependent on the sugar industry. A few were very rich, but the majority were poor, and without political rights.

In 1917 Congress made minor reforms to the Puerto Rican Constitution. The Governor and leading officials would still be appointed by the President of the United States, but Puerto Ricans would be allowed to elect their own Senate which would have sole legislative power in internal matters. Puerto Ricans were granted United States citizenship, but their island was referred to by the Supreme Court as an 'unincorporated territory of the United States'.

1917 to 1952

The 1917 reforms marked the beginning of party politics in Puerto Rico. By the 1930s, political issues were explosive. The Nationalist Party wanted immediate independence. Intellectuals led by Campos formed a small private army and attacked United States officials. After the murder of the American Chief of Police, they proclaimed a republic. In 1937 they demonstrated in Ponce in the south of the island in defiance of police orders, and nineteen students were shot. The Republican Party, on the other hand, wanted Puerto Rico to become a full state of the United States (henceforth known as 'statehood' policy). The Socialist Party stuck to a policy of economic and social reform, considering constitutional issues unimportant. In the depression of the 1930s, better conditions seemed to be the most pressing need.

The Legislature was dominated by a coalition between the Republicans and the Socialists until 1938. Then Luis Muñoz Marin formed the Popular Democratic Party, which won the election of 1940. Muñoz Marin wanted economic reforms which would benefit the majority of Puerto Ricans. When these had been achieved, he would move on to constitutional proposals. Large American-owned sugar estates would be broken up, and smallholdings and 'proportional benefit' farms created. This won him much support from the rural peasant population. Social services, such as water supply, sewerage, health and education, would be put under semi-autonomous government bodies.

During the Second World War, through the Industrial Development Corporation and the Puerto Rican Development Bank, his government expanded the economy and diversified industry very successfully. The Popular Democratic Party won the election of 1944 and Muñoz Marin became President of Puerto Rico. The economic advances made in Puerto Rico diverted people from constitutional issues which is exactly what he intended. He sought the attainment of economic stability and a foundation for future prosperity while still under the protection of the United States. The great achievement of his government during the War was to convince Congress that a native Puerto Rican administration could carry out its programme efficiently and with political stability.

This prompted President Harry S. Truman to appoint the first Puerto Rican Governor, Jesús T. Piñero, in 1946, and in 1948 Congress allowed the Governor to be elected. Because of the political and economic progress of Puerto Rico, Congress proposed major constitutional changes in 1950. The Puerto Ricans, aided by favourable circumstances, had done well. The United States market was expanding rapidly and taking all that Puerto Rico could produce. People with money in the United States were looking for investment opportunities overseas and Puerto Rico was attractive because it enjoyed the protection of the United States without the disincentives of federal taxation. Luis Muñoz Marin proved himself an outstanding leader and one with whom the Americans were happy to work because he was a force for unity and his regime was relatively free from corruption.

The Commonwealth of Puerto Rico, 1952

In 1950, a Constitutional Convention in San Juan drafted a constitution for self-government which was submitted to a referendum of the people of Puerto Rico. It was adopted by a four to one vote in Puerto Rico and then passed to Congress and was duly approved. On 25 July, 1952, the Commonwealth of Puerto Rico was established, and Luis Muñoz Marin became its first elected President. Puerto Rico became the first 'free and associated state of the United States', or in Muñoz Marin's words, *Estado libre asociado*.

Puerto Rico's position under the Commonwealth Constitution is unique. It is not recognised as an independent state, but neither is it a full state of the United States. Its people can be citizens of Puerto Rico, and of the United States if they want to be; they are allowed 'dual citizenship'. They do not have to pay federal income taxes if the money is earned in the island. Puerto Rico has representation in the United States Congress, but no vote. It seemed such a good constitution to Puerto Ricans that, in a referendum in 1967, over sixty per cent voted to retain it. It is like the French policy of assimilation, but with a difference. Puerto Rico is able to keep its cultural and ethnic identity and almost complete autonomy, while modelling its institutions on those of a state of the United States. It enjoys the protection and other benefits of its guaranteed permanent association with the United States.

Puerto Rico adheres to the doctrine of the separation of powers in that the executive, legislative and judicial branches of government are kept completely apart. The Constitution of Puerto Rico must not conflict with the Constitution of the United States and cannot be changed without the consent of the people of Puerto Rico and the United States Congress.

1 The Governor is head of the executive branch. He is elected by universal suffrage for a four-year term. He is assisted by an Advisory Cabinet of fourteen Secretaries who are appointed by the Governor and approved by the Senate. The Secretaries are heads of government departments. The highest executive department is the Department of State whose Secretary becomes Acting-Governor in the absence or death of the Governor. Puerto Rico also has many semi-autonomous government departments, known as 'authorities'. Many of these are concerned with public utilities, such as water, electricity and transport.

2 The legislative branch consists of two Houses: a Senate of twenty-seven members, eight senatorial districts electing two members each, and eleven others coming from the island as a whole; and a House of Representatives of fifty-one members, one each from forty districts, and eleven others from the island as a whole.

Election is by proportional representation which insures that minority parties have some representation in the Legislature.

3 The judicial branch is headed by the Supreme Court of Puerto Rico. The justices are appointed

by the Governor with the advice and approval of the Senate. There is a Chief Justice and six Associate Justices. Under the Supreme Court is the Court of First Instance which is sub-divided into a Superior Court and District Courts. The Chief Justice assigns judges to these courts. Because the administrative work cannot be handled by one man, the Chief Justice is assisted by an Office of Court Administration.

Decisions of the Supreme Court can be reviewed by the United States Supreme Court because the 1952 Commonwealth Constitution does not allow any Puerto Rican law to conflict with the United States Constitution. This is one way in which complete autonomy in Puerto Rico is limited.

Constitutionally Puerto Rico is not an independent country because the United States government controls Puerto Rico's defence, internal security, foreign relations, inter-state trade, coastguard and lighthouse, Post Office and currency. Federal Law applies in these affairs and in Puerto Rico there is a United States District Court and a United States Attorney, as in any other state of the United States. Puerto Ricans do not pay federal income tax, but they pay federal customs duties which are collected by United States customs officials and handed over to the Commonwealth government.

Puerto Ricans elect a Resident Commissioner to the United States Congress. He sits in Congress and can speak, but he cannot vote. Puerto Ricans do not have a vote in United States presidential elections.

Politics

Luis Muñoz Marin was able to carry out his progressive economic programmes in the 1940s and 1950s because he had the support of the United States administration, even though many of his reforms were against American interests. For example, he broke the stranglehold of the giant American corporations on the sugar industry. American-owned estates were reduced in size by the Land Authority. On the other hand, some of his measures favoured American interests. With business booming in the United States just after the war, investors wanted overseas outlets for investments. Muñoz Marin granted tax 'holidays' (periods of freedom from taxation) to new American-owned industries.

Puerto Rican immigrants in New York

His policies were so successful that Puerto Rico experienced a boom in the late 1940s and 50s. Costs were lower in Puerto Rico chiefly because wages were lower, but Puerto Ricans were content because their wages were rising and unemployment was declining. Muñoz Marin kept the trade unions on his side with minimum wage legislation and a Labour Relations Board.

In spite of the incentives and favouritism shown to foreigners, there was little anti-United States sentiment among the masses. The peasants were being given smallholdings, the workers more jobs and higher wages. There was also the opportunity to emigrate to the United States where wages were very high. This was a safety valve which relieved the pressure of unemployment in Puerto Rico. It also brought much money into the island from repatriated wages. Therefore, in 1952, Puerto Ricans were happy with their constitution, their association with the United States, their own government and, particularly, with their President.

However, there were minority groups which were dissatisfied with the constitution. It failed to satisfy those who wanted complete independence and those who wanted full statehood in the United States Union. From the early 1950s the Independence Party was second in strength to the Popular Democratic Party, but the Republican Party (later the New Progressive Party) was gaining strength. The latter party favoured statehood and, by the early 1960s, it was the second party and the Independence Party was third by a very long way.

The Popular Democratic Party of Luis Muñoz Marin had been in power since 1940, enjoying, on average, sixty per cent of the vote. This ended in 1968 when the New Progressive Party won about forty-five per cent of the vote against forty-two per cent for the Popular Democrats. Since 1968 there has been a two-party system in Puerto Rico. The election in 1972 was won by the Popular Democratic Party. Perhaps this was because the New Progressive Party, in its four-year term, had made no constitutional changes, the main feature of its programme, but merely adopted the highly successful economic policies of its rival.

In 1976 there was a swing back to the New Progressive Party who captured just over forty-eight per cent of the vote against forty-five per cent for the Popular Democratic Party. Carlos Romero-Barcelo became Governor. The New Progressive Party still favours statehood but, with such a slender majority, it does not feel that it has the necessary mandate to press for a constitutional change which would have to be approved by the majority of Puerto Ricans in a referendum. Moreover it does not know how the United States Congress would view any proposal for constitutional change. In 1976 the Independence Party had just under six per cent of the vote. Most pressure for Puerto Rican independence comes from outside, chiefly led by Fidel Castro of Cuba. In 1980 it seems that a clear majority of Puerto Ricans still favour the 1952 Constitution and that the United States is against independence.

7
Regional co-operation

T. A. Marryshow

Early attempts at unification

Stapleton and the Leewards

In the seventeenth century the British government aimed at administrative convenience in colonial government in the West Indies. They wanted as few officials and as little expense as possible, and only two or three local assemblies to deal with. At first Barbados and all the Leeward Islands were under the command of the Earl of Carlisle. He appointed separate officers for each island, which enabled the British government to pass over its colonial reponsibility to Carlisle, a very convenient and cheap arrangement. In practice, before 1660, Barbados was kept separate from the Leewards which were governed by Thomas Warner. When William, Lord Willoughby was made Governor of Barbados and the Leewards in 1660, he exercised authority over the Leewards also and all the Eastern Caribbean was controlled by one Governor for roughly the next ten years. Barbados's influence over the Leewards was strengthened in this period because of the help she gave them in the Second Dutch War, 1665–1667. However, the Leewards complained that this help was not enough and that Barbados was holding back their development. Therefore, after the war, the Leewards asked for separation from Barbados under their own Governor.

In 1671 Sir Charles Wheler was appointed Governor of all the Leeward Islands and governed them as Warner had done. Wheler was a failure and was replaced by Sir William Stapleton in 1674. He inaugurated the first federation in the British West Indies. His motive was administrative convenience. The Leewards were spread over an area of about 240 kilometres from north to south, and 160 kilometres from east to west. Communication by sailing ship was not difficult and he saw no reason why there should not be one assembly for all the islands in St Kitts. In 1674 he called the first meeting of the 'General Assembly of the Leeward Islands', consisting of two representatives from each of the four major islands, Antigua, Montserrat, Nevis and St Kitts. The General Assembly met fairly regularly until 1711, but after that it did not meet again until 1798. Thereafter it was never called again. An attempt to revive it in 1837 was a failure.

The idea of federating under a common government was unpopular in the islands, but while Stapleton was Governor from 1674 to 1685, the first assemblies were attended because of his dynamic leadership. However, they rejected his plan to strengthen the federation by giving all the islands one government and one set of laws in 1683. St Kitts, supported by the other islands, insisted that each island should make its own laws.

The Leeward Islands Federation, 1871 to 1956

The individual islands of the Leewards maintained their own legislatures throughout the eighteenth and first half of the nineteenth century. They were too close geographically not to have some common offices. There was one Governor for all the Leewards and each island had its own Lieutenant-Governor. From the early eighteenth century they shared an Attorney-General. They were grouped for defence under the naval base at English harbour, Antigua. However, they each had their own assemblies and their own laws.

Between 1816 and 1833 there was a short-lived experiment which divided the Leewards into two groups, again for administrative convenience and not because the islands themselves wanted it. One Governor administered a north-western group consisting of St Kitts, Nevis and Anguilla, and

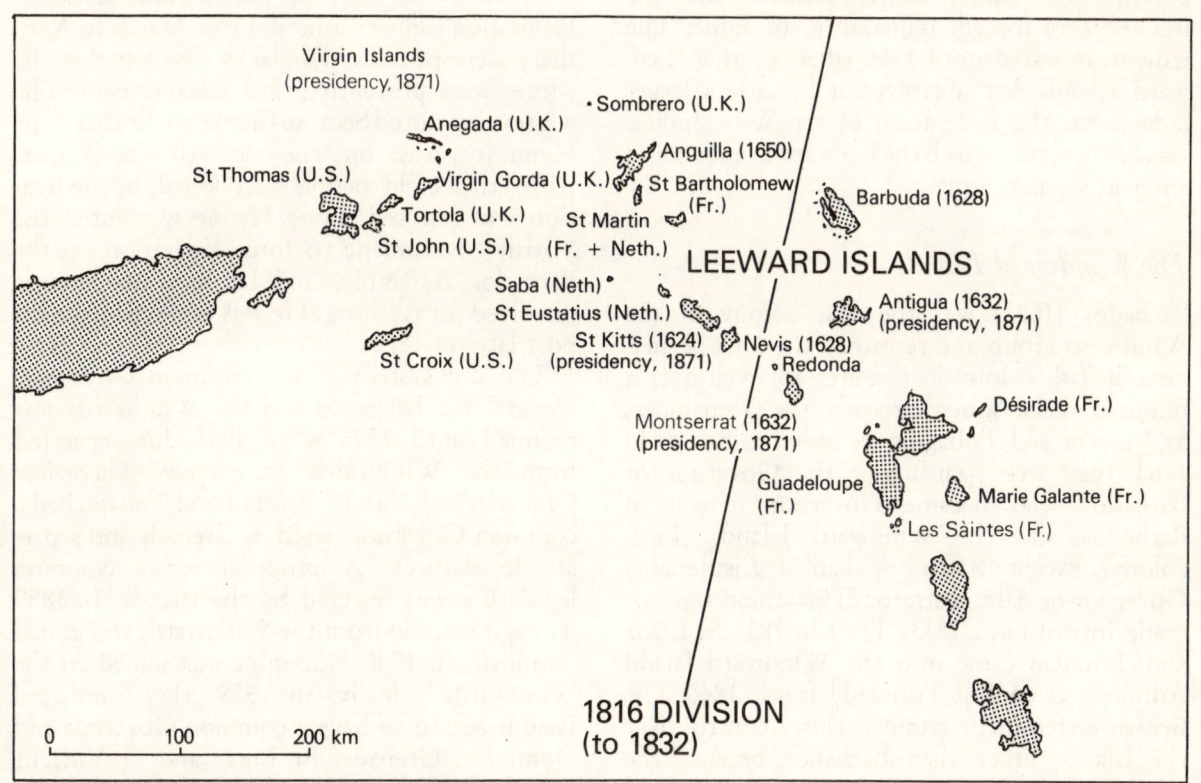

Map 5   Leeward Islands (Federal Colony 1871–1956)

another governed the south-eastern group of Antigua, Barbuda and Montserrat. In 1833 all the Leewards were joined together again. In that year Dominica was added to the Leewards instead of being administered as a separate colony.

After emancipation the British government came into conflict with the island assemblies, as we saw in a previous chapter. The Leeward Island assemblies were extremely unrepresentative, one member seldom representing more than twenty voters. With the assemblies so weak, so unrepresentative and so neglectful of the black population, the British government decided to establish a federation. In 1871 it passed the 'Leeward Islands Act' setting up the 'Federal Colony of the Leeward Islands'. The units, called 'Presidencies', were: Antigua (including Barbuda), Dominica, Montserrat, Nevis, St Kitts (including Anguilla) and the Virgin Islands. There was one Governor for the Leewards Federation and separate administrators or commisioners for each Presidency. One Assembly passed laws for all the islands.

This federation was unpopular with the individual islands because it meant a loss of independence. But the British government was pressing for administrative reforms and the islands were forced, reluctantly, to agree. The federation lasted until 1956 when another 'Leeward Islands Act' dissolved it because a larger federation, the Federation of the West Indies, was being set up, which the Leeward Islands could enter as separate units.

The Windward Islands

Barbados (1627) was the first colony of the Windward group and remained the only permanent British colony in the area for well over a hundred years. When Grenada, the Grenadines, St Vincent and Tobago were ceded to Britain in 1763 they were put under the Governor of Barbados who became Governor-General of Barbados and the Windward Islands. Each colony, except Barbados, had a Lieutenant-Governor or Administrator. This union was not made formal until 1833. Then in 1838 St Lucia and Trinidad came into the Windward Island Administration, but Trinidad left it in 1840. The British government retained closer control over the islands other than Barbados because the salaries of the Lieutenant-Governors were paid from Britain.

With the exception of St Lucia and Trinidad, the islands had their own assemblies. They were scattered over a wider area than the Leewards and west-to-east communication with Barbados was very difficult until the coming of steamships. They did not want any closer federation, not even for defence, because after 1815 the danger from France had passed. Barbados always held herself aloof from the other islands because of her much longer colonial history and the strength of her government institutions.

However, the British government proposed federation for Barbados and the Windwards in 1868 in order to create a stronger unit in the wave of administrative reform after Morant Bay. The Windward Islands resisted federation chiefly because of the determination of Barbados to stay out. The whites there even set up a Defence Association to preserve their ancient Assembly and legislative independence. In 1875 John Pope Hennessy arrived as Governor just when white public opinion against federation was very strong. He failed to appreciate this. The blacks on the other hand wanted federation as they thought it would bring them increased wages.

In 1876 the issue of the Windward Island Federation came to a head. From March to April there were riots by the blacks who felt that the whites were preventing their advancement. The whites also rioted because they thought that Pope Hennessy was on the side of the blacks. Altogether eight people were killed, but federation was rejected. Pope Hennessy wanted the British government to force federation on the Barbados Assembly, and he tried to have it dissolved for resisting. He was removed from his post later in 1876.

The old system of the common Governor-General for Barbados and the Windwards was retained until 1885 when Barbados separated from the Windwards completely. Thereafter Grenada, St Lucia, St Vincent and Tobago had a common Governor based in Grenada and separate legislatures. A proposal for a common legislature was rejected by the islands. In 1889 Tobago seceded from the Windwards and joined Trinidad. In 1940 Dominica was joined to the Windwards. Finally, in 1958, the Windward Islands ceased to have a common Governor and Dominica, Grenada, St Lucia and St Vincent joined the Federation of the West Indies as separate units.

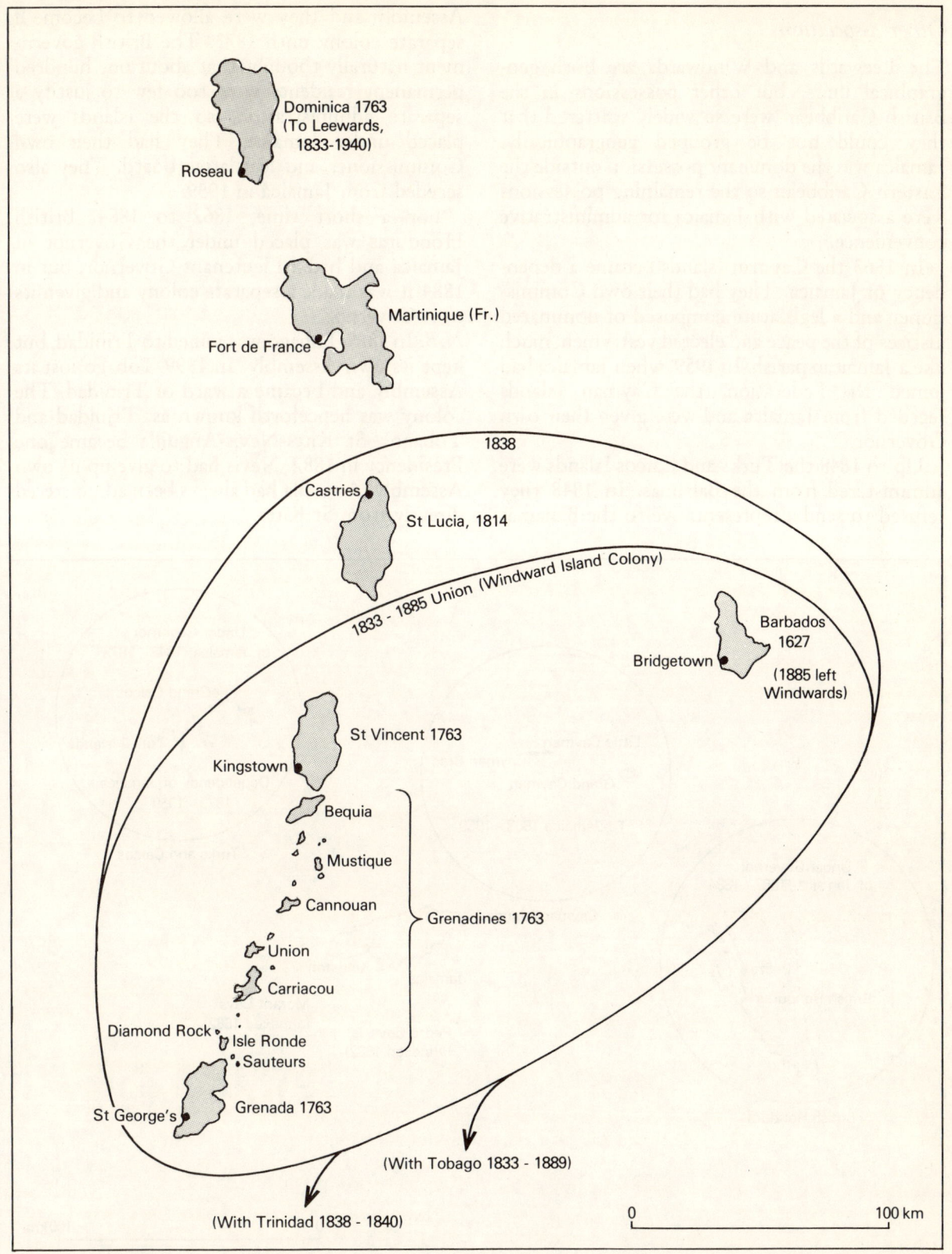

Map 6 Windward Islands (Federal Colony until 1885)

Other associations

The Leewards and Windwards are both geographical units, but other possessions in the British Caribbean were so widely scattered that they could not be grouped geographically. Jamaica was the dominant possession outside the Eastern Caribbean so the remaining possessions were associated with Jamaica for administrative convenience.

In 1863 the Cayman Islands became a dependency of Jamaica. They had their own Commissioner and a legislature composed of nominated justices of the peace and elected vestrymen, much like a Jamaican parish. In 1959, when Jamaica had joined the Federation, the Cayman Islands seceded from Jamaica and were given their own Governor.

Up to 1848 the Turks and Caicos Islands were administered from the Bahamas. In 1848 they refused to send a representative to the Bahamas Assembly and they were allowed to become a separate colony until 1873. The British government naturally thought that about one hundred permanent residents were too few to justify a separate administration, so the islands were placed under Jamaica. They had their own Commissioner and legislative board. They also seceded from Jamaica in 1959.

For a short time, 1862 to 1884, British Honduras was placed under the Governor of Jamaica and had a Lieutenant-Governor, but in 1884 it was made a separate colony and given its own Governor.

N.B. In 1889 Tobago was joined to Trinidad, but kept its own Assembly. In 1899 Tobago lost its Assembly and became a ward of Trinidad. The colony was henceforth known as 'Trinidad and Tobago'. St Kitts-Nevis-Anguilla became one Presidency in 1882. Nevis had to give up its own Assembly. Anguilla had always been adminstered directly from St Kitts.

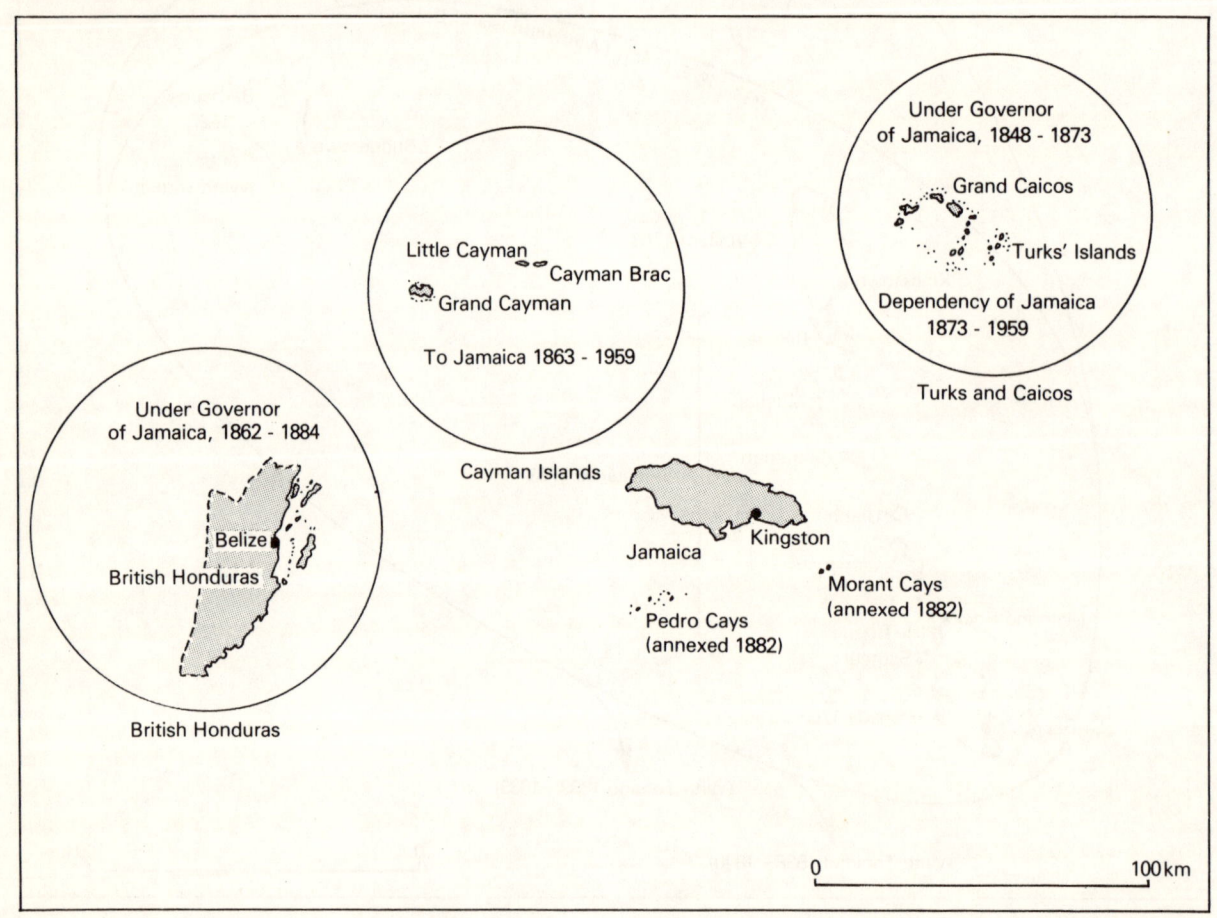

Map 7 Jamaica and her associated territories

Unifying forces, 1897 to 1947

Tendency to disunity

In all the federations and associations before 1900, the initiative had come from the British government and it had been met with reluctance by West Indians. The federations were unpopular and the forces pulling them apart were stronger than those holding them together. For example, St Kitts and Nevis, two islands separated by only four kilometres of sea, could not work in harmony; Nevis felt that St Kitts tyrannised her.

Insularity and parochialism were present in the islands from the very beginning of British colonisation. St Kitts was jealous of Barbados because of her faster development. Barbados felt that the Leewards were always begging for help. As the years went by, island pride and separateness grew stronger. People did not feel that they were West Indians, but thought of themselves as Barbadians, Jamaicans, Antiguans and so on.

The separation between the east and west Caribbean possessions was most difficult to bridge. Before the nineteenth century this was partly due to lack of communication. Jamaica was about 1600 kilometres from the Eastern Caribbean islands and the west to east voyage was never undertaken because of contrary winds and currents. Thus Jamaicans were completely ignorant of the Eastern Caribbean. Some even believed that the languages and peoples of the eastern islands were different. Nearly all thought that they were backward.

Before the twentieth century the British islands were producers of the same crops and competed for the same markets. They knew that a poor crop in another island would lead to the easier sale of their island's crop, and that prices would be higher. So great was their rivalry, that the islands began to wish disasters on each other. They were also in competition for the supply of slaves. Jamaican planters were very upset when the Ceded Islands began producing sugar and needing slaves because it drove up the price of slaves in the Kingston market. In commercial affairs the rivalry between the British islands themselves was as keen as that between the British and French islands in peace-time.

Emancipation contributed to the separate development of the British islands. In some islands, for example Barbados, the plantation system remained strong. But in others, for example Jamaica, peasant agriculture developed and the plantations quickly declined. Some islands developed different crops for export, others had more subsistence agriculture. Emancipation developed the separate character of the islands and increased their insularity and parochialism.

The rivalry between the British islands as sugar producers was broken down in the nineteenth century by the difficulties they all experienced. This gave them the feeling that they were 'all in the same boat' and in the twentieth century there was no longer cut-throat competition in agriculture, but far more co-operation between the islands.

Forces contributing to unity

There were some links binding the British islands together. The first was, of course, history. They were all British colonies and owed allegiance to the Crown. The Crown was very unpopular at times, but it was accepted as the common ruler. The strength of the Crown as a unifying force was strongest in time of war when Britain was fighting in the Caribbean against her European rivals. When the British islands were threatened by invasion or economic ruin, they all looked to the Royal Navy for help.

From their common history they inherited common political institutions. The assemblies sensed their unity in defiance of the Crown over such issues as emancipation. The British islands also shared common social systems. They were plantocracies based on the slave system. There was more social mobility between the same classes from different islands than there was between different classes in the same island. Slaves, of course, had a common loyalty, but it could seldom be demonstrated. For the plantocracy, Britain was the common home. Planters were often educated there, visited there, took up permanent residence or retired there at the end of their working lives. Absentee planters created a special social group in eighteenth-century England. The West India Committee in London united the interests of the planters throughout the islands. Emancipation gradually weakened the plantocracy and the West India Committee.

In the nineteenth century the British government was the greatest force towards unity. British

Guiana, St Lucia and Trinidad had their laws from Britain by Order-in-Council and the British government found this administrative system much more convenient and efficient. They began to see that it would be much easier to enforce unpopular legislation by Orders-in-Council for the British West Indies as one unit. When the British government enforced amelioration on the Crown Colonies by Order-in-Council, they expected the other islands to legislate for themselves to bring in amelioration but they refused. With emancipation, the British government expected the same laws to be carried out in all the islands and refused to allow the islands to adopt their own alternatives to apprenticeship. In major legislation, no variation or exceptions were allowed. As one, the British islands had to pass certain laws. Another example of legislation which embraced the whole British West Indies as one unit was the Sugar Duties Equalisation Act, 1846. There were very strong protests against this Act from British Guiana and Jamaica, but no exception was made. The different territories were united by being treated as one by the legislators.

Abolition, amelioration, emancipation and the Sugar Duties Equalisation Act also served to unite the colonies because they brought common problems and hardships and called forth common protests. After the 1846 Act, Jamaica tried to persuade the other islands to join her in sending a delegation to London to try to have the Act repealed.

Towards the end of the nineteenth century the practice of treating all the islands as one unit was normal. The Royal Commissions of 1883 and 1897 were sent to deal with all the problems of the islands together – the problems caused by the decline of sugar in the British West Indies.

In the nineteenth century the British government had tried to establish federations and other large units. In the twentieth century they still favoured the policy of larger political units, but they realised their unpopularity with West Indians. They therefore waited for a favourable reaction towards closer union to come from West Indians themselves. In 1921 Major Wood tested public opinion on federation and reported that it was too unpopular to be considered. In 1936 another commission reported an unfavourable reaction to closer union between Trinidad and Tobago and the Leeward and Windward Islands.

Yet two years later the Moyne Commission was in favour of federation.

Signs of growing unity

In the twentieth century there were several developments which brought the islands closer together. The Norman Commission of 1897 led to the establishment of an Imperial Department of Tropical Agriculture in Barbados which was linked to the Botanical Departments in all the islands and sent out lecturers and demonstrators throughout the area. In 1924 the Imperial College of Tropical Agriculture was established in Trinidad to serve all the British islands. Another common body, founded in 1919, was the West Indies Court of Appeal.

In 1926 the West Indian Standing Conference on Federation first met in London. It was held every year until 1929 when the last one was held in Barbados. This appeared to be a great step towards federation but, in fact, almost nothing was achieved. Also meeting in Barbados in 1929 were the Associated West Indian Chambers of Commerce and the West Indian Press Association. The Chambers of Commerce met regularly and became a permanent force in the movement towards federation. It was the Caribbean counterpart of the West India Committee in London. It had been meeting for over twenty years and urging permanent committees for the British West Indies as a whole. A free trade area was its first demand, but political federation usually went with it.

The British government saw encouraging signs that West Indians were thinking of federation from the West Indian Unofficial Conference in Dominica in 1932. It was attended by East Caribbean politicians who saw that the best chance for independence lay in federation. They told the British government that they would only consider federation if the British government would promise independence for it. The delegates went as far as to suggest a constitution and list the subjects which the federal government would control. They wanted a strong federation with wide powers over island development. Unfortunately this suggested federation was for the Eastern Caribbean only.

The champion of federation at this time was T. Marryshow of Grenada who was in London at the time of the Dominica Conference. He rejected the conference's report chiefly because it wanted to achieve federation before self-government and he wanted it the other way round. Marryshow had made federation his life's goal from about 1915, but he wanted self-government first so that the islands could take themselves into federation and not have it imposed on them by a colonial government. He was wary of the aims of the planters and Chambers of Commerce in wanting to create standing associations or even a federation because he thought that they would cheat the people of representation. He wanted a 'People's Parliament' based on universal suffrage and rejected the idea that each island should control its own elections to a federal parliament. Marryshow was a dynamic force in the struggle for federation for thirty years and died in 1958, the year in which that goal was achieved.

The British islands were united once more by the troubles of 1935 to 1938 and the Royal Commission which was sent out to investigate them. The Moyne Commission dealt with the British West Indies as one unit, just as the earlier commissions on economic problems had done. It was presented with demands for federation from people of all walks of life, from business leaders to trade unionists. The report, when it was published after the Second World War, encouraged the British government to work for federation.

The most important single unifying force which resulted from the Moyne Commission was the Colonial Development and Welfare Act of 1940. This treated the British West Indies as one unit with a common fund for all the islands to draw on. The administration of the Act was in the hands of a Comptroller for Development and Welfare with a staff of advisers. The permanent headquarters of the Development and Welfare Organisation was in Barbados. This office co-ordinated the development plans of the colonies and built up a large body of experienced workers in inter-island matters which the Federal Government inherited in 1958.

The British Guiana and West Indian Labour Conference which met in Georgetown in 1938 was attended by important labour leaders and politicians. When this conference demanded federation the British government knew that at last West Indian leaders, with the support of the working classes, were in favour of federation.

The two World Wars and emigration to the United States and Britain had served to throw people from all parts of the British Caribbean together. This had created comradeship and given them a common identity in foreign lands. Ignorance and mistrust had been dispelled by mixing together. The West India Regiment had served in both world wars and its soldiers returned home with broader outlooks and an increased readiness to work together. The emigrants did not usually return, but the difficulties of facing a new life in strange lands drew West Indians together. For example, Trinidadians and Jamaicans intermarried more frequently in Britain than they would have done in the Caribbean. Correspondence from emigrants told of this new 'West Indian identity' which had developed overseas.

The attitude of the British government

From the seventeenth century onwards, the British government had tried to persuade the West Indian colonies to accept larger units of government, for example, one governor instead of six, one set of colonial servants, one body of laws and one local assembly. The financial saving would have been great because there would have been far fewer salaries to pay and offices to run. The Colonial Office could have co-ordinated its administration and introduced reforms more easily. Moreover, the British government felt that federation was realistic because many of the colonies were too small to be administered efficiently with the manpower available. One of the British objectives in the founding of the University College of the West Indies was to provide the islands with trained administrators.

The British government had been discouraged by the early response of West Indians to federation. By 1920 they had decided not to propose any further moves towards federation. However 'feelers' like the visit of Major Wood in 1921 and the Moyne Commission in 1938 were put out, and between those two dates it became obvious that the West Indian attitude to federation had changed. Perhaps it was the economic problems of the 1920s and 1930s that brought about this change – a realisation that small units could not cope with such problems as the Great Depression by themselves.

However, it was also clear to the British government that, although West Indians viewed federation favourably, leaders like Marryshow would reject 'Crown Colony Federation'. At the Labour Conference, West Indian leaders made self-government a necessary condition for accepting federation. Marryshow put self-government first. Others were prepared to accept federation first provided there was a guarantee of self-government to follow. Therefore the British government had to accept the idea of self-government. This was not difficult because, as we saw in the last chapter, their attitude to decolonisation in general was changing.

By 1945 there were a number of West Indian groups of importance urging federation:
a) the West Indian Labour Conference which had been meeting regularly since 1938 and which, by 1945, was led by Marryshow;
b) the Barbados Progressive League led by Grantley Adams;
c) the People's National Party in Jamaica, led by Norman Manley;
d) the Jamaica Legislative Council;
e) the Associated West Indian Chambers of Commerce.

All these, representing a cross-section of West Indian public opinion, convinced the British government that West Indians wanted federation. In 1945 Colonel Oliver Stanley, the Secretary of State for the Colonies, asked colonial governments to consider federation again. This time the response was enthusiastic and the Secretary of State then advised the colonial governors of the proposed establishment of a federation for the whole of the British West Indies.

8
Federation and after

Grantley Adams

Progress to federation

The Montego Bay Conference

Arthur Creech Jones, the newly-appointed Secretary of State, followed up his predecessor's proposals by calling a conference of members of the legislatures of all the islands at Montego Bay, Jamaica, in September, 1947. Calling the conference in a West Indian town instead of London implied that the focal point of the West Indies was no longer London, although the subsequent conferences reverted to London. All colonies except the Bahamas sent delegates and they all approved of the idea of closer union or federation. The Montego Bay Conference was an exploratory one, which set up committees to work out the details of federation. The two most important committees were the Standing Closer Association Committee which was to draft a federal constitution and the Regional Economic Committee which was to consider such basic problems as a customs union.

The Standing Closer Association Committee presented a draft constitution in March, 1950. Its recommendations were accepted by ten colonies which were to become the units of the federation. They were: Antigua, Barbados, Dominica, Grenada, Jamaica, Montserrat, St Kitts-Nevis-Anguilla, St Lucia, St Vinćent, and Trinidad and Tobago. The mainland territories, British Guiana and British Honduras, rejected the federation. As

Montego Bay Conference

large land areas they feared that they would have to accept widespread immigration from the densely-populated islands if free movement of people within the federation was allowed. British Guiana, half of whose population was Indian, feared that large-scale immigration of Africans would turn the Indians into a suppressed minority. British Honduras felt that her future lay in closer contact with her Central American neighbours rather than eastward to the Caribbean. The third territory to reject federation was the British Virgin Islands which did not want to disturb their close relationship with the United States Virgin Islands.

The Montego Bay Conference allayed the fears of Jamaica and Trinidad that federation would slow down their own progress to self-government. The conference passed a resolution that internal political developments would not be affected by membership of the federation.

The general arguments in favour of federation put forward at Montego Bay were political in that they followed the British government's case for federation:
a) it would bring more efficient administration;
b) a larger electorate would mean purer democracy;
c) there would be greater scope for talented West Indians in government;
d) the government would be more talented in federation.

The economic arguments put forward were from the West Indians:
a) it would create a larger market;
b) there would be the free transfer of goods and services;
c) there would be greater impetus for rapid development for the area as a whole and for the individual units.

There was no further need to discuss the desirability of federation and it was decided that the next conference would discuss the details.

Other conferences

By 1953 all the committees set up at Montego Bay had drafted their reports which were put before a conference in London. All the reports were accepted and then circulated to the island legislatures for ratification. At this stage British Guiana and British Honduras formally notified the conference that they would not take part in federation.

Another conference was called in London in

1955 to discuss federal finance, in particular, the question of revenue. The administration of the federation and the composition of the civil service were also discussed. However, the problems of finance were not solved before the federation actually began because the final conference in 1956 also failed to settle conclusively what the federal government's powers in raising money were to be. Grantley Adams seemed to think that the federal government would eventually have the power of taxation. Norman Manley felt that the 1956 conference gave it no such power. The problems arising out of this confusion were heightened by the fact that the exact position of the federal government was not clearly stated either. Trinidad thought the federation would have more power than it actually had in 1958.

At the 1956 conference the federal constitution was formally agreed by the representatives of each unit and the British government. The British Parliament then passed the 'British Caribbean Federation Act' and the Federation of the West Indies was set up by Order-in-Council. It was hoped that British Guiana and British Honduras would reconsider membership later.

Lord Hailes

The Constitution

The 1956 Act set up a colonial federation. The Crown could legislate by Order-in-Council on foreign affairs, defence and the maintenance of financial stability. The Crown also appointed a Governor-General (Lord Hailes) who had more power under the constitution than the elected leader.

The legislature consisted of a Senate of nineteen members, one for Montserrat and two each for the other units, and a House of Representatives of forty-five members to be elected by universal adult suffrage. Jamaica was to have seventeen seats, Trinidad and Tobago ten, Barbados five and the others two each, except for Montserrat which had one. Another colonial institution was that the government would be headed by a Council of State, not a Cabinet. It would be presided over by the Governor-General and consist of the Prime Minister and ten other Ministers. A federal civil service was established with John Mordecai of Jamaica as Federal Secretary. Most of the civil servants came from the colonial government and had been engaged in such projects as the administration of the Colonial Development and Welfare Act. Provision was made for a compulsory review of the constitution within five years.

One of the drawbacks of the constitution was that even when it was introduced in January, 1958, it was out-of-date as far as constitutional development in Barbados, Jamaica and Trinidad and Tobago was concerned. Ten years had passed since the Montego Bay Conference and in that time the constitutions of those islands had outstripped that of the Federation. By 1958 Barbados, Jamaica, Trinidad and Tobago had partial self-government. To them, the federal constitution was a step backwards and naturally some dissatisfied politicians in those islands called it a 'Crown Colony Federation'.

In 1957 the site for the federal capital was discussed. Barbados, Grenada and Jamaica offered sites, but Trinidad was chosen after heated debate. The Chaguaramas peninsula would be available after the completion of negotions with the United States to remove some of their naval base. The site was not ready by January, 1958, so Port of Spain provided temporary headquarters. Britain promised £1,000,000 towards the building of the federal capital.

The federation at work

Politics

The federal elections were held in March, 1958. They resulted in a narrow victory by twenty-six seats to nineteen for the West Indies Federal Labour Party, sometimes referred to as the 'Federalist Party'. This was an association of socialist parties throughout the West Indies and its leaders were the politicians who had been most in favour of federation. The chairman was Norman Manley who did not stand in the elections. Also in the party, but not standing for election, was Eric Williams of Trinidad. The leader of the W.I.F.L.P. in the House of Representatives was Grantley Adams of Barbados. Thus the chief ministers of the two largest units in the federation did not join the federal government. This made it lose prestige immediately in the eyes of West Indians, who felt that it could not be important if the two most important West Indian politicians did not bother to join. Norman Manley's absence was the more significant because he was nearly 2,000 kilometres away from the federal headquarters. At least Eric Williams was on the spot in Trinidad.

The narrowly-defeated opposition was the Democratic Labour Party. This party won eleven out of seventeen of the Jamaican seats and a majority of the Trinidad seats. Therefore the victorious party, the West Indies Federal Labour Party, did not have a majority in the largest units, but relied on its support from the smaller islands. Consequently, when the government was formed, most of the ministers were drawn from the smaller islands (the Prime Minister, Grantley Adams, came from Barbados). Jamaica and Trinidad felt under-represented, not only in the House of Representatives, but also in the Council of Ministers. Because of this and the absence of Manley and Williams, federal politics were dominated by the smaller islands.

Finance and other affairs

Federations are called 'strong' or 'weak' according to the powers of the federal government. If the unit governments hand over most of their powers to the federal government and only keep the residual powers themselves, the federation is strong. But if the unit governments keep most of the powers themselves and hand over the residual powers to the federal government, then the federation is weak. Australia is a strong federation because the state governments have only residual powers. At its foundation the United States was a weak federation because the state governments were reluctant to hand over power to the federal government. Over the years the federal government in the United States has gained strength at the expense of the state governments and it is now a strong federation.

The federation of the West Indies was extremely weak. It was given residual powers only; anything considered important was retained by the unit governments. In fact, the federal government merely took over matters which were inter-island concerns before, like the West Indies Welfare Fund, the University College and the West India Regiment. It had no power to levy taxes because the unit governments would not yield this power, just as they had refused to do in the Leeward Islands Federation of 1871 to 1956. Federal government revenue came from 'unit contributions' which were fixed in proportion to the unit's resources. Jamaica at forty-three per cent, and Trinidad at thirty-nine per cent, of the total revenue, were easily the biggest contributors. The revenue of the federal government was only about £2,000,000, or $9,000,000 (local dollars). Of this one-third was earmarked for the running costs of the University College of the West Indies. This left only about £1,300,000 for all the other expenditure of the federal government. With virtually no money at its disposal, there was little it could contribute towards any development programme. Financially, the federation was extremely weak; not a 'federation of paupers' as Bustamante had labelled it at Montego Bay, but a 'pauper federation'.

The government affairs, over which the federal government was given control, were relatively unimportant to the unit governments. They were:
a) the allocation and administration of funds under the Colonial Development and Welfare Act;
b) the West India Regiment;
c) the administrative costs of the University College of the West Indies;
d) the Federal Civil Service and the Supreme Court of the West Indies.

Library of the University of the West Indies

It also controlled federal shipping, meteorological services, control of emigration and immigration from outside the Federation, the maintenance of Federal High Commissions in Canada, Britain and Venezuela and exchange control, but these involved little expenditure. Important affairs such as taxation, education and economic development in industry and agriculture were retained by the unit governments. Therefore, the federal government was very weak both in its scope of business as well as in its finance.

Constitutional revision, 1959

Jamaica and Trinidad soon asked for a revision of the constitution although they had agreed that it would not be amended for five years. The British government accepted this and a constitutional revision took place in September, 1959.

Jamaica and Trinidad together contributed seventy-seven per cent of the population, eighty-three per cent of the land area, and eighty-two per cent of the revenue. They were under-represented in proportion to their population and demanded increased representation. Since the federation could not continue without their support, their position was very strong. However, the smaller units resisted their demands and there was heated debate before Jamaica and Trinidad were given what they wanted. The House of Representatives was increased to sixty-four seats with Jamaica's share being thirty and Trindad's fifteen.

There were more demands for other constitutional changes. Trinidad had never liked a weak federation. Outside the Constitutional Revision Conference Eric Williams was demanding that power to levy taxes should be given to the federal government together with the control of economic development and a customs union. He had no hope of these demands being accepted because of Jamaica's opposition. However, Trinidad did ask the Conference for cabinet government and for a definite date to be fixed for the independence of the federation before April, 1960. At first the British government resisted these demands, but in August, 1960 it gave the federation full internal self-government. The Council of Ministers was replaced by a Cabinet. The Governor-General had to accept the Cabinet's decisions on all matters except foreign affairs and defence. Thus, by the end of 1960, the federation had reached the same stage of constitutional development as Barbados, Jamaica and Trinidad.

Breakdown of the federation

These latest changes in the constitution, however, could not save the federation. One of the provisions of the first constitution had been that individual units could negotiate separately with the British government about their own constitutional progress. Neither Jamaica nor Trinidad had shown much enthusiasm for the federation and in January, 1960, Norman Manley visited London to request independence for Jamaica if she left the federation. Trinidad also had separate negotiations with the British government.

In May, 1961, Sir Alexander Bustamante, leader of the Democratic Labour Party in Jamaica, declared that his party was opposed to federation and asked for a referendum. In retrospect, Manley was foolish to agree to this because he lost the subsequent general election. With a poll of only fifty-four per cent of the population in the referendum, the Jamaican people rejected the federation. After Jamaica had seceded, Trinidad decided to withdraw also because she held that the federation was either all the ten units or nothing. Early in 1962, the British Parliament passed an Act dissolving the Federation of the West Indies. This came into force in May, 1962.

General reasons for the breakdown

In the British West Indies the small islands had been most enthusiastic for federation because they saw it as their only hope of winning independence. The large islands such as Jamaica and Trinidad had less to gain, and indeed felt that association with the smaller islands might delay their own independence.

Their discontent was heightened by the fact that the small islands were proportionally over-represented in the federal parliament, especially in the Senate where Antigua had the same representation as Jamaica. The small islands dominated the Cabinet because the party they supported was the majority party in the federal government. Thus Jamaica and Trinidad found that they were dominated by the small islands. If the federation were to be given increased powers of government, this domination would increase. In the opinion of Jamaica and Trinidad, the constitutional changes in 1959 and 1960 did not go far enough to prevent this happening. The rift between them and the Eastern Caribbean became deeper. They decided to withdraw before their own development was affected adversely by the policies of the small islands.

One of Jamaica's original fears about the federation was that the British government was supporting it in order to transfer the liability for the small islands from Britain to Jamaica. After two years of federation Jamaica was convinced that this fear was justified and that she was supporting the Eastern Caribbean. Bustamante appealed to the electorate on this issue and won.

Another reason for the breakdown of the federation was its weakness:
1 The units had opted for a weak federation and kept tight control over their own affairs. The Federation of the West Indies was so weak that there was little point in its continuation.
2 Inadequate revenue limited what the federal government could do. Most of its meagre revenue was already committed, and there was little left for anything constructive. Moreover, it could not increase its revenue because it had no control over taxation.
3 The British government weakened the federation indirectly by allowing the units to make their own constitutional progress outside the federation. Jamaica and Trinidad had political leaders who did not join the federal government and they put the constitutional development of their own islands before that of the federation.
4 The Federation of the West Indies was still a colony. Few West Indian politicians knew what was expected of the federation to begin with, and Britain did not give a lead. Yet the West Indian politicians could not act without Britain's approval. This state of affairs changed with internal self-government for the federation, though too late to save it.
5 The two major powers in the federation, Jamaica and Trinidad, were at loggerheads.

Trinidad favoured a strong federation, Jamaica a weak one. This difference of opinion sharpened as time passed, thus condemning the federation to failure.

Specific causes of breakdown

1 *Freedom of movement* The freedom of people to move from one part of a federation to another is essential. It is unthinkable that a United States citizen could not move from one state to another. However, there were objections to freedom of movement in the Federation of the West Indies. British Guiana and British Honduras had not joined for this reason. After the federation began, the small islands, especially Barbados whose density of population was about 610 per square kilometre, insisted on freedom of movement. Trinidad resisted it vigorously. Her *per capita* income was twice as high as that of the next richest country and she feared a wave of immigrants coming in looking for jobs and lowering her standard of living. This issue was acute in 1961 and was a major factor in Trinidad's withdrawal.

2 *Customs union* Another ideal of federation is that of free trade and movement of goods within the federation and uniform tariffs on goods from outside it. On this issue Jamaica and Trinidad were opposed to each other. Most of Jamaica's revenue came from customs duties, and she would not consider lowering or abolishing them. Trinidad wanted the goods she produced to be able to move freely throughout the federation. Most of the units envisaged the federation becoming a free trade area in which the flow of goods would increase and trade and production would thereby expand. The policy of the federal government was to create a customs union. This was a major cause of Jamaica's withdrawal.

3 *Chaguaramas* In 1957 the Chaguaramas peninsula in Trinidad was chosen as the site of the federal capital. However, under the Destroyer/Bases deal between Britain and the United States in 1940, Chaguaramas had been leased to the United States for ninety-nine years. Eric Williams, Trinidad's Chief Minister, claimed the peninsula because the Trinidadian people had never been consulted about the agreement. He

Crowded living conditions in Barbados

said that the United States occupation was restricting the expansion of Port of Spain and cutting the people off from some good bathing beaches. When the British government agreed to provide £1,000,000 for the building of the federal capital, Eric Williams wanted the Americans to move out quickly.

This led to a quarrel between the Trinidad government and the federal government because Williams negotiated independently with the United States and United Kingdom governments. The federal government held that it was a federal issue and that Williams had no right to negotiate by himself, especially as he had caused friction between the United States and the federation over Chaguaramas. Williams behaved as if it was a domestic issue and he used the siting of the federal capital as an excuse to score a political victory for himself.

4 *Control of economic development* This was, perhaps, the chief cause of conflict between Jamaica and the federal government. The latter wanted to control the economic development of the whole area and did not want any unit to develop faster than, or at the expense of, the others. Jamaica insisted on controlling her own economic development. Her economy was expanding faster than that of the Eastern Caribbean, except for Trinidad, and she did not want it to be held back by the smaller islands.

This issue came to a head in 1960. Jamaica allowed a company to build an oil refinery in the island, granting the company tax concessions in return. There was strong objection from the federation. Firstly, Jamaica was acting in a matter of economic development without first consulting the federal government. Secondly, the oil refinery would contribute to Jamaica's economic development at the expense of the other units. Thirdly, Jamaica was competing with Trinidad who considered that oil refining was her preserve. Fourthly, the tax concessions which Jamaica had promised were considered illegal by the federal government.

Grantley Adams, the federal Prime Minister, took up this last issue. Unit governments had kept control over income tax and customs duties, but this was a special tax arrangement to secure industrial development and was, therefore, a federal matter.

5 *Retroactive legislation* This proved to be the 'last straw' for some Jamaicans in their quarrel with the federal government. Grantley Adams claimed that taxation would become a federal subject and that, after 1963, legislation could be made retroactively, that is a law could be passed to undo or change a measure previously taken. He would, therefore, make Jamaica's tax concessions to the oil company illegal, and claim back the unpaid taxes. At first the Jamaican government tried to obtain constitutional changes which would ensure that the federal government could have no control over taxation or economic development. However, Bustamante was so annoyed that he demanded secession.

British account of the breakdown

When the British Parliament asked the Secretary of State to account for the collapse of the Federation of the West Indies he gave the reasons in reverse order to that outlined in this section. He started with the disputes over specific issues, emphasising freedom of movement, control of taxation and control of economic development. Then he mentioned the different views of Jamaica and Trinidad on the scope of the federation. Finally, he came to the general point about the insularity of West Indian islands, saying that the West Indians still put allegiance to their own island before allegiance to the West Indies as a whole. He added a more controversial explanation that personalities had played a part in the collapse of the federation. Grantley Adams had always been under attack from the other leaders. Williams and Manley would not join his government and criticised it from the outside. They themselves would not yield their personal power to a central government. Moreover, Bustamante used the problems of the federation to further his own personal and political ends inside Jamaica.

With so many problems, the Federation of the West Indies was doomed to failure. It lasted only four years and was so weak that it has been labelled 'the federation that never was'.

Inter-regional co-operation after 1962

When the British government dissolved the federation in May, 1962, the small islands were still anxious for some kind of closer union. In May, 1962, Antigua, Barbados, Grenada, Montserrat, St Kitts-Nevis-Anguilla, St Lucia and St

Vincent attended a conference in London to discuss the possibility of federation. Barbados was the dominant member by population and resources and, at first, there was a chance of a federation developing. Further talks were held in Barbados in 1963 and 1964, but in 1965 Barbados decided to seek separate independence and the 'Little Eight' broke up.

CARIFTA

The breakdown of the federation discouraged the British Caribbean territories from further attempts at closer union, especially any political union, for some years. However, most of the territories realised the benefits which a larger economic unit could bring. Therefore, in 1965, exploratory talks were held between Antigua, Barbados and Guyana to consider a trading association. In December a preliminary agreement for a Caribbean Free Trade Association was signed and final agreement was reached by the Treaty of Antigua in May, 1968. The first signatories were Antigua, Barbados, Guyana and Trinidad. In the next three months they were joined by Dominica, Grenada, St Kitts-Nevis-Anguilla, St Lucia, St Vincent and, finally, Jamaica and Montserrat. In 1971 British Honduras completed the twelve in CARIFTA.

Its aims were to foster the economic development of the whole association, and of the individual members, by increasing trade and by diversification of products. All customs duties on goods traded between member countries would be removed which would stimulate the movement of goods. Obviously the aim was to create a common market at some time in the future. The members hoped that economic development would bring full employment and a better standard of living throughout the area.

The organisation of CARIFTA was:
a) a Heads of Government Conference which would outline general policy;
b) a Council of Ministers which would translate that general policy into specific schemes and which would meet whenever the need arose;
c) a Commonwealth Regional Secretariat which would be a permanent body based in Georgetown, Guyana. It would keep the association together and organise the trade and economic development schemes that the Ministers had decided upon.

The constitution allowed for new members to join by applying to the Council of Ministers.

The most difficult problem CARIFTA faced at the beginning was to remove customs duties. This could not be done outright in 1968 because so many countries depended on customs duties for their revenue. This had been Jamaica's problem over the federation's proposed customs union. A period of adjustment from customs duties to other sources of revenue had to be given. Therefore, duties on some goods were lifted immediately, others were to be removed over a five-year period in the case of the developed countries and over a ten-year period in the case of the less developed. In fact it was not such a serious problem as it appeared because in 1968 less than ten per cent of CARIFTA's trade was between members. After five years most barriers to trade were down, a wider market had been achieved and the flow of goods between member countries was increasing. By 1974 the members of CARIFTA were ready to make a bolder step towards the creation of a common market.

CARICOM

In 1974 the CARIFTA Heads of Government signed the Treaty of Chaguaramas which set up the Caribbean Common Market (CARICOM). This step bridged the gap between a purely economic association and a political union. It was twelve years after the failure of the federation, but even so the measures taken were very tentative.

The machinery of government was almost the same as that of CARIFTA; that is, a Heads of Government Conference to lay down general policy which would be executed by a Council of Ministers and member governments. The current administration would be in the hands of the Secretariat which would negotiate with foreign governments and other external bodies. There would be free trade within CARICOM and common duties against goods originating outside the area.

In attempting political integration CARICOM experienced similar difficulties to the federation. The members still had different resources and different rates of growth, but there was more willingness by the richer members to yield to the interests of the poorer for the good of the community as a whole. Closer political union is still regarded with great suspicion and so far the only wider subjects that have come under CARICOM's control have been health, meteorology, agriculture and transport.

CARICOM is dependent on outside investment for new development. Much help was given by the International Monetary Fund. More recently (1977) the European Economic Community has provided financial assistance. Three projects which have been developed with outside help have been a Regional Food Plan, a West Indian Shipping Federation, and a Fisheries Project. However, at a time of rising oil prices and a world recession in trade, most of the financial assistance has to be used to reduce budget deficits and there is little left for investing in development projects.

Other inter-regional bodies

The University of the West Indies The Irvine Commission of 1945 recommended the setting-up of a University College of the West Indies and this was founded at Mona in Jamaica in 1948. It was affiliated to London University. From about two hundred students initially, numbers grew fast so that it was decided to open another campus at St Augustine, Trinidad. This incorporated the old Imperial College of Tropical Agriculture. The two campuses in 1960 were complementary, not overlapping. Some faculties were in St Augustine, while others were in Mona, so both campuses were still inter-regional. By 1963 there was need for a third campus and this was built at

Caribbean Development Bank

Cave Hill, Barbados. In 1962 the University College of the West Indies was given the full status of an autonomous university. It became known as the University of the West Indies and was able to award its own degrees.

The University has played an important role in integrating the West Indies in four ways:

1 Its running costs have always been borne by the individual governments. Fourteen separate territories made the first contributions.

2 One of the original aims of the British government in promoting a university was that it would train administrators for the West Indies Federation and, in some cases, help to prepare for self-government. Many leading West Indian politicians and civil servants trained together there.

3 By bringing together students from all over the Commonwealth Caribbean it has broken down barriers, dispelled ignorance of other territories and forged lasting links.

4 It acts as a body for research and consultation for governments and other institutions throughout the Commonwealth Caribbean.

The Caribbean Development Bank This is a specialised agency for financing development in the territories of its members. It was founded in 1969 with its headquarters in Bridgetown, Barbados. Unlike CARIFTA and CARICOM, which were both open to all Caribbean countries but which did not attract any non-British members, the Caribbean Development Bank accepted Venezuela and Colombia in 1972. The Bank's funds come from internal sources and it can channel investment from one area into a development project in another. So far its funds have chiefly been used for the benefit of the smaller islands.

9
Colonial churches

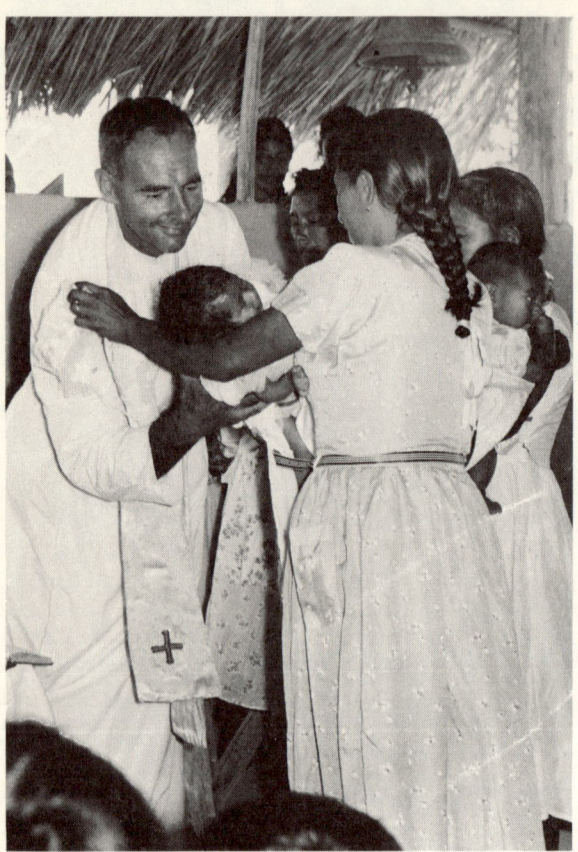

A christening in Guyana

Amerindian religion

In almost all societies there are religious beliefs. Some may seem very primitive, but they are nevertheless religious. For example, man has always wondered about his origins and thus developed creation stories. Man has always felt powerless against the forces which affect his life, like good health or illness, storms or drought, fertility and infertility, thunder and lightning, fire and death. He has, therefore, invented stories about these forces and attributed them to spirits which resided in living and non-living things like rocks, stones, wood, trees, earth, sea and sky, or in man-made objects like idols. Death, and life-after-death, was another puzzle which led man to invent stories of heaven and hell to explain it.

A religion in which power over human life is attributed to spirits in living or non-living things is known as animism. The Arawaks and Caribs in the West Indies had animistic beliefs which were so important to them, especially the Arawaks, that their religion was also a social force. The *caciques* who ruled them were semi-divine. Priests had a social role and religious ceremonies provided the people with their festivities and their singing, dancing, drinking and smoking.

Arawak religion can be traced back to the cultures of the northern tribes of South America through folk tales and myths. One link is 'shamanism', or the belief in a central figure with the power to heal the sick and otherwise control men's lives. The chief shaman of the Arawaks was represented by the *zemi* (idol) of the *cacique*. However, there were many such *zemis* amongst the Arawaks and in this they were different from other primitive tribes.

Each family had its own *zemi* and the power of these *zemis* helped to stratify the society. Making crops grow, healing the sick, bringing illness and death, causing hurricanes and other powers were attributed to *zemis*. Therefore they were worshipped and prayed to, typical practices in an animistic religion.

The Arawaks had their myths also. Their creation myth involved the sun escaping from a cave when the guardian was unwary (the story was not exactly the same amongst all Arawak tribes). They had other creation stories for man, plants and animals. In fact, they probably had a rich religious folklore which we know little about because the Spaniards did not concern themselves with it before they destroyed Arawak civilisation. It was many years before the Spaniards even realised that the Arawaks had a religion.

Spanish Catholicism

Because Spain was the spearhead of colonisation in the New World, she was expected to carry Christianity to the pagans there. Spain and Portugal succeeded in converting two-thirds of the Americas to Roman Catholicism and it is still the church to which the vast majority of the population of the Americas belong; 200,000,000 claim to be Catholic. In the Caribbean, too, Catholicism is dominant.

Colonising expeditions would not dare to leave for the New World without the blessing of the Pope as head of the Roman Catholic Church. The Pope imposed the condition that the colonisers had to convert the heathen to Christianity. Although most of the early Spanish settlers had little regard for religion and still less for converting the native peoples, sometimes natives were sent back to Spain or Portugal to be converted; for example, the Portuguese sent back Africans from the Rio de Oro in West Africa in 1446, and Columbus sent back Arawaks on his second expedition, 1493–6.

The settlers felt that conversion was the responsibility of the clergy but, initially, they did very little beyond establishing a church for settlers. The Roman Catholic Church in the Indies was established and organised on European lines. As soon as the population warranted it and parish priests had laid the foundations, a bishop was sent out and a diocese established. As the empire spread, sub-bishoprics and new dioceses were created. The diocese of Santo Domingo was founded first in 1511; then a subordinate bishopric was founded at Baracoa in Cuba in 1518 (later moved to Santiago de Cuba); the diocese of New Mexico was established in 1530 and that of Lima in Peru, in 1541. These dioceses were the settler capitals in the New World. The bishops and the cathedrals were intended for the settlers.

The conversion of the Americas was undertaken by the 'regular' clergy, not the secular. 'Regular' means those clergy who have taken vows to keep to the rules of a certain order in the Church. In the Roman Catholic Church there were missionaries belonging to special orders who made apostolic work their aim. They went to live among the heathen, to preach to them and convert them. The five most famous orders were the Franciscans, the Dominicans, the Carmelites, the Augustinians and the Jesuits. They all played a part in the Spanish empire, but the most powerful of them was the Dominicans.

When Dominican friars came to the Caribbean they could preach where, and to whom, they wanted; in the cities to the settlers, as Montesinos did in Santo Domingo, or on the frontiers to the Indians, as las Casas did in Venezuela, Guatemala and Costa Rica. Montesinos and las Casas were both Dominicans. Their independence brought them into conflict with the settlers who wanted to use the natives for labour, while the missionaries were trying to win souls for the church. The Dominicans frequently condemned the settlers and were hated for it. Montesinos antagonised the settlers of Santo Domingo in 1511, and las Casas the settlers around Chiapas in Guatemala in 1545.

The Church and the Indians

In the early Catholic Church racism was unheard of. When a person of whatever race became baptised, he became a human being and a Christian, an equal with all his fellow Christians. The Portuguese showed less regard for race than any other Western European coloniser. The Spanish, in theory, held no racial barriers in

Santa Maria de Menor, Santo Domingo

religion and marriage. The Spanish monarchs, from Isabella to Philip II, favoured the rapid economic development of the empire and they were persuaded that the exploitation of Indian labour was essential for this. Thus little effort was concentrated on converting the Indians. The secular clergy did not oppose their exploitation, but the Dominican missionaries frequently did.

The Church had the greatest interest in the Indian problem for humanitarian and self-interested motives:

1 The missionaries wanted to convert the heathen to Christianity;
2 They wanted to save the Indians from exploitation and extermination;
3 By saving the Indians they would have more pagan souls to convert, which would please God and the Pope;
4 They themselves needed Indian labour for the construction and maintenance of their churches and monasteries.

The settlers were destroying the Indians by *encomienda* and *repartimiento*. Thus their interests and those of the Church were completely opposed. With the settlers on one side and the Church on the other, the Crown was in a dilemma. It favoured the economic development of the empire, but it also had a duty to protect the Indians who were among its subjects and to support the Church in the conversion of souls. By the four 'Bulls of Donation' from 1493 to 1506, the Pope had given the Indies to the Crown of Spain. Therefore it was the sacred trust of the King to see that the Indians were converted to Catholicism. Bartholomew de las Casas argued that the sole purpose of the donation was conversion. The settlers' case was argued by a lawyer named Ginés de Sepulveda. He said that the Indians were a sub-human race who should be conquered and exploited.

Las Casas and the Church fought to resist these ideas and though they may have won the argument in Spain, they lost it on the frontier. The Laws of Burgos in 1512 attempted to define the relations between the settlers and the Indians. They illustrated the King's dilemma clearly because, while they stated that the Indians were free men, they allowed *encomienda*.

Montesinos and las Casas

Among the Dominican friars who protested in 1510 was Montesinos. He preached a sermon in which he accused the settlers in Hispaniola of enslaving the Indians, and compared them to the Moors, who as Moslems and heretics were much despised by the Spanish. The settlers complained to the Governor about Montesinos, and the split between the Church and the settlers widened. King Ferdinand could not ignore the issue when Montesinos returned to Spain in 1512 to put the case before him. Ferdinand's Grand Inquisitor was Cardinal Jiménez de Cisneros who had been Isabella's principal religious and political adviser. Ferdinand had an obligation to Jiménez because he had supported Ferdinand's claim to the throne in 1504. Jiménez had been responsible for reforming the Spanish clergy earlier in his career and had then given his attention to the conversion of the heathen. With such an ally at court, Montesinos had to be listened to, and

Map 8 Roman Catholic missionary activity in the West Indies

Ferdinand issued the Laws of Burgos. Unfortunately Montesinos did not return to the Indies, the Laws of Burgos hardly helped the Indians, and Jiménez, who might have made such a difference to Indian policy, died in 1517.

The leadership of the Indians' cause was taken over by las Casas as we saw in Book 1. He was born in Seville in 1474, the son of a merchant, and served as a soldier in Granada. In 1502 he went to Hispaniola with Ovando and was given his first *encomienda*. In 1512 he took holy orders and was perhaps the first person to be ordained in the New World.

The turning-point in his life came when he accompanied Velasquez on his conquest of Cuba in 1511. After witnessing the needless massacre of Caonas, he turned against the Spanish treatment of the Indians. Therefore, in August, 1514, he renounced his *encomienda* and returned to Spain where he was supported by Cardinal Jiménez in his efforts to save the Indians. Under the *Plan para la Reformación de las Indias* (plan to convert and save the Indians), las Casas was sent back to the Indies in 1516 as a commissioner to report on their condition. On his return to Spain in 1518, las Casas developed two practical plans for helping the Indians:
a) to attract farmers as settlers;
b) to establish 'towns of free Indians', where Spaniards and Indians could work together.

Neither of these schemes was successful. In 1520 las Casas took some farmers to start a colony on the Gulf of Paria. There were not enough farmers and, after an attack by the local Indians, the colony was abandoned in 1522.

Las Casas was disillusioned and joined the Dominican Order in 1523 to study and to write. In 1527 he wrote *Historia Apologética* which was the forerunner of his famous *Historia de las Indias*, in which was recorded all he had seen in the Indies. His aim was to reveal to Spain the horrors and injustices of the settlers' treatment of the Indians. After his experiences in Central America he wrote *De Único Modo* (The Only Way [of conversion]). He tried to put his ideas into practice at Tuzutlan on the Golfo Dulce in Costa Rica, where he converted the Indians to Christianity without *encomienda*. This was his most successful practical venture and he went to Spain in 1540 to explain his new ideas.

In 1542 he wrote his second great work, the *Brevisma Relación de la Destrucción de las Indias* (A Brief Account of the Destruction of the Indians). His influence on Charles V was so great that the King passed the new laws in the same year. The Church was supported against the settlers over *encomienda*.

In 1544 las Casas took forty-four Dominican friars to Chiapas in Guatemala where he had been appointed bishop. But he aroused strong opposition among the settlers by ordering the priests not to hear the confessions of those who held *encomienda*. He finally returned to Spain in 1547. Las Casas became adviser on Indian affairs to Charles V, a position he held until his death in 1566, and he continued to devote himself to the cause of the Indians. His history, published against his wishes in 1562, had a great impact on Europe, but not so much on Spain or the Spanish Church. In the second half of the sixteenth century the Dominican and Franciscan friars were lax in their efforts at conversion, but with the arrival of the Jesuits as part of the Counter-Reformation, there were renewed campaigns for conversion in North and South America.

After las Casas' death, Philip II ordered all his works to be collected and published. He was referred to as 'the Apostle of the Indies' and ranked with the greatest of the early European missionaries. His writings influenced the leaders of Latin American independence movements, among them Simon Bolivar.

The Roman Catholic Church and slavery

The Laws of Burgos and the New Laws stated that the Indians could not be enslaved because they were the subjects of the Spanish Crown. This attitude was not extended to African slaves, who were taken to the West Indies in great numbers from about 1515. Even las Casas saw nothing wrong with African slavery. By about 1650 all the Arawaks in the West Indies had been wiped out. The problem now facing the Church was slavery. It accepted slavery in the West Indies, but tried to make it compatible with Christianity.

Roman Catholicism is a highly centralised religion, receiving orders and advice from Rome. Their slave policy was basically the same in the colonies held by both the Catholic powers, France and Spain, with only local variations.

The Spanish had justified the taking of slaves from Africa by arguing that they were subjects of foreign princes who were at war with Spain. Both the Spanish and the French argued that slavery was desirable in the West Indies because it enabled Africans to be brought up as Christians. Thus, whereas the British denied Christianity to their slaves, the Spanish and French, officially, encouraged it. The Spanish slave code, *Las Siete Partidas*, required a master to baptise his slaves, instruct them in the Christian faith and allow them time to go to church. Slave marriage was allowed but not encouraged.

The French *Code Noir* of 1685 was even more definite. Slaves had to be made Christians and be allowed all the rights of Christians. The *Code* laid down that only Roman Catholics could own slaves.

On paper, therefore, the attitude of the Roman Catholic Church to slavery was very different from that of the Church of England. However, in practice the difference was much narrower. In the Catholic islands baptism was usually only a token gesture. Thereafter there was little attempt to instruct the slaves in Christianity. Most Spanish and French slave owners agreed with their British counterparts that Christianity taught ideas which were dangerous to the slave system. In the final analysis the treatment of slaves in all the islands very much depended on the individual owner. A British owner might encourage his slaves in Christianity against official policy.

However, the fact that the Church officially welcomed the slaves in the Catholic islands meant that it won over the slaves, and when emancipation came they were already church members. This explains why the Roman Catholic Church had almost total support from the black masses in the Spanish and French islands, whereas the Church of England was largely shunned by the masses in the British islands.

Protestant churches in the British West Indies

The British West Indian colonies were founded mainly by Anglicans, i.e. members of the Established Church, the Church of England. Often they were religious only in so far as all people in England in those days were regular church-goers whose lives were bounded by the parish. Dissenters, people who disagreed with the Church of England, were often deported to the West Indies. The Quakers are the best example. The seventeenth century was a period of great religious turmoil in England, but this had comparatively little effect on the British West Indian colonies.

The first determined move to establish the Church of England in the British islands was made in 1641 by Captain Philip Bell, the Governor of Barbados. He made attendance at church every Sunday compulsory and punished Dissenters. Lord Willoughby continued this policy. Thus one of the pillars of royalism, the Church of England, was established in Barbados before the English Civil War. Consequently, during the Civil War and the Protectorate period from 1642 to 1660, many Church of England loyalists emigrated to Barbados and the other British islands.

A series of Acts, passed in England between 1661 and 1665 and known collectively as the Clarendon Code, tried to force Dissenters and Nonconformists back into the Church of England. As a result of this many Quakers were deported to Barbados, Nevis and Jamaica. Serious religious dissension reached the colonies. As the number of Quakers increased, the Church of England, through the government, began to persecute them, especially in Barbados. However,

Children going to church in Barbados

when religious toleration was granted in 1689 in England, it also applied in the colonies. Dissenters enjoyed a period of freedom, but later in the eighteenth century persecution returned, chiefly of the Quakers, because it was felt that their numbers had grown to dangerous proportions.

Jamaica was conquered by Cromwell's army which was accompanied by seven Puritan chaplains but it never became a Puritan colony because the soldiers were largely an irreligious rabble. Systematic government began in Jamaica after the Restoration and therefore the Church of England became the first established church there.

The organisation of the Church of England

The Church of England is an episcopal organisation, in which bishops are the key figures. The church is divided into dioceses which are under the bishops. The dioceses are then sub-divided into parishes which are under rectors or vicars.

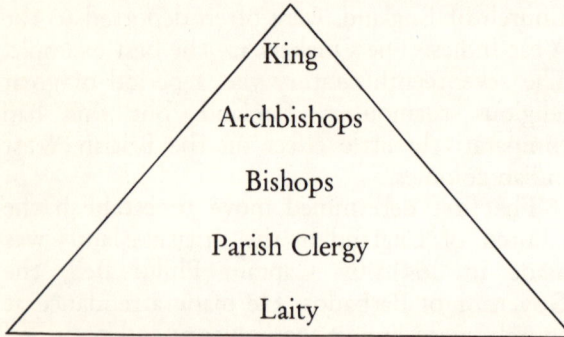

The Bishop of London assumed responsibility for the West Indian colonies from about 1634, although historians can find no documents assigning the colonies to him. His chief function was to appoint clergy to the colonies. Thereafter he had little influence in the colonies and the local legislatures were against any extension of his authority. They allowed the governors to issue licences to preachers without consulting the Bishop, and the governors installed the clergy in their parishes. This was known as the induction. The Bishop of London never visited the West Indies and sent only four representatives there between 1634 and 1800.

The Church at home, the Church in the colonies, even the Bishop of London himself and the Society for the Propagation of the Gospel, asked for a local bishop in the West Indies, but none was appointed until 1824. The following reasons were put forward for this:
1 The colonies felt that a bishop would lessen their autonomy;
2 The Church in the islands did not need close episcopal control;
3 A bishop would deny the independence of the local church;
4 The episcopacy was the agency of the Crown and would thus hasten the separation of the colonies.

The episcopacy was finally introduced when the Church of England realised that it was necessary to improve its organisation before emancipation.

From the earliest days the British islands were sub-divided into parishes. If the church received an income from land in the parish, as many West Indian churches did, the incumbent was known as a 'rector'; if not, a 'vicar'. However, the parish went beyond a mere church division. As the people in the parish received baptism, marriage and burial from the church, the parish was responsible for keeping registers of its parishioners. Because of this, the central government relied on the parishes to collect taxes, hold elections and publish laws. Thus the parishes became institutions of local government. In modern times, this government role has become much more important to most local people than the church role.

The parish needed its own government to deal with its administration as well as its church functions. This body was known as the vestry. Clergymen sat on vestries *ex officio*, but other members were elected by the parishioners. The vestry thus provided the local government.

The central governments voted money for the parishes, thus the salaries (stipends) of the clergy were paid partly by the central government. By 1870 one-tenth of all government expenditure in the British West Indies went to the Church. However, Church of England clergymen had other sources of income also. They received money from the Mother Church in England, from bequests, donations and alms and, possibly, from parish lands. In the seventeenth and eighteenth centuries Church of England clergymen received fairly generous stipends, especially if the parish held rich lands. A figure of not less than £300 per year was general for a vicar. It is not surprising that the clergy aspired to mix with the highest levels of society.

Weakness of the Church of England before 1800

The Church of England had a very poor record in the British West Indies before 1800. Perhaps the general irreligiousness of the people was beyond its control, but some of its failure was due to poor organisation and the rest to the poor quality of the clergy.

1 *General irreligion* Christianity did not attract the settlers, and non-attendance at church was the rule, especially by men. Port Royal was the 'Sodom and Gomorrah' of the British islands. One clergyman said of it that there was 'no more ungodly people on the face of the earth'. Another said of the West Indies in general 'I am in the Devil's country; women and drink carry all before them'.

2 *Poor organisation* Some of the reasons for this are listed below.

a) The British West Indies were in the diocese of London, 6,400 kilometres away. Apart from the initial recruitment, the Bishop had no power over the clergy in the West Indies. However incompetent or immoral a clergyman was, there was no bishop or archdeacon to remove him. Governors had the power of suspension or deprivation, but never used it.

b) There were no Synods as in England, so there was no local discussion of church matters and no corporate spirit among the clergy. There was also no direction or instruction from a superior on doctrine or liturgy which was often subject to local variation. Clergy were often ill-informed on such basic matters as the Articles and Creed.

c) There were too few clergymen. In 1800 there were only forty-eight in the whole of the British West Indies.

d) Some parishes did not even have a parish church. In others the church was too small or was located in an inaccessible part of the parish.

e) The clergy were not backed up by lay auxiliaries such as lay-readers, catechists, Sunday School teachers or parish visitors as they were in England.

f) There was no recruitment of locally-born clergy until the nineteenth century. Christopher Codrington the Younger in 1710 willed part of his Barbados estate for the setting up of a college for training students for the ministry, to be administered by the Society for the Propagation of the Gospel. It was not until the nineteenth century that the provisions of his will were carried out. The first ordinations from Codrington College took place in 1834.

3 *Poor quality of the clergy* Of course, there were many exceptions to the following generalisations. Moreover the clergy faced an almost impossible task in an hostile environment.

a) The Bishop of London applied lower standards in recruiting of clergy for the West Indies than for England.

b) Clergymen were often attracted by the high stipends and social status enjoyed in the British West Indies.

c) There was an absence of the evangelical zeal which was needed to spread the Gospel in the West Indies.

d) The clergy were slack in the colonies because they knew there was no likelihood of deprivation.

e) A few of the clergy were so immoral that they were despised or were social outcasts.

The greatest condemnation of the Church of England in the West Indies before the nineteenth century was its almost total rejection of the slaves. They were the vast majority of the poulation and were eager to join the Church. In this the Church of England upheld the existing social order and the clergy even disobeyed the directions of their superiors. In 1685 King James II said that Christianity should be taken to the slaves. In 1723 the Bishop of London urged slave owners to have their slaves instructed in Christianity. In 1737 Bishop Berkeley asked missionaries to go out among the slaves and convert them.

Some of the reasons for this are listed below.

1 The clergy were weak and apathetic and it needed courage to oppose the plantocracy.

2 Orders from England were never strong enough and, in any case, could not be enforced.

3 The clergy accepted the prevailing colonial view that slavery was necessary for economic development and social stability. Christianity, by undermining the slave system, would endanger the prosperity of the colonies.

4 (the most crushing indictment of all) The clergy in the colonies enjoyed the slave system and liked the high social status it gave them. The clergy put forward many excuses for not accepting slaves into the Church, among them, that slaves were unfit to become Christians and that it was contrary to the law of the colonies, quoting a law of 1676.

Thus the Church of England neglected the slaves until it was too late. When emancipation was inevitable it attempted some reforms, but by then the Nonconformist churches were active in converting the slaves. Consequently, when emancipation came, most of the freed slaves rejected the church which had rejected them, and remembered the churches which had welcomed them in their slavery days.

Church of England missions

The Society for the Propagation of the Gospel, founded by Royal Charter in 1701, did try to do something about converting the slaves, although they were too weak to act against the vested interests in the British islands. In 1794 the Society for the Conversion and Religious Instruction and Education of the Negro Slaves in the British West Indian Islands was founded as a counterweight to the evangelical work of the Nonconformist churches. The Church Missionary Society (1799) and the British and Foreign Bible Society (1803) were primarily directed at Africa, the East and the Pacific but did some work in the West Indies.

The Nonconformist churches

The Quakers

The Society of Friends was founded by George Fox between 1647 and 1666. It was given the nickname 'Quakers' in 1650 by Mr Justice Bennet when George Fox told him to 'tremble at the word of the Lord'. The Quakers held that the personal knowledge of God by each individual was the foundation of belief, and that there should be no formal creeds, prayers, clergy or ritual in the church. The basis of Quaker worship was the meeting at which the assembled worshipped God and waited for his word to come to them. In Quaker terminology, after 'silent waiting' an 'inward light' would come to someone which would lead to a 'concern' to the rest of the meeting who would debate it. If it was acceptable it would be adopted unanimously. This is how Quaker opposition to slavery arose. Any dealing with, or owning, slaves became a 'concern' to a single group of Quakers at first, but then spread to the whole Quaker movement. Any Quaker disobeying the Society was disowned.

The first Quakers arrived in the West Indies in

A Quaker meeting

1658. They had often been deported from England as indentured servants and were made to work extra long periods of indenture (up to seven years) to pay back the cost of their passage. The Quakers became outcasts because they rejected so much of the West Indian way of life. They refused to join the militia because Quakers must not bear arms or fight. They refused to attend Church of England services or to pay tithes to it. They taught reading, writing and Christianity to their slaves and often gave them their freedom. They would not marry non-Quakers. They adopted a special language and dress to show their special honesty, purity and equality.

The Quakers were most active in Barbados. In 1658 Quaker missionaries visited the island, and in 1671 George Fox himself came. This gave the movement much encouragement and numbers grew. Eventually, in 1676 the Barbados Legislature passed an Act against Quakers and persecution of them grew. They were particularly hated for making their slaves Christians, for their refusal to patronise the Church of England and join the militia.

The Moravians

Moravianism began in East Bohemia about 1417 and the movement was unified in 1727 at Herrnhut in Moravia, which is now in East Germany. It was founded on the belief that the Bible was the authority for all conduct in life. Its members sought to imitate Christ in gentleness, poverty, patience and love of one's enemies. They aimed at extending Christianity to the ends of the earth, so missionary work was of the utmost importance to them.

Their first missions arrived at St Thomas in the Danish West Indies in 1732. They lived in close-knit communities which aimed at self-sufficiency and their piety was very obvious. In fact, because of this, they aroused little opposition. The British Parliament passed an Act in 1749 encouraging Moravian missions in the British Islands. Following this, a Moravian mission was established in Antigua in 1754.

A typical Moravian community in the West Indies would take over a sugar estate, or estates, and cut themselves off from the world outside. The blacks were made Christians and were equal in status with the whites. Whites and blacks worked alongside each other in the fields. This caused some offence to other white planters who felt that whites should never do manual labour in a slave society. The Moravians remained numerically small and their ideas were confined to their communities. Only in Antigua did the Moravians form a significant proportion of the population, reaching 9,000 by 1800. They were also active in Jamaica and Barbados.

Their importance lies in the impact that they had on the missionary movement in other churches. The reports from their world-wide missions stimulated Protestant churches to send out their own missions. Moravian missionaries were leaving Herrnhut throughout the eighteenth and nineteenth centuries and, by the end of the period, other churches had begun to follow them, firstly the Nonconformist churches and later the Church of England.

The Wesleyan Methodists

'Methodists' was a nickname given to a group of students led by John Wesley at Oxford University in 1729 because they were so earnest about their worship. They attended church regularly, studied the Bible in groups and put their Christianity into practice by visiting the Oxford prisons. Methodists simplified worship and insisted on a personal relationship with God. They stressed the power of the Holy Spirit to help a person believe in God. They had a ministry, but not an aloof hierarchy like the Church of England ministry. Methodist ministers worked in partnership with the laity. They also laid emphasis on good works, which consisted of helping the poor and underprivileged and on improving social conditions. Missionary activity was very important in Methodism. John Wesley and his brother, Charles, preached countless sermons on both sides of the Atlantic to people in all walks of life, but chiefly to the underprivileged who felt rejected by the Church of England. John Wesley himself kept the movement, theoretically, within the Church of England until 1784, but others had broken from the Church well before that.

Methodism proved very attractive to the slaves. It had missionary emphasis, concern for the oppressed, refusal to be held down by the social system, relegation of the status of the clergy, informal meetings as well as formal services and emphasis was placed on the personal relationship between the believer and God. Therefore it is not surprising that it took root in the British West Indies. Methodism was introduced in Antigua in 1770 after Gilbert, the Speaker of the Assembly, had met John Wesley in England. It had spread to other islands by 1789 when Thomas Coke visited the West Indies. This led to the Methodist Missionary Society sending out twelve more missionaries. By 1800 there were about 7,000 Methodists in Antigua, nearly all of whom were slaves. By 1838 the Methodists were next in number to the Roman Catholics and Anglicans in the West Indies, in spite of being persecuted for teaching Christianity to the slaves.

The Baptists

The Baptist Church had its origins in the Puritan movement in seventeenth-century England. Their churches were based on the New Testament churches. Each church had to be a self-governing body composed of believers only, not based on a territorial parish which included non-believers.

Within the early Baptist movement, there was a split. The Particular Baptists felt that Christ died only for an elect, 'The Chosen', and only these were predestined for salvation. This belief was strongly Calvinist. The General Baptists felt that Christ died for all men. It was associated with Jacobus Arminius, a Dutch theologian, who emphasised man's free will and salvation by good works. Therefore these Baptists were sometimes called Arminians.

Some Particular Baptist groups went to North America, but the American Loyalists who brought the Baptist Church to the British West Indies in 1776 were General Baptists. The following beliefs still form the basis of Baptist worship:

1 The Bible is the supreme authority for all conduct and belief;
2 The baptism of infants is not favoured. A person must be a believer before he can be baptised;
3 A church is composed of believers only, all those who place their trust in Christ;
4 All believers have an equal part in the life of the church;
5 Each church is self-governing and does not have to look to any outside authority;
6 The Church and State are separate. Religion is a matter for each man's conscience and there must be no outside interference.

Baptist worship is distinguished by:
1 Plain, simple chapels;
2 A sermon based on the scriptures as the central part of the service;
3 Little ritual and very few set prayers;
4 Prayers are extemporaneous and often consist of different words each time;
5 The importance of hymn singing;
6 Monthly communion which takes place in the pews, not at an altar;
7 The baptism of believers by total immersion, usually in a river or the sea.

The first Baptists settled in the Bahamas and Jamaica. George Lisle, a coloured Baptist deacon from Virginia, was given a licence to preach in Kingston and built a huge chapel. He suffered imprisonment for preaching to slaves, not just in his chapel, but in the fields also. He converted another American, Moses Baker, and together

Baptists undergoing total immersion

they built up the Baptist Church in Jamaica. They were not helped by the Baptist Church in Britain or the United States for many years. However, their success was so great they could not be ignored and the Baptist Missionary Society of Britain sent out missionaries in 1814. The Baptist Church became easily the most popular church in Jamaica for the ex-slaves.

Persecution of Nonconformist churches

Nonconformists were regarded with suspicion by the ruling classes in the British West Indies. This was basically because they taught slaves the Christian doctrines of equality and brotherhood which the planters considered would undermine the slave system.

At first Nonconformist preachers were issued with licences fairly easily, but as feelings against them grew, the licences were hedged about with conditions which rendered them useless. For example:
1 Preachers could not preach on estates unless invited by the owners or attorneys;
2 Preachers could not preach between the hours of sunrise and sunset. This effectively meant they could not reach the slaves;
3 Baptism could only take place with the permission of the parish authorities after prior notice had been given;
4 Licences would not be issued unless the preacher had been resident in the island for a certain length of time.

These restrictions reflected the worry of the plantocracy at the success of Nonconformist missionaries. Towards the end of the eighteenth century and in the early nineteenth century, the planters' attitude hardened into violence, due to abolition and emancipation. The planters blamed the missionaries for the end of the slave system. Violent persecution was most common in the large islands. In Barbados the Methodist chapel in Bridgetown was stoned and the meetings stopped in 1789. The slaves who attended were flogged. Methodist and Baptist ministers were beaten up in Jamaica.

As emancipation drew nearer, the cases of violence became more frequent. Among the best known was the burning of William Shrewsbury's Methodist Chapel in Bridgetown. However, the persecution meted out by the Colonial Church Union in Jamaica in 1832 was the climax. Fourteen Baptist and six Methodist chapels were destroyed and an unrecorded number of preachers beaten up. After emancipation the violent persecution died out, but social persecution of Nonconformists continued throughout the nineteenth century. An example was the ejection of George William Gordon from St Thomas' Vestry in 1863 on the grounds that he was a Baptist.

10
Religion and emancipation

Voodoo priestess

Preparation for emancipation

Evangelicalism concentrated on practical Christianity. It emphasised the need to perform good works in order to be a good Christian, and denied the emphasis put on sacraments, liturgy and ritual. Converting the slaves provided it with the perfect opportunity for doing good works.

The evangelicals in England, known as the 'Clapham Sect', were only active in the abolition of the slave trade. They agreed with converting the slaves, but expected the Church of England to emphasise the doctrine of obedience so that the master-slave relationship could be maintained.

Other evangelical groups in the Church of England also stopped short of emancipation at first. The missionary societies, like the Society for the Propagation of the Gospel and the Society for Promoting Christian Knowledge, had worked within the framework of a slave society as if slavery was a permanent institution. The new societies, like the Church Missionary Society (1799) and the British and Foreign Bible Society (1803), were not concerned with changing society. In any case, apart from the Society for the Propagation of the Gospel, these societies had little influence in the West Indies. The slaves themselves certainly felt little impact from the Church of England societies. The ruling classes would not co-operate with the evangelicals and the local clergy of the Church of England wanted to preserve the existing social order.

Nonconformist missions

Nonconformist churches were basically evangelical because they were against the excessive emphasis placed on church government, liturgy and ritual by the Church of England. Their early goals were to help the oppressed and spread the Gospel to the underprivileged. They appealed to the lower classes and attracted their support because they were prepared to go among them. In 1792 the Baptist Missionary Society was founded. The Methodists had no formal missionary society at this stage (the Wesleyan Mission was founded in the nineteenth century), but John Wesley sent out individual missionaries across the Atlantic in 1771, of whom Francis Asbury was the most famous. Later Thomas Coke, the greatest Methodist missionary, joined him. The Nonconformist missionary efforts to reach the masses had begun to have an impact on the slaves before the end of the eighteenth century.

With the approach to emancipation they made genuine efforts to better the conditions of the slaves and end slavery. Their position was difficult because they were preaching equality and the brotherhood of all men while the law was denying these Christian principles. When passions were at breaking point they had to restrain the slaves from violence in order to keep within the law. It was not until 1815 that the Jamaican Assembly acknowledged the right of the slaves to receive Christian instruction. Before that the missionaries had really been acting illegally. The demands for baptism and marriage from the slaves gave them a tremendous amount of work and many died in the attempt. They were constantly persecuted by the ruling classes and, most disheartening of all, they were accused by the slaves themselves of being on the side of the whites when riots broke out. This was the experience of the Reverend John Smith in Demerara and William Knibb in Jamaica.

In 1815 opposition to the Nonconformist missionaries diminished as some islands agreed to operate parts of the amelioration policy. Methodist chapels were reopened in Antigua and Jamaica and there was a sharp rise in the number of slave baptisms and marriages. However, there was a reaction against this in 1823 and persecution of Nonconformists was renewed in Barbados and British Guiana. By doing this, the plantocracy was acting against its own interests because public opinion in England became convinced that complete emancipation was the only solution. The death of John Smith in prison caused a great outcry in England.

The ruling classes in Jamaica made a last effort to suppress the Nonconformist missions between 1828 and 1833. In 1828 the Assembly made a bitter attack on the Methodists and Baptists, saying that their only object in converting the slaves was to make money.

The violence of the Colonial Church Union increased so much in 1832 that it had to be outlawed early the next year. Once again the efforts of the persecutors were counter-productive. William Knibb, Thomas Burchell and the Reverend J. M. Phillippo, who had all suffered in violent incidents, led a Baptist delegation to England. Their reports brought evangelicals together in their denunciation of the slave system. This formidable body of public opinion ensured that Buxton would carry the Emancipation Bill.

Conclusion

The Church of England did very little to bring about emancipation. Typical Church of England preaching stressed the obedience of man to God, sons to fathers and slaves to masters. In answer to their critics who accused them of doing nothing to bring about emancipation, the Church of England said that their work had been to prepare all classes to accept the changes peacefully. The Nonconformists, on the other hand, were openly in favour of emancipation and agitated for it at home and in the West Indies. The slaves understood the different attitudes taken by the Church of England and the Nonconformists and it influenced their choice of denomination in the emancipation and post-emancipation period.

Reforms in the Church of England

In response to competition from the Nonconformists, the Church of England attempted to improve its organisation in the British West Indies. It tried to ensure that every parish had a church building in good repair and a resident clergyman. This was easier said than done. In 1800 Bishop Porteus of London set up a Commissiary Court of five rectors in Jamaica to discipline the clergy. However, little was done and the first Bishop of Jamaica, Christopher Lipscomb, concluded in 1824 that it was necessary to wait for the old clergy to die before standards could be improved. Bishop Porteus also tried to encourage Sunday Schools in the West Indies but it was almost impossible without lay volunteers. The most valuable reform before 1824 was the reduction in fees for baptism from over twenty shillings to two shillings and sixpence. Later, in 1824, no fees were charged to slaves for baptism.

The creation of two dioceses

In 1824 an Act was passed which proposed the creation of two full dioceses in the British West Indies, paid for by the British Treasury. The diocese of Jamaica, including British Honduras and the Bahamas, and the diocese of Barbados, including St Vincent, Grenada, the Leewards, Trinidad and British Guiana, were established. It was hoped that this would improve the organisation of the church. The first two Bishops were Christopher Lipscomb in Jamaica and William Hart Coleridge in Barbados. Their instructions were to instruct and discipline the clergy and report on what had been done for the slaves.

This was accompanied by other reforms. The grant to the West Indian Church was increased to about £20,000 per year, which enabled the two bishops to appoint more clergy. In the diocese of Jamaica the number of clergy was increased to forty-five, and in Barbados to twenty-seven. However, it was difficult to raise the numbers and standard of the clergy immediately. The Church was still dependent on English-trained clergy. The first locally-ordained clergy graduated from Codrington College in 1834. Most of them went to Barbados and Jamaica continued to rely heavily on English recruits.

By 1833 Bishop Coleridge was able to report an increase in the number of church buildings, clergy, congregations and the taking of the sacraments. The number of Church of England schools also increased. However, the reforms of 1824 came too late to attract the slaves to the Church of England, except in Barbados.

Codrington College

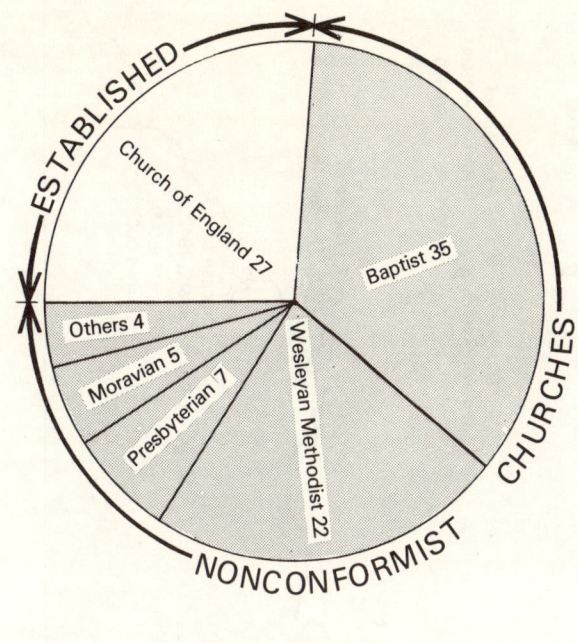
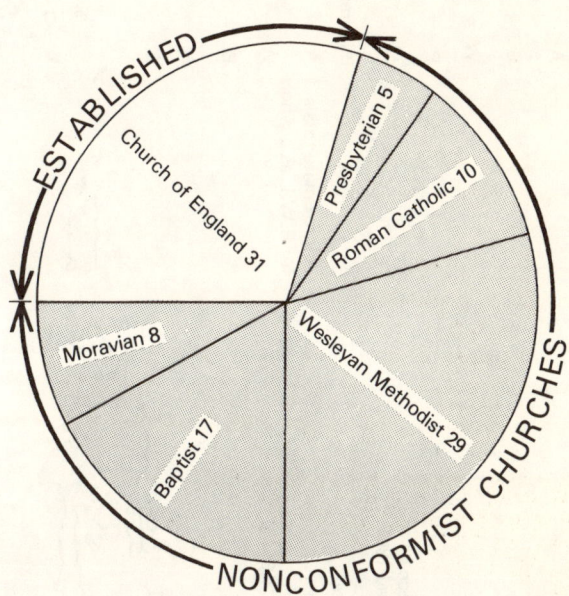

Pie charts of the Christian denominations c 1850

Post-emancipation period

The same trends were followed in the post-emancipation period. From 1834 the Negro Education Grant paid £30,000 per year (later £40,000) for schools in the British West Indies. The Church of England's share of this was channelled through the Society for the Propagation of the Gospel. The Society was also authorised to take collections in church to help towards its missionary work. In the decade following emancipation it had funds totalling nearly £200,000 at its disposal, most of which went on education. Money from England was matched by local grants. The local vestries voted so much for the recruitment of new clergy that the bishops were at a loss to find the men. The island governments also increased their grants to the Established Church. In 1841, the Jamaican Assembly voted it £66,000.

The number of Church of England clergy in the post-emancipation decade more than doubled. In the diocese of Jamaica there were about ninety clergy by 1845 and about seventy in the diocese of Barbados. Spread over such a vast area as the Caribbean they could not be effectively supervised by only two bishops, even though the size of the flock was very small by English standards.

Inevitably more bishops and new dioceses had to be created. In 1842 the diocese of Antigua and the diocese of Guiana were created; in 1861 the diocese of Nassau (Bahamas); in 1872, the diocese of Trinidad; in 1879, the diocese of the Windward Islands; and in 1883, the diocese of British Honduras. In this year the Archdiocese of the West Indies was also established. Thus, by the end of the nineteenth century, there was better supervision of the clergy and some improvement of standards.

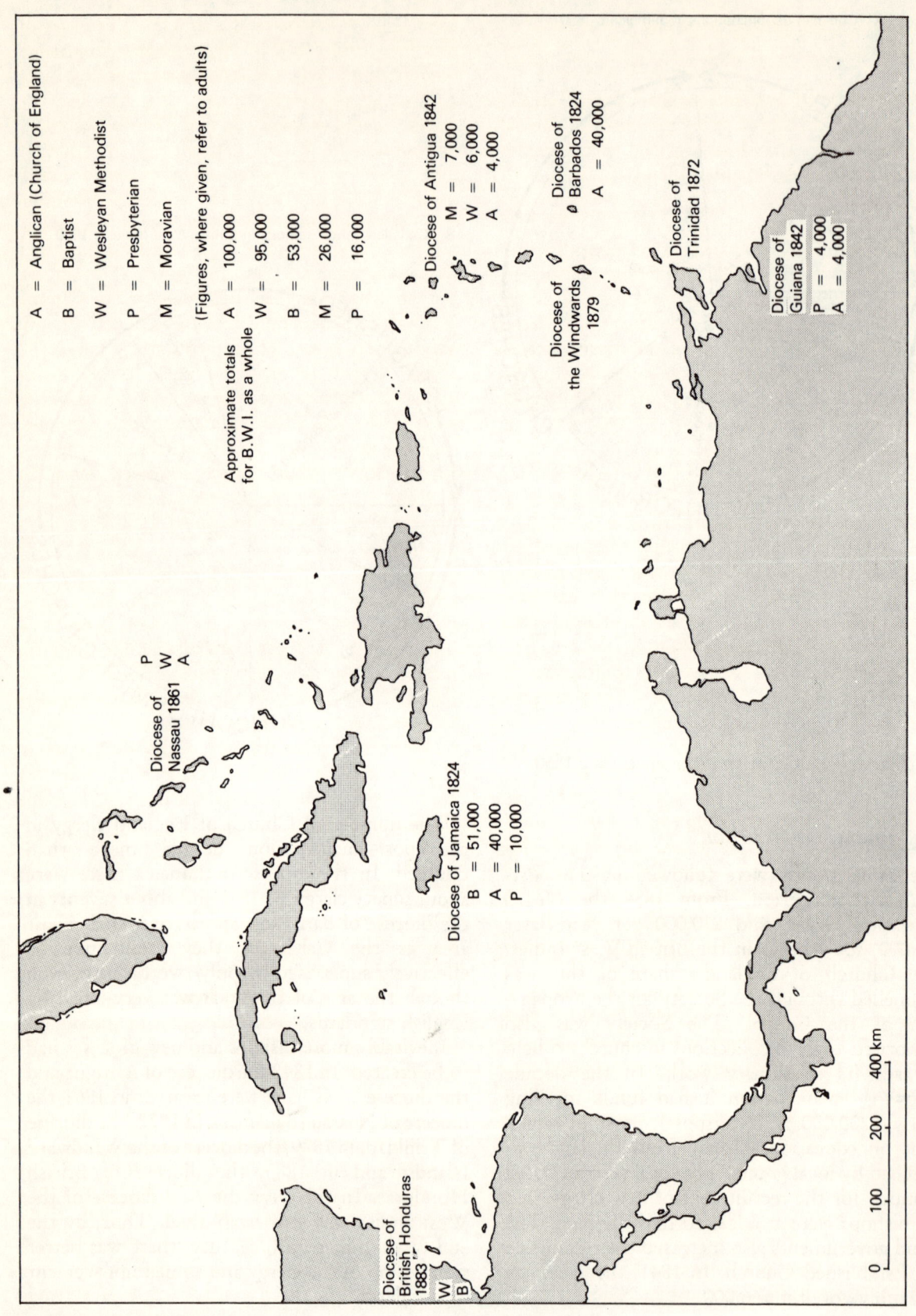

Map 9 Protestant churches in the British West Indies, 1848

The disestablishment of the Church of England

The Church of England as the 'official' church enjoyed a privileged position in the British islands. It was the church of the ruling classes. However, establishment did not interfere with freedom of choice in religion. There was no legal disability for not being a member of the Established Church, except that occasionally a Nonconformist was excluded from vestry membership. A Nonconformist could vote, sit in the legislature, hold government office and serve in the armed forces. Often a person aspiring to rise in society would transfer from a Nonconformist church to the Church of England but this was for social reasons only.

Reasons for disestablishment

The proposals to disestablish the Church of England came from the British government, but the final decision was left to the island governments. It met with no open opposition, except in Barbados, and therefore disestablishment took place between 1868 and 1870.

Disestablishment was not only confined to the British West Indies. The reasons which prompted it applied in a world-wide context:
1 The British government wanted to stop paying grants to the Church in the colonies;
2 It was felt that local churches could, and should, pay for themselves;
3 The theory of 'one state, one church' had been an essential in the days of absolute monarchy but had no validity in democratic times. Freedom of religion was almost universally accepted;
4 Establishment caused unwanted social and racial divisions;
5 (Without doubt the strongest reason) In many parts of the empire, the Church of England, although the state church, was a minority church. In 1870 in the British West Indies the Church of England had the support of about one-third of the population; in Jamaica, just over one-quarter. Only in Barbados was the Church of England the church of the majority.

Procedure for disestablishment

In the early 1860s, governors were sent out to the British West Indies with instructions to assess local feelings on disestablishment. The reaction was favourable, and in 1868 the British government stopped the £20,000 per year grant to the Church in the West Indies. This measure was called 'disendowment'. It was pointed out that disendowment would amount to disestablishment and it was opposed in the House of Lords until the colonies themselves said that the grant was no longer needed.

Then the island governments passed their own Disestablishment Acts. In Jamaica, when the government withdrew support from the Church of England, the property of the Church was not nationalised, but still belonged to the Church. To enable it to hold property legally it had to be made a corporation. By the Jamaica Disestablishment Act of 1870, all churches, rectories, vicarages and schools were transferred to the new corporation. Other islands followed, with St Vincent, in 1883, the last to do so because the Church there could not support itself as easily as the others.

Disestablishment brought little change to the Church, except financially. Stipends were paid by the governments while the incumbents were alive, but as they died the parishes had to find the money for the new clergy themselves. Therefore the death of a rector cost each parish between £300 and £400 and many parishes could not afford to support a rector. In spite of disestablishment, the Church of England continued to be the church of the ruling classes, the upper classes and the whites.

Barbados

The exception in the West Indies was Barbados, where disestablishment was resisted for the following reasons:
1 The Church of England was the church of the majority. About seventy per cent of the population belonged to it;
2 There was little social division on the grounds of religion;
3 There were so many blacks in the Established Church that it could not be called 'the church of the whites';
4 Codrington College was in Barbados. The clergy of the Church of England there were locally born and locally trained. The Barbados government wanted to support its church;
5 The influence of the early bishops, Coleridge

and Parry, and the principals of Codrington College, Finder and Rawle, ensured that the Church was well founded and popular;

6 Barbados had successfully resisted Crown Colony government. This gave it the independence and strength of mind to resist disestablishment which it considered Britain was trying to force on it;

7 State endowment ensured that absentee proprietors contributed to the upkeep of the Church which they would not do if it became a voluntary matter.

Therefore, in 1872, the Barbados Legislature confirmed the Church of England as the Established Church by passing an Act which fixed the appointments and stipends of a Bishop, an Archdeacon and clergy. Stipends would be paid by the government monthly. The parish vestries would continue to be responsible for the maintenance of churches, rectories, vicarages and schools, and for the expenses of church services. The Church of England has remained the Established Church in Barbados.

Immigrant religions

Apart from the Christian religions already mentioned, there are a number of other religions firmly established in the West Indies. Among these are Hinduism and Islam, the religions of the Indian immigrants who arrived in large numbers in Trinidad and British Guiana in the nineteenth century. These faiths are more than religions, they are social systems as well. The British government and the Christian churches accepted this and allowed the Indians religious freedom. However, there was more conversion of Indian immigrants in the West Indies than in other comparable areas of Indian immigration like Fiji or East Africa where the Eastern faiths remained almost completely unaffected.

The Indian immigrants were discriminated against more on racial than on religious grounds. However, they were disadvantaged because their marriages were not recognised and thus their children were classified as illegitimate and were unable to inherit property. They were also deprived of education because they did not belong to a Christian denomination. However, even when education became secular, Indian children were still kept away from school because their parents did not want them to have contact with 'immorality'.

The Church of England looked on the immigrants as a challenge and, in British Guiana, the Society for the Propagation of the Gospel opened up seven missions among the Indian community and appointed three missionaries and ten catechists. In Trinidad the Society spoke of a 'missionary country' and welcomed the chance to win souls, but here the Canadian Presbyterian Church was far more successful. It established schools especially for the Indians and converted many of the young to Christianity.

However, Hinduism and Islam remain the predominant religions of the Indians to this day. The proportion is roughly six Hindus to one Moslem. To understand their resistance to Christianity it is necessary to know something about their faiths.

Hinduism

Hinduism is not simply a religion. It is a set of social customs and a structuring of society as well as being a body of religious belief. It is much older than Christianity, having its origins in the sixth century B.C.

Originally there were three equal and identical gods in the Hindu Trinity, Brahma, Vishnu and Siva. In about 800 A.D. Brahma declined in importance and Vishnu and Siva became the chief deities. All Hindus hold one of these two as the highest form of existence and worship him with supreme devotion. Siva is the god of destruction, but also of creation because everything must be created before it can be destroyed. He is regarded as a bloodthirsty god who inspires fear and wonder. He can work miracles. His followers, called 'Sivaites', come from the extremes of society; from the highest caste Brahmins and the lowest caste Harijans. Vishnu is the Protector and Preserver who upholds order in the world. His followers are called 'Vishnuites'. Both these gods are pantheistic. Their followers believe that god is everything, and everything is god. Hinduism is also polytheistic. There are many gods. Some of them are Vishnu and Siva in other forms, others are minor gods. Perhaps the best known of the others are Rama, Krishna and Laksmi.

Hinduism affects social life through its mysticism. Devout Hindus do not consider material things, especially money, important. The caste system is extremely important and has resisted all attempts to break it down in India. It is not so rigidly practised outside India, but it is still apparent when it comes to occupation and marriage.

Bound up with caste are the Hindu doctrines of reincarnation and the transmigration of souls. Hindus believe that the soul does not die but passes from one form of life to another in its earthly cycle. A soul can pass from an animal to a human and up through the castes. Eventually, if its life on earth has been lived in a godly and moral way, the soul can pass into 'Nirvana', or 'Everlasting Bliss'. This belief reinforces the sanctity of all forms of life and accounts for vegetarianism, the non-taking of life and other Hindu principles.

In the midst of Christian communities the most conspicuous evidence of Hinduism is the festivals. In the British West Indies only some of the festivals can take place because others involve pilgrimages to shrines which are in India itself. The following are ones which are well known in Guyana and Trinidad:

1 *Diwali* takes place in late October. This is a celebration chiefly for the merchant community in which Laksmi, the goddess of wealth, is honoured. Lighted earthenware oil lamps line the parapets and balconies of houses, shops and temples, or float on rivers and ponds, in memory of the return of the god, Rama. A new financial year starts as merchants open new account books. Every one wears new clothes, decorates his house, feasts and gives presents. Westerners call Diwali 'the Hindu Christmas'.

2 *Holi* is the Hindu Spring Festival in February or March. It is a joyous festival in which coloured waters and powders are thrown at people, and there are bonfires, fireworks and special songs. Images of the gods are carried in processions. Worshippers of the god Krishna recall when he played with the wives and daughters of the cowherds. On the day of this festival caste divisions are forgotten.

3 *Mahasivarati* or the 'Great Night of Siva' falls in the first three months of the Christian calendar. It is a solemn festival for the first day of fasting and night of vigil, but the following day is joyous with feasting and exchanging presents. It is the major festival for Sivaites.

The authorities in the British West Indies tried to confine these festivals and celebrations to Indian villages at first, because there was rioting on one occasion when they were held in the public streets. However, more understanding of Hinduism has helped the masses to be tolerant of the festivities and they can now be enjoyed in the towns and cities of Guyana and Trinidad.

Islam

Islam is the religion preached by Muhammad. It is summed up in the belief 'There is no god but Allah, and Muhammad is his prophet'. Muhammad laid down the five pillars of Islam which are the compulsory doctrine of Moslems throughout the world.

1 *Belief in one God* In Islam Allah is one and must be obeyed. Muhammad was entrusted to teach and explain God's message and he is the greatest prophet.

2 *Prayer* There are five prayers a day which can be said in a mosque or wherever a believer finds himself. A prayer mat is placed towards Mecca for the delivery of the prayer. The midday prayer on Friday in the mosque is the most important service of the week.

3 *Alms-giving* This is like a religious tax. It is scaled according to the wealth of the believer.

4 *Pilgrimage* 'Haj' is the Islamic word for the

Mosque in Trinidad

pilgrimage to Mecca which every believer should make once in his lifetime. Then he is entitled to place 'Haji' before his name.

5   *Fasting in Ramadan.* A Moslem must undergo a month-long period of atonement in which he makes peace with Allah and begs forgiveness for all his sins.

Like Hinduism, Islam is more than just a religion. It is a system of law and social conduct. Moslems living in western societies have to observe the laws of the land, but in Moslem countries Islamic laws prevail except in the case of commercial law which involves international transactions. According to the Koran, Moslems are allowed up to four wives and Moslem women are not emancipated. They only have rights as permitted by their husbands and legally a woman can only inherit half as much as a man.

Apart from the mosques and other outward symbols of Islamic architecture, Moslems are not so conspicuous in their way of life as Hindus in a western society. The Moslem festivals are not as many nor as riotously gay as the Hindu ones, with the exception of Ramadan. This is a month of fasting fixed by the moon so calendar dates cannot be given. During this month Moslems are not permitted to eat, drink or have sexual intercourse between dawn and dusk. This abstention is for atonement. It is an extremely solemn period. The twenty-seventh day of Ramadan is known as the Night of the Decree to commemorate the time when the Koran was given as guidance to believers. Ramadan ends with a joyous festival, *Id-el-Fitr* (the breaking of the fast). This can be called the Moslem 'Christmas' as people exchange presents, visit friends and decorate themselves and their houses.

American revivalism

The Christian churches originally came to the Caribbean from Europe. However, in the twentieth century there were revivalist movements in the Protestant churches in the United States which had a small but dramatic impact on religion in the Caribbean.

There had been revivalist movements in Europe such as Puritanism and Anabaptism in the sixteenth-century and German Pietism (e.g. the Moravians) and Methodism in the eighteenth. Twentieth-century American revivalism shared many common ideals with earlier movements:
1   The Bible is the supreme authority for belief and conduct and cannot be wrong;
2   By following Jesus Christ man can reconcile himself with God;
3   Jesus Christ will return to earth again. This is known as the Second Coming;
4   Man has control over his own salvation by free will and good works;
5   By prayer a believer can have certain knowledge of God.
Believers should abstain from wordly practices like drinking liquor, smoking, dancing and going to the movies.

American revivalism has its closest links with Wesleyan Methodism. Indeed many revivalist leaders were once Wesleyan ministers, and it is strongly Methodist in feeling.

American revivalist churches can be divided into two groups.
1   *Holiness Churches* These include the Church of God, the Church of the Nazarene, the Church of Christ and Pilgrim Holiness which are all common in the Caribbean. They emphasise the belief that the Holy Spirit can enter the heart of a believer in prayer and give him a second blessing or 'holiness'. Their church services are simple and subdued and their way of life is restrained. Members should have a commitment to serve the community, especially the poor and deprived. However, in the Caribbean, they have tended to cut themselves off from the rest of the community. This has allowed the Salvation Army to win many of the souls which might have gone to the Holiness Churches.
2   *Pentecostal Churches* They also believe in a second blessing which comes some time after initial conversion to the faith. The split with the Holiness Churches occurred because of the nature of the Pentecostal church services which are very boisterous with much body movement, loud shouting and stamping in prayers and generally very active participation by the congregation.

The great upsurge in American revivalism was between 1933 and 1963. It came to the Caribbean in the 1940s. American missionaries penetrated Cuba, Haiti and Puerto Rico. Then they made a great impact on Jamaica and finally spread through the Eastern Caribbean as far as Guyana. The churches have only small followings, but they are growing. The Church of God in Jamaica

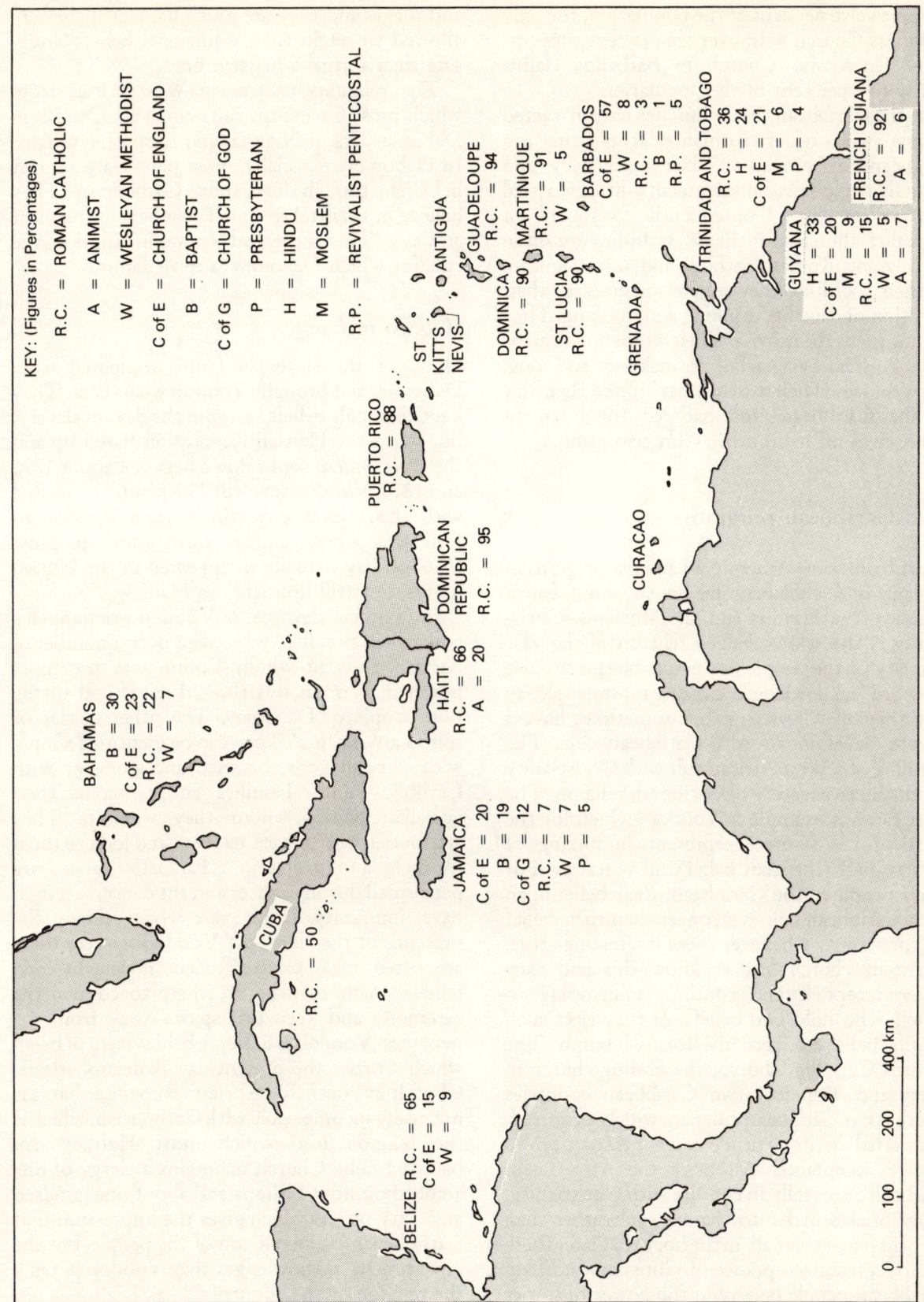

Map 10 Religions and religious denominations in the principal Caribbean territories, c 1970

claims twelve per cent of the population, the only Holiness Church with over ten per cent support. The Pentecostal Church in Barbados claims nearly five per cent of the population.

In the Caribbean these churches have attracted people who reject Roman Catholicism and Anglicanism because of their episcopacy and excessive emphasis on sacraments, liturgy, ritual and adornment. Consequently members of revivalist churches in the West Indies are often fiercely anti-Roman Catholic and anti-Anglican. In their social life they are conspicuous for their rejection of dancing, drinking and smoking. They do not go to the movies. Their womenfolk can be distinguished by wearing no make-up and long, plain dresses. Their attitude has limited their size in the Caribbean, and had led them to cut themselves off from other Christian groups.

Afro-Caribbean religions

Apart from some Amerindian animist religions in Guyana and elsewhere in South and Central America, the Hindus and the Moslems, Christianity is the acknowledged religion of the vast majority of the people in the Caribbean. We use the word 'acknowledged' because most people say that they are Christians, but sometimes have a private belief in an Afro-Caribbean cult. The blending of a West African cult with Christianity is a distinctive feature of Caribbean religion. The most famous example is Voodoo, which for the most of its devotees represents a mixing of African and Christian belief and practices. For many people in the Caribbean, their belief in an Afro-Caribbean cult is stronger than their belief in Christianity whenever there is a testing crisis. Christian church leaders know this and they either accept it and continue ministering to people who hold two beliefs, or they eject such double believers from the formal church. The Roman Catholic Church, the leading church in Haiti and Trinidad, two Caribbean countries where Afro-Caribbean cults are widely practised, has varied in its attitude from persecution to passive acceptance. Although the Afro-Caribbean cults are really in conflict with Christianity, many priests prefer to share a soul rather than have no part in it at all, in the hope that later there will be a total acceptance of Christianity. Many Caribbean people believe in the power of spirits and magic and they are much happier if they are allowed to retain their traditional beliefs alongside their formal Christian ones.

The religious centres in West Africa from which most Caribbean cults come are Ouidah in Dahomey, Ife in Nigeria, and Kumasi in Ghana. In Dahomey, especially, most people are animist in belief although they profess Catholicism. They believe in a central spirit which is held in great fear and awe. This is the god Vodun in Voodoo, the cult for which Dahomey is most famous.

Voodoo in Haiti

Many of the slaves in Haiti originated from Dahomey and brought Voodoo with them. They kept their cult beliefs secret in the days of slavery, but when the Haitian Revolution flared up and the slave system broke down between about 1790 and 1820, Voodoo revived. The planters who fled with their slaves unwittingly took Voodoo to Louisiana where another form grew up. Now Voodoo has virtually disappeared in the United States, but still flourishes in Haiti.

In Haiti the devotees of Voodoo worshipped a god called 'Bondieu' who ruled over a number of African gods of whom Vodun was the most powerful. Vodun was the old tribal god of the Fon people of Dahomey. The other deities or spirits are the 'loa'. They can be identified simply with African gods, or with ancestors, or with Catholic saints. Families adopt loa as their guardian deities whom they worship. They attribute magic powers to them and look to them for help and protection. Fantastic dances are performed during trances and the dancers seem to have immunity from pain which shows the presence of the spirit. At Voodoo services there are often male priests, called 'hourigans' and female 'mambos' who are there to control the ceremony and keep evil spirits away from the devotees. Voodoo is a deeply held system of belief which worries the present-day Roman Catholic Church in Haiti. Some priests recognise that it is not really incompatible with Catholicism which is the religion into which most Haitians are baptised. The Church maintains a clergy of one archbishop, four bishops and about one hundred and sixty priests which gives the impression that Catholicism is the religion of the people, but the government acknowledges that Voodoo is truly the religion of the country.

Other Afro-Caribbean cults

Many blacks in Trinidad are followers of Shango. This practice derives from the Yoruba of Western Nigeria whose god of thunder and lightning is Shango. The Yoruba had other gods like Ogun, the god of war and iron, and Orisha Oko, the goddess of fertility, but Shango was the god the slaves remembered. Shango is also a powerful belief amongst the blacks of Grenada. Rada, another cult from Dahomey, is practised in Trinidad where it is linked with Catholicism.

In Jamaica, African religious beliefs were preserved by the Maroons, the runaway slaves. In the bush they were cut off from any contact with Christianity and had animist religions as their substitutes. Kumina is such a cult. Its devotees can be possessed with spirits who can save them from sickness and death. However, in the last hundred years Pocomania has taken over as the chief Afro-Caribbean religion in Jamaica. Spirit possession is essential to it, accompanied by much drumming and dancing, but it also embodies many Christian beliefs.

Throughout the Caribbean, obeah magic has believers, some serious, others not so serious. It cannot be classed as a religious cult. The word obeah derives from *obi*, the Ashanti word for priest. In the Caribbean an obeahman is capable of working spells for good or ill. Superstitious people attribute mysterious happenings to obeah.

Rastafarians

Today, Rastafarianism is more of a social and political movement than a religion, although this was not so originally. In the 1930s Marcus Garvey, recently returned to Jamaica from the United States, instilled pride in the black race by extolling the virtues of black civilisations in Africa. The Rastafarians adopted many of his ideas. They worshipped the Emperor of Ethiopia, Haile Selassie I (*Ras* means 'prince' and *Tafari* was his name as a prince). To the Rastafarians he was the Messiah of the black race. They believed that blacks were subjected to the whites because of their past sins, but that Haile Selassie would come and lead them back to Africa where they would make a heaven on earth.

In the Jamaica of the 1930s they rejected the way in which the blacks copied the whites. They became anti-white and adopted an African culture with their own black ideals and goals. They sincerely believed that Haile Selassie would lead them out of their subjection in Jamaica and called this event the Exodus. At this stage the Rastafarian movement had followers in the towns and in the countryside. When the Exodus never came they grew disillusioned and the rural followers dropped out of the movement. The visit of Haile Selassie to Jamaica disappointed his devotees. He did not seem to them to be the 'Lion of Judah', but just a Head of State, giving no acknowledgement to their movement.

Current Rastafarian belief in its pure form consists of the following tenets:
a) black pride
b) rejection of western medicine
c) rejection of contraception
d) rejection of Christian marriage and burial
e) no wearing of second-hand clothes
f) no physical contact with whites
g) no eating of pork (Some Rastafarians are convinced that Haile Selassie was a Jew because he was descended from Solomon.)

Rastafarianism is a strong social and cultural force in Jamaica today and has spread to the Jamaican immigrants in Britain. However, now it is mainly an urban movement among the youth and has lost its appeal to the peasantry.

A Rastafarian

11
Social life

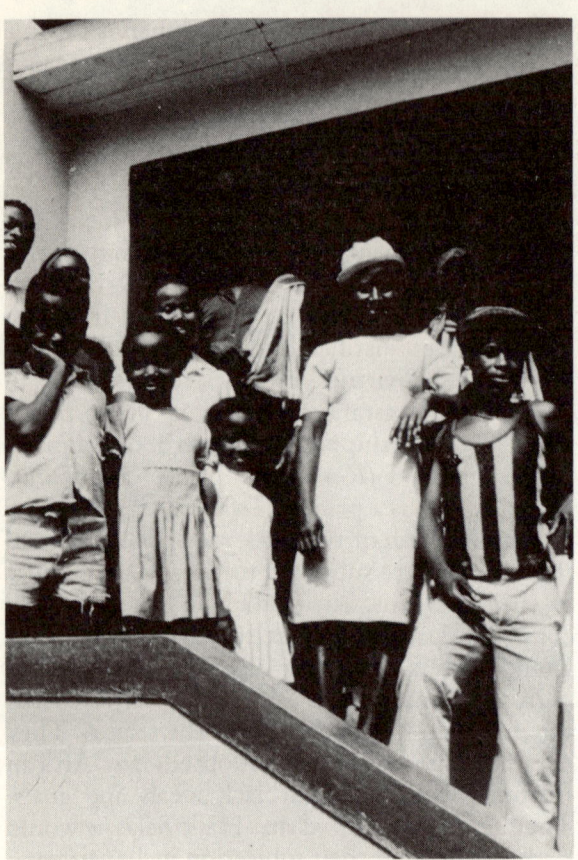

A Jamaican family outside their house

After emancipation

The structure of society in the West Indies did not change radically in the nineteenth century. Emancipation effected a great legal change by freeing the slaves, but in every other way their life style remained unchanged.

Life altered only in minor ways. The changes that occurred were gradual and almost unnoticeable, although they were to provide the basis for the major social changes of the twentieth century. For example:

a) blacks acquired land and formed a peasant class;
b) in some islands immigrants became labourers on the sugar estates;
c) educational opportunities for blacks and coloureds improved;
d) a few became teachers, lawyers and journalists etc., thus improving their social status;
e) the black and coloured populations increased while the white population declined;
f) alternative sources of wealth to sugar were developed;
g) communications improved and this, together with the opportunities for emigration, brought a new consciousness to the West Indies towards the end of the period.

However, the basic form of West Indian society, with the whites on top and the blacks at the bottom, remained unchanged.

There are a number of reasons for this somewhat surprisingly static situation.

1 Emancipation was a bloodless revolution, effected by reformers in England rather than by the blacks themselves. It was not a violent class or race struggle in which the classes attempted to reverse their positions in society. On 31 July, 1834, the blacks were slaves and at midnight, by the stroke of a pen, they were free. There was little disruption and life, especially in the Eastern Caribbean, went on as before. In Jamaica, the situation was more difficult but, even there, violence was rare and there was an orderly exodus from the plantations.

2 The slaves were resigned to their position in society. They soon realised that freedom had not brought them material benefits: indeed sometimes they were worse off. However, they did not rebel. They were long-suffering, perhaps as a result of three hundred years of slavery, and they accepted that changes could only come about gradually.

3 West Indian society was very conservative at all levels. Conservative people are reluctant to change their way of life. This is a common feeling where society is based on land and, certainly, the landowners did not want change. The peasants, who depended on the land for their livelihood, were also reluctant to risk their security.

4 The slaves had been indoctrinated with the idea that 'white is right'. Whites were the leaders economically, politically and socially. Because of this the blacks tried to copy them. This did not change in 1834. The blacks knew of no other life than that of the plantation, and had no other ideas than those instilled into them by their former owners. Indeed, emancipation reinforced the desire to copy the whites because it made it possible to do so.

5 Colonialism, which became a much more conscious force in the nineteenth century, reinforced all the values of West Indian society. Between 1865 and 1867, all the British territories, with the exception of Barbados, became Crown Colonies. Local assemblies disappeared and there was more direct control from Britain. Governors regained their powers and more British civil servants were appointed, which reinforced the idea that the white man ruled. The hold of the plantocracy on society was strengthened because the white planters were associated with the white administrators. The planters welcomed colonialism because it strengthened their position in society. In the 1960s Kenneth Kaunda, President of Zambia, trying to rid Africans of the idea that the white man still ruled after independence, coined the phrase 'psychological colonialism'. The black people in the West Indies certainly felt and saw that the white man ruled after emancipation.

Nobody was deceived about how little difference emancipation had made to society. In 1848 Lord Harris, Governor of Trinidad, wrote to Sir Charles Grey, the Governor of Jamaica: 'A race has been freed, but a society has not been formed.' A peasant, talking to another about slavery and emancipation, said: 'one kind they abolish, but they forget to abolish the next kind.'

Colour

Before emancipation there was one basic division in society; that between slave and free. Later, the dividing line was colour. But there were innumerable shades of colour and thus social distinctions became less clear. This was further complicated after 1838 by the entry of southern Europeans and immigrants from the East.

Between whites and blacks came the intermediate group of coloureds. For reasons of security and economic self-interest, whites and coloureds had tended to support each other, and both had despised the blacks. After emancipation the whites despised the coloureds because having 'colour' became a taint; a coloured had some 'blackness' in him which grouped him with the blacks. On the other hand, the blacks felt the coloureds had some 'whiteness' in them which kept them apart from the blacks.

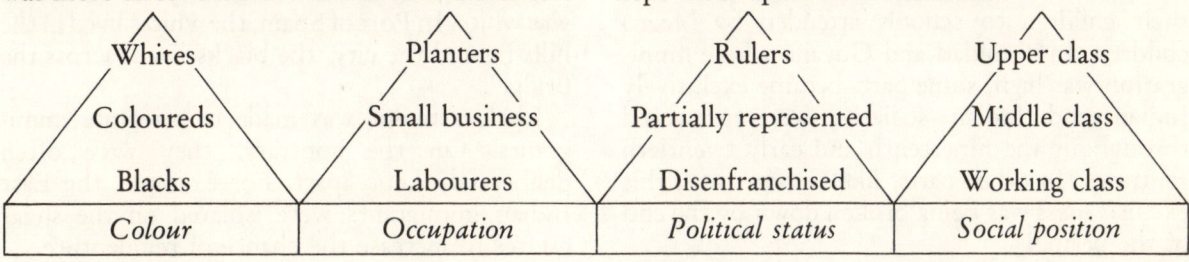

Whites	Planters	Rulers	Upper class
Coloureds	Small business	Partially represented	Middle class
Blacks	Labourers	Disenfranchised	Working class
Colour	*Occupation*	*Political status*	*Social position*

In the nineteenth century the division of society by colour began to coincide with the division of society by occupation and political status as can be seen in the diagram on page 121. There were few places in the Caribbean where societies were not mixed. As colour and racial identity increased in importance so did racial prejudice. Its hold on society was so strong that it was rarely questioned in the nineteenth century.

Marcus Garvey was one of the first blacks to reject white values and take pride in being black.

He said in 1914:

> I was a black man and, therefore, had absolutely no right to lead; in the opinion of the coloured element, leadership should have been in the hands of a yellow, or a very light man... There is more bitterness among us Negroes, because of the caste of colour, than there is between other peoples.

The older plantation colonies of Antigua, Barbados and Jamaica were predominantly black at the end of the nineteenth century, unlike Trinidad and Guyana which had a large population of East Indians.

Colour and kin were not as important to these immigrants as their own cultural traditions. The East Indian immigrants were either Hindus or Moslems and few of them were converted to Christianity. Both the Hindu and the Moslem religions exert a powerful influence on the everyday life of their followers.

The Hindus retained the caste system they had known in India and thus remained a separate group in West Indian society. A cross-caste relationship, i.e. the mixing of classes, was impossible. Caste determined everything. For example, certain menial jobs were confined to sweepers, and, at one time, only Parsees played cricket. Indian girls were very strictly brought up and marriages were arranged by their parents. Although they attached great importance to education, East Indians were unwilling to send their children to schools attended by Negro children. In Trinidad and Guyana where immigration was high, some parts became exclusively Indian and Indian societies were preserved throughout the nineteenth and early twentieth centuries. In other parts, like Georgetown, this exclusiveness was being broken down by the end of the period.

The various groups of immigrants, by their diverse cultures and races, contributed to West Indian development in many ways. They gave a rich cultural heritage and provided a middle strand between black and white.

As we have seen, they enabled the sugar estates to continue and increased the growing number of small farmers producing new export crops. The East Indians were responsible for the growth of the rice industry in Trinidad and Guyana. They also brought with them knowledge of irrigation which was useful in growing not just rice, but also sugar and other crops.

The Chinese became shopkeepers, traders and businessmen. All the immigrants who succeeded in making a little money were aware of the importance of educating their children and thus provided many future leaders. In 1909, the Trinidad Immigration Department said:

> We have now, in practice and at work here, clergymen, lawyers, solicitors, merchants, shopkeepers, proprietors, managers, overseers, bookkeepers and tradesmen, some of whom came to Trinidad under indenture, the rest of whom had indentured fathers.

Society divided

As a result of slavery, plantation society, emancipation and immigration, the West Indies was a society where the races mixed but did not combine. This had advantages, but it also had disadvantages. Friction, both dormant and evident, existed and indeed increased. The answer was integration, but little attempt to achieve this was made by either the British government or any of the individual groups.

Towns are usually great melting pots where integration happens inevitably. This was not so in the West Indies, where towns were quartered by race. For example, in the nineteenth century West Kingston became black, North Kingston was white. In Port of Spain, the whites lived in the hills behind the city, the blacks lived 'across the bridge'.

Little attempt was made to integrate immigrants. On the contrary, they were often deliberately kept apart. For example, the East Indian immigrants were isolated on the sugar estates to increase the chance of reindenture.

There was little or no social mobility. Administrative posts were held by whites. Later, coloureds of light skin could aspire to a high position, but definitely not a black. There was no law against it, but it simply did not happen. Social forces were too strong. Blacks did menial jobs. No matter how lowly, illiterate or unsuited for any other job a white might be, social forces would not let him labour in the nineteenth century.

Some writers have argued that the island governments positively discouraged integration so that it would be easier for the whites to retain control. Certainly white domination would have ended if the opposition to it had ever united. Even in the days of slavery, in the British West Indies and in St Domingue, the planters feared the possibility of an alliance of free coloureds and slaves.

It is true that the divided society enabled the whites to keep their dominant position, but it is not clear that it was deliberately engineered by the whites. Non-integration in the nineteenth century seemed natural to both the upper and the lower classes. The example of British Honduras makes this clear. British Honduras had never been a plantocracy, but it was a very small forestocracy. Relationships between slaves and masters were very good by British West Indies standards. Throughout the nineteenth century it remained very small in spite of attempts to attract immigrants. However, society there was made up of more distinct groups than practically anywhere else in the British West Indies. There was no conflict between the groups, but by choice they never integrated. As the whites only numbered between 200 and 400, any alliance could have ended their dominant position, but society was so conservative, and so politically naïve, that integration did not take place.

British Guiana was much larger. It had a very mixed society in which there was a legacy of hatred between blacks and whites. Here there is a real case for saying that the policy of 'divide and rule' was a deliberate one. In the days of slavery the whites had played off the Amerindians against the blacks by means of a white/Amerindian alliance. After emancipation, this policy was continued. One racial group was played off against another to prevent integration; East Indians against blacks, Portuguese against coloureds and blacks.

Social patterns

Marriage

Monogamy, i.e. having one wife, was most common among the upper classes. Often it was a marriage of convenience, to join two plantation families, or for money, rather than a love match. In such cases the husband often had a number of concubines from among the slaves on his estate. Promiscuity was widespread among all classes.

Serial monogamy, very common among the middle class, was a social practice particular to the West Indies. The couple concerned did not undergo a marriage ceremony, but lived together for a considerable period of time, on average about six years. Then the man would change his partner and be equally loyal to the new one for about the same period.

The social acceptability of having many partners varied, according to how strongly Christianity was followed. Undoubtedly there were double standards; outward conformity to religion on Sundays combined with unchristian unions in everyday life was common. Towards the end of the period such unions tended to become less socially acceptable to the upper and middle class.

Economic considerations made formal marriage among the poor uncommon. A man could not marry because he did not have the money to buy or build a house, support a non-working wife and raise a family.

Often a couple would have a common-law marriage, i.e. one recognised by society, not by the Church, for most of their lives and only formalise it at a very late stage. Apart from economic considerations, there were other reasons for such a late marriage: to legitimise children, often under pressure from the children themselves; desire on the part of the partners to honour each other by a formal marriage; and the desire to satisfy the Church before death. Formal marriage was more common in small communities or where the Church, especially the Catholic Church, was a strong force.

Socially, if not legally, common-law marriages were just as binding as formal ones. The children were 'legitimate' in a social sense and grew up with obligations of support from their parents, and obligations to support their parents in old

A Jamaican wedding

age. They owed their first allegiance to the mother but, if the union had been permanent or very long-lasting, there was also a natural allegiance to the father.

Illegitimate births varied from a low figure of two out of three to a high figure of figure of four out of five. Perhaps, three-quarters of the children were born illegitimate. This is an important distinction because many were legitimised later.

Legally a man was not obliged to support his illegitimate children, but socially and historically he was. An illegitimate child could not inherit in most islands, unless his father had willed him property. This had been common during slavery and continued after emancipation.

Matri-focal families

Among the manual workers and, to some extent, the middle class, West Indian families were matri-focal, that is, centred around the mother or grandmother. This was not the case among the upper classes, because economic considerations of property and inheritance made for patriarchal families, controlled by the father.

Because of historical and social developments within the West Indies, the mother often took the place assumed by the father in Western and West African societies. This had begun during slavery and social forces after emancipation encouraged its continuation:

1 Irregular unions, as in the days of slavery, left women with children of fathers unknown, or unwilling to contribute to their support.
2 Economic considerations prevented marriage.
3 Serial monogamy meant that the father might leave the children dependent on their mother.
4 Migrant labour forced the husband to leave home.
5 A woman who had passed through two or more regular, or semi-regular unions, would want to keep all her children.

6 A daughter, who worked for the support of her family home, would leave her children in the care of her own mother.

Segregation of the sexes

In the West Indies men and women may have lived together, but they were apart most of the time. This was due, firstly, to Victorian ideas and practices copied from their colonial rulers. Secondly, with so little formal and permanent marriage, both sexes preferred the freedom this allowed. Therefore in leisure activities, in their clubs, sports and other recreations, the men kept together. They drank, played dominoes, played cricket or just talked together. Women's activities took place in the home, or in connection with the church. Even at mixed gatherings, church meetings or more formal social functions like weddings, the men and women segregated themselves soon after arrival.

This underlined the lack of companionship and even affection between men and women, compared with the affection felt between children and their parents, especially their mother.

Kinship

Large family groups developed because of ties of kinship. However if support was received under this system, the recipient was expected to contribute his share either at the time, or in the future. It seemed a very loose system, but it was not. Who could receive benefits, and what obligations each member owed, were clearly defined.

The 'yard'

This was a larger group than the family and arose out of the slave quarters or the 'barracks' of the indenture system. It seemed a natural way to live after emancipation and was transferred from the rural communities to the towns to become the accepted pattern for West Indian living.

Houses, huts, shacks, whatever the form of dwelling, they clustered round a yard. The yard gave social security, mutual service and benefit to all its members. It prevented loneliness, cared for the sick and aged, and gave recreation to children and adults.

The spirit of co-operation engendered by the yard served the community well. In the nineteenth century, if a church, village hall or school had to be built, the labour was done in common. Unpleasant tasks, like scrub-cutting, were tackled together, and when the task was finished there was the inevitable celebration and party.

Social change in the twentieth century

Life in the British Caribbean changed little in the nineteenth century but this was not so in the twentieth century. Customs, recreations, occupations, dress and education changed far more quickly than before. The following section deals with three aspects of everyday life:
1 The contrasting positions of black and white and the ways in which these changed;
2 Newspapers which are such an important feature of island life;
3 Cricket which is the major sporting interest for West Indians.
Social change makes an interesting individual study and in the questions at the end of the book we have suggested that students study other aspects of this topic as a project.

White élite/urban blacks – a study in contrasts

British West Indian society with its two extremes makes an interesting social study. It consisted of a white élite who, though not aristocratic by birth except in the case of some of the French creole families in Trinidad, were still able to live like aristocrats, unlike some of their counterparts in Europe; and urban blacks who were living in some of the worst conditions of squalor and poverty anywhere in the world. It was a society resulting from slavery, the plantation economy and the decline of sugar.

The white élite

In most of the British islands this consisted of two distinct classes; the old creole families and the top expatriate officials. They despised each other yet mixed socially and defended their exclusiveness against the lower classes.

White élite

Certain creole families like the de Verteuils (French) and the Warners (British) in Trinidad, the Beckfords and later the Tates in Jamaica, the Drax's and the Clarkes in Barbados, determined island society and maintained their position by intermarriage and business acumen. In a large island like Trinidad society was determined by some fifty families. In a small island like Cayman there were only four or five important families. Colour and birth were of the utmost importance. The élite had to be free of the taint of colour. Endogamy (marriage within a clan or class) was rigidly practised. Within a group of fifty families the dangers of in-breeding might be avoided but in the smaller islands this was not possible. Marriage outside these families led to social ostracism unless it was to a high-ranking expatriate official.

Élite status could not be maintained without property and wealth. Originally, the élite were the plantocracy but the change in economic conditions in the nineteenth century made commerce and the professions acceptable. The kinship of the leading white families helped to maintain their prosperity. The family successful in commerce would help the planter with favourable terms: the lawyers would provide their services without fee and the magistrates and judges would overlook breaches in the law in the case of a fellow white.

The quality of life of the aristocracy depended on cheap labour. In the late nineteenth century a domestic servant could still be employed for $5 to $6 a month. When domestics asked for $8 to $10 per month it caused an outcry. Domestic servants like cooks, cleaners, washerwomen, seamstresses, butlers, grooms, drivers, gardeners, nannies, governesses and maintenance men were necessary to maintain the estate and leisured life of the aristocrat. Such an establishment could be conducted in a paternalistic, feudal sort of way but this was rare in the British islands where a strict master-servant attitude was more common and the domestic servants were treated very much like dispensable paid labour.

The leading families educated their children in Europe in the nineteenth century and some continued to do so even up to the present day. As noted in an earlier book, this practice contributed to absenteeism through the ties established between planters and the home country. Visits to Europe were common not so much for business but just to keep in touch with European society.

The life of the menfolk outside their profitable occupations consisted of visits to friends, attending receptions, dinners and other formal functions, and taking their wives to balls and parties in the evenings. Their circle was small and unchanging apart from the inclusion of one or two prominent coloureds towards the end of the nineteenth century. An exclusively male activity was going to the club, perhaps the Liguanea Club in Kingston, the Union Club in Trinidad or the Ice House restaurant in Barbados. There members would drink, play cards and billiards, or perhaps cricket and golf. Visits to mistresses were common.

The daily life of the womenfolk was very leisurely. They supervised their households and might engage in charity work but otherwise the whole day was free apart from social engagements. Their education was directed towards a life of leisure. They were taught dancing and music and how to be witty and well-mannered in company.

The white élite behaved as if the other social classes did not exist. They recognised blacks only as servants and regarded them as possessing every vice imaginable. In Jamaica, Trinidad and British Guiana they preferred to deal with Indians wherever possible. They were extremely snobbish and nasty petty jokes and smirks about colour were common sources of humour. The élite were very important as trend-setters and arbiters of taste and fashion, manners and morals, recreations and sports. Although their position has declined in the twentieth century and they no longer hold their former economic power, they are still influential.

The economic rise of the blacks and coloureds has led to the creation of black and coloured élites which the lower classes gladly imitate. In the 1930s it became more fashionable to display one's blackness and African traditions. Finally in the 1960s the idea of black power has led to an outright condemnation of white culture, religion and society by many blacks.

Urban blacks

In the major cities of the West Indies, especially Kingston, Port of Spain, Bridgetown, Georgetown and St John's, Antigua, the lower classes were very poor and lived in very squalid conditions. A recent book has referred to them as 'the urban labouring classes', but in truth many of them had no work. Since over ninety per cent of them were black it is better to call them 'the urban blacks'. The attractions of the cities for ex-slaves were:

1 They were as far removed from the plantations as possible;
2 Social mobility was more possible and more rapid in the cities;
3 There was a greater likelihood of finding a paid job;
4 There was more opportunity for street trading, 'huckstering' or 'higgling' in local terminology;
5 More casual work was available;
6 There was a greater chance of subsistence through charity;
7 There were better educational facilities;
8 There were better health services;
9 There was more opportunity for crime;
10 Cities seemed more exciting and adventurous to the young.

The urban drift continued throughout the nineteenth century. By 1900 Port of Spain and San Fernando held a quarter of Trinidad's population. In the twentieth century, especially since the Second World War, the urban drift has accelerated. By 1960 Kingston held a fifth of Jamaica's population, and today the proportion is a quarter.

Urban blacks

In most of the British islands the urban population has grown at a faster rate than the rest of the country. The poor blacks have settled in certain areas of the cities, notably West Kingston and Trench Town; in Port of Spain, Laventille, Belmont and East Dry River; in Bridgetown, Lower Green and Golden Square. As the black population increased there was much money to be made in renting out property. Landlords favoured the barrack-type accommodation where more people could be housed at lower cost. These were often built against the back walls of shops fronting the main streets. Between six and ten wooden partitions divided a typical barracks, making cubicles about three metres by four. They were roofed with corrugated iron. Sometimes six people slept in these cubicles. The whole barracks shared one tap and one pit latrine. The doors opened onto a yard, and similar barracks were built on the other three sides of the yard if possible. The average rent for such a room at the end of the nineteenth century was between $3.00 and $4.00 per month. Sometimes a room could be let for about 15 cents a night. Usually occupancy was far from permanent! The authorities tried to limit the expansion of the cities by prohibiting new building, especially wooden building, but this put more pressure on the barracks.

Overcrowding contributed to disease, immorality, crime and despair amongst the urban blacks. The cities did have better medical services than the rural areas, but the pressure on city hospitals was intolerable. They became overcrowded and the staff overworked. Education facilities were totally inadequate in dealing with the vast numbers of young children who came from the urban slums. They turned to petty thieving and fighting, and the young girls often became prostitutes. Many adults seemed to prefer to remain unemployed. Vagrancy was a major problem because it led to street gangs, violence, gambling and crime. It became even more acute after the decline of sugar around 1884-5. More blacks drifted into the towns and gang fights became common. For example, Trinidad's carnival presented an open invitation for the street gangs to fight each other in support of rival favourites. In the years 1880-4, Trinidad's Chief of Police Baker waged a vigorous and successful campaign to break up the gangs. They reappeared in the yards and streets of Port of Spain in the late 1940s and early 1950s with the rise of steel bands, and their fighting gave this type of music a very unsavoury reputation. Vagrancy rarely led to starvation and death because communal living made it possible to 'hang round' the common cooking pot and be fed, or to exist off charity hand-outs of food from the 'soup kitchens'.

Gambling was often at the root of crime because money was stolen for the stakes or to pay off debts. In the last three decades of the nineteenth century the crime figures in British West Indian cities increased greatly, but then the rate receded because:
a) emigration became a safety valve;
b) there was revival of the sugar industry during the First World War;
c) alternative crops succeeded for a time.
The police in the cities had great problems.
1 Black police did the street patrols and they tended to mingle with their own race. This led to the upper classes accusing the police of corruption and consorting with criminals and prostitutes.
2 The police were naturally sympathetic towards their own race and were especially unwilling to arrest vagrants whom they pitied.
3 Many blacks felt great hostility towards the police. It was dangerous for the police to enter some areas of some of the cities; for example, Belmont in Port of Spain in the last century, and Trench Town in Kingston in recent times.

The courts treated the urban blacks harshly, even unfairly. Under British law a man is assumed innocent until he is proved guilty. An urban black was often assumed guilty until he could prove his innocence. Harsh penalties still existed and were used in the British West Indies.

In spite of all this the urban drift continued. Cities offered hope of betterment whereas the blacks regarded rural life as drudgery. There was greater social mobility in the cities and the occasional 'success story' was enough to inspire hope. By the twentieth century many blacks were entering the professions and the higher ranks of commerce through education, hard work, thrift and successful huckstering.

Newspapers

Newspapers in an island society are more important than in a larger country. In many West Indian islands there is only one newspaper published weekly. Thus it has a great responsibility to report the news fairly and accurately.

Newspapers have always had a relatively wide circulation. For example, the *Cayman Compass* in one of the smallest islands, has a weekly circulation of nearly three thousand out of a total Cayman Island population of nearly fourteen thousand. One has only to be on the streets around publication time about 4 p.m. on Fridays to see how avidly the paper boys scramble for their copies and dash off to their favourite selling points. People stop work to rush out to buy their copies; others drive into town and cause traffic hold-ups while they buy their copy. The cry goes out, 'The *Compass* is out'; people say to each other, 'What's in the *Compass?*' This is typical of press day in any British island.

In spite of the high rate of illiteracy in the nineteenth century which still prevails in some places, newspapers have proved very successful. Even people who could not read bought their copy and took it to someone who could read. The reader soon had a crowd around him thirsting for the latest news.

Newspapers in political and social conflicts

The press has played an important part in Caribbean history. The first newspaper is reputed to have been the *Jamaica Courant*, first published in 1722, followed in 1731 by the *Barbados Gazette*. Many of the early newspapers were called 'Gazette' showing that they were the voice of the government. They were often more like advertising sheets than modern newspapers, recording new appointments in government, new laws and new policies. Because the governments of the day were plantocracies, the only opinions reflected by the newspapers were those of the planters. Where social news was reported it was restricted to white society and other races and the lower classes were ignored. Typical of such newspapers were *The Royal Essequibo and Demerary Gazette* and the *Port of Spain Gazette*.

In the nineteenth century they began to take sides in political and social controversy and to reflect anti-government opinions. For example, in 1811 the St Kitts' newspaper reported the Edward Huggins' case, expressing an opinion contrary to that of the local Assembly.

The chief dividing issue in the early nineteenth century was emancipation. The older newspapers, such as the *Colonist* and the *Guiana Chronicle*, reflecting planter opinion, attacked the British government's policy of emancipation. The new newspapers which appeared often took the side of the slaves and the coloureds. In 1829 *The Watchman* in Jamaica was established by the free coloureds and edited by Edward Jordan, a mulatto. It criticised the Jamaican Assembly and advocated the abolition of slavery. Freedom of the press had not been an issue earlier because the government had never been so openly attacked. In 1832 Jordan was charged with sedition and treason, and was arrested. The charge came to nothing and *The Watchman* survived as the voice of the coloureds. It could be called an opposition newspaper. For some time George William Gordon was its owner.

Gazettes were the voice of the local government only and they frequently attacked the British government, for example, over emancipation and, at the end of the century, over Crown Colony government. They often favoured constitutional reform and united creole races and classes in opposition to the colonial government. For example, about 1890, the *Port of Spain Gazette* was strongly anti-colonial in its editorial policy, although in domestic affairs it still reflected the attitudes of the white élite. Among the newer liberal newspapers in Trinidad which expressed the views of the blacks and coloureds were the *Recorder* and the *Palladium*. Newspapers took part in race and class conflict. They had become a vital part of colonial society and were in the thick of most controversies.

Newspapers and party politics

Many pressure groups in West Indian society began to produce their own newspapers early in the nineteenth century. We have already seen the example of the coloureds and *The Watchman* in Jamaica. In Barbados the trend was even more apparent. In 1818 two opposing white groups founded their own newspapers. The 'Yeomanry of Barbados' under James Sarsfield Bascom, formed the Salmagundi party and produced the *Globe* newspaper. The white élite, nicknamed 'Pumpkins', answered with the *Western Intelligence*.

The coloureds in Barbados also produced their own newspapers. The first was *The Times* but it was soon overtaken in popularity by the *Liberal* which was closely allied to the Liberal Party. This had been formed by Samuel Jackman Prescod to represent the Ten Acre Men. He was also editor of the *Liberal* for twenty-five years. He took issue with the Barbados Assembly in his newspaper on behalf of the black working classes over the Masters and Servants Act in the 1840s. The reasonable support of the coloureds and blacks through the *Liberal* was an important contribution towards the acceptance of coloureds into politics in Barbados.

In the twentieth century, newspaper support for political parties in Barbados became clearcut. Two good examples are the *Herald* which supported the Democratic League and C. A. Brathwaite in the 1920s, and the *Beacon* which was produced by the Barbados Labour Party and supported Grantley Adams in the 1940s.

In the 1970s even the small population of St Vincent has been able to support two newspapers which are divided on party lines; the *Star* is the organ of the St Vincent Labour Party, and the *Tree* that of the Democratic Freedom Movement.

The number of newpapers in circulation in the British Caribbean today proves that the press is very much alive. This is reinforced by the vigour and determination with which the press and the people of the West Indies resisted any threat to the freedom of the press.

Cricket

An outsider cannot easily appreciate the importance of cricket in West Indian life. It is the national sport of the British Caribbean, uniting races and social classes, black, brown and white, rich and poor, men and women. On the field of play at least all are equal. Women must be included because their passion for the game in the West Indies has no parallel amongst women in other parts of the world. Cricket excites more passion among West Indians than soccer among Brazilians or rugby among New Zealanders – that should give some measure of its popularity! It divides also, not socially, but nationally. This division can be good for the game when the rivalry is sporting and produces keen competition and higher standards. On the other hand, it can be harmful when it becomes nationalistic and political.

Cricket was not always a unifying force socially. The white élite made it fashionable in the mid-nineteenth century, and the Indians and blacks copied them. Whites, blacks, coloureds and Indians confined their games to their own races and colours. Amongst the Indians there was even a caste division, as cricket was meant to be a Parsee game, although this soon broke down outside India.

The most famous club in the development of the game in the West Indies was the Queen's Park Cricket Club in Trinidad. At first all its cricketers were white. It controlled cricket in Trinidad and influenced the development of the game throughout the British West Indies. As it was one of the first to break down racial barriers on the cricket field at the turn of the century, its example was followed throughout the islands. The rest of the club remained exclusively white, but the cricket section admitted some coloured members who belonged to the professions. However, its representative teams remained all white. Then in 1895 the All-Trinidad team to play the visiting English team included five non-white players. This seems to have been the first racially mixed representative team in West Indian cricket. Among the non-whites was Lebrun Constantine, the father of Lord Learie Constantine.

Non-white cricket was held back not only by racial prejudice, but also by economic circumstances and lack of opportunity. The facilities of the white clubs could not be matched by those of the other racial groups. Indians tended to play their cricket on vacant estate lands and blacks had to play wherever they could, often on vacant city lots. However, poor facilities and equipment could not hide the natural talent of the blacks, coloureds and Indians. Cricket is a game where there is much room for improvisation; bamboo canes for wickets, a piece of wood for a bat, even a small coconut for a ball. There was plenty of enthusiasm and therefore plenty of improvisation.

Right up to the 1960s, representative teams reflected a disproportionate number of whites. This would suggest that the teams were not selected entirely on merit. The economic position of most whites made it easier for them to take time off work for cricket matches and tours. They were better able to support their families while away on tour, and of course, in the days of strict amateurism, they could pay their own expenses. The full potential of non-white cricketers began to be recognised after the Second World War with the dominating batting performances of the three Ws, E. D. Weekes, F. M. Worrell and C. L. Walcott, all Barbadians. Yet the very successful West Indies touring party of 1963 still had three whites out of eighteen players altogether.

National prestige in cricket

Inter-colonial matches began in 1865 with a match between Demerara and Barbados. In 1891 the first inter-colonial tournament was played between Demerara, Barbados and Trinidad. These inter-colonial matches were not regular fixtures and rivalry was not great because they were more like friendly matches between the white élite of each colony. The first visiting English team was led by R. Slade Lucas in 1895. It could not play a combined West Indian team because there was no such thing. It played the leading white teams in the south-eastern Caribbean, with the exception of the All-Trinidad team already noted. In 1900 the first West Indian touring party visited England. Several black players were included in spite of opposition from Barbados and British Guiana.

Gradually cricket in the British West Indies became more organised. In 1926 the West Indian Cricket Board of Control was formed to organise and control inter-colonial competition and organise foreign tours. Henceforth intense national rivalry developed over who would win the inter-colonial competition, how many representatives each territory would have in a West Indies side, and especially, who would be appointed as the national captain. This brought out the unifying force of cricket – the West Indies Board of Control and the combined national team – and the divisive aspect – fierce rivalry often leading to violence and political antagonism. Reasonable West Indians acknowledge that the national team is selected on merit, but there are arguments and each naturally supports his fellow islanders. The masses are often unreasonable and cannot accept the exclusion of their own island players or a predominance in the team of rival islanders. The national captaincy confers such a great honour and responsibility that it provokes the strongest nationalism. In most recent times the unquestionable stature of such cricketers as Worrell, Gary Sobers of Barbados and Clive Lloyd of Guyana has removed much of the controversy from the choice of captain. The organisation of inter-island competition under the Shell Shield which began in 1965 has made team selection easier. Guyana, Trinidad, Barbados, the Windward and Leeward Islands and Jamaica have played each other at least once a year since 1965.

However, at the national level cricket is still a topic to be approached with caution socially. It can produce a cheerful debate, but it can also provoke deep-felt passions and resentments which can cause much unpleasantness and even violence.

The international status of West Indian cricket was enhanced between the wars by two great black cricketers. Learie Constantine of Trinidad, a great all-rounder, first toured England with Austin's side in 1923. George Headley of Jamaica was the West Indies' answer to Don Bradman. From the Second World War onwards the West Indies have had a succession of great teams. Goddard's team which toured England in 1950 contained the three Ws and two spin bowlers, A. Valentine of Jamaica and Sonny Ramadhin of Trinidad. This was the first West Indies side to win a test match and a series in England.

West Indies touring team at Adelaide 1980
Back row, left to right: Haynes, Marshall, King, Croft, Garner, Holding, Gomes, Parry
Front row, left to right: Murray (D. A.), Richards, Kallicharran, Rodriguez (Manager), Lloyd, Murray (D. L.), Rowe, Roberts, Greenidge

The 1963 side under Worrell began a period of international supremacy for the West Indies which has continued into the 1980s. Worrell's side was the most popular touring side to visit England because of the 'bright' cricket they played. It included Garfield Sobers, the greatest all-rounder ever, who was knighted by the Queen in Barbados in 1974 for his services to cricket. The social consequences of West Indian cricket supremacy have been far-reaching, ranging from black pride within the West Indies, to international understanding and helping better race relations in Britain.

Society in the Spanish islands

For most of the nineteenth century there was slavery in the Spanish islands. The Cuban slave trade continued until 1865 and slavery existed there until 1886. Therefore any comparison between the British West Indies and the Spanish islands must exclude the slaves.

There were far more Europeans in the Spanish colonies than in the British, and in Cuba especially they were of a different class from the planters of the British islands. In the eighteenth century tobacco was the great export crop of Cuba. Fine tobacco needed individual care and a large class of yeoman farmers known as *vegueros* existed in Cuba. They were the backbone of society, but had little political, economic or social influence. They were at the mercy of the tobacco buyers who paid little for their crop. The incentive to produce tobacco became less and, with the difficulties of the French Wars, tobacco production in Cuba declined at the beginning of the nineteenth century. The *vegueros* almost disappeared, sugar became increasingly important, and with it slave labour. Society was changing in Cuba and, to a lesser extent, in Puerto Rico.

There was another split in white Cuban society, that between the Creoles (Cuban-born Spaniards) and the Peninsulares (Spanish-born Spaniards). The Spanish empire had strong central government and this led to the presence of many Peninsulares in high administrative positions in Cuba. They considered themselves the leaders of Cuban society and tended to behave as colonial masters, superior in breeding and education, if not in wealth, to the Creoles. The Creoles resented them and felt that as planters they should be the leaders of society. The continuation of slavery complicated the issue between Peninsulares and Creoles. The slave trade was in the hands of the Peninsulares and, of course, they wanted it to continue. The Creoles were undecided. They feared that the continuation of slavery would lead to risings and perhaps bloody revolution, but they also feared emancipation, having seen its results in Haiti and in the declining sugar production in Jamaica. Cuban liberals wanted emancipation because slavery was a blot on their society. Even some sugar plantation owners wanted emancipation. The conservatives wanted to keep plantation society and some of them even considered annexation by the United States.

The abolitionists won the day. They were supported by the liberals, by Cuban exiles in North America willing to supply arms, by some creole planters who resented the Peninsulares and their support of slavery, by coffee farmers who did not need slavery and by Cuban patriots who did not want the experience of Haiti. To win over all those who feared for the future of Cuba, the abolitionists promised that a large-scale white immigration movement would accompany the freeing of the blacks. The Ten Years War, 1868–1878, ensured emancipation, but it came about gradually between 1878 and 1886, so fears of a black republic came to nothing.

Before the change to sugar gained momentum, the whites were in the majority. By 1820 there were 350,000 blacks to 300,000 whites, but two-thirds of the blacks were slaves. The 1899 census showed a large white majority, making up about sixty-seven per cent of the population. The authorities probably exaggerated the white figures but, nevertheless, they show the success of the white immigration policy. This policy was followed vigorously in the first quarter of the twentieth century and Cuba remained a white-dominated society. The whites not only had numerical strength, but they also monopolised the economy, education and culture.

Between 1853 and 1874 Cuba had a Chinese immigration scheme, but it had a very small impact on Cuban society, unlike the East Indians in British Guiana and Trinidad. The reasons for this were:

a) Cuba was so large that the entry of 125,000

Chinese over twenty years could not affect the social pattern;
b) they were confined to the sugar estates;
c) they were treated so badly that only 14,000 survived in 1899;
d) the immigrants were exclusively male and they intermarried so quickly that very few pure Chinese survived.

In the nineteenth century there was no attempt at integration, but due to the liberal Latin attitude towards miscegenation there was a very large mestizo population, nearly twenty per cent of the total. It was probably higher but the census transferred many mestizos to the whites to boost their figures. In Cuba the whites were more ready to receive the mestizos into their ranks than the whites in the British islands. The integration of whites and coloureds became more complete in the twentieth century. This liberal attitude did not, however, extend to the blacks, who remained oppressed until the 1959 revolution.

12
Social conditions and the Moyne Commission

'Barracks' in British Guiana

Social conditions prior to the Moyne Commission

By the 1930s the British government was facing a major breakdown in law and order in the West Indies. They realised that social distress was the underlying cause of labour unrest and political agitation. All previous attempts to solve this by Secretaries of State and Royal Commissions had failed or gone unheeded. For example, the Norman Commission of 1898 had recommended crop diversification but with the exception of cocoa in Trinidad and fruit, especially bananas in Jamaica, these crops had failed to arrest the economic decline. The British West Indies were still dangerously dependent on sugar. In 1930 Lord Passfield (Sydney Webb) as Secretary of State, urged colonial governments to reform trade union law in order to make trade unions in the islands more effective, but without success.

Both the Norman Commission and the Olivier Commission of 1929 had advocated the transfer of land to small independent farmers. The latter said:

> No reform affords so good a prospect for the permanent welfare in the future of the West Indies as the settlement of the labouring population on the land as small peasant proprietors.

However, this was resisted by the planters who refused to sell off fertile estate land, maintaining that a plentiful supply of cheap labour was essential for the sugar industry. The declining sugar industry and the stubbornness of the plantocracy were major causes of rural distress. The 1929 Commission noted the relatively high standard of living of the smallholders compared with the squalor and degradation of the sugar workers. However, the West Indian governments took little notice.

Much of the blame for the distress of the rural poor must be laid on West Indian employers, in particular, the directors of the sugar companies and the oil companies in Trinidad. While their workers were suffering they were drawing large profits and paying out generous dividends to shareholders. These companies should have cut down on their profits and paid the workers more. The social results of their continuing exploitation were appalling; terrible working conditions, unemployment, bad housing, ill-health and inadequate opportunities in education.

This local distress was made worse by world economic depression beginning in 1929 and continuing into the 1930s. It meant that foreigners had no money to buy West Indian products and no money to invest there. Thus the slump spread to the West Indies, and hardship and suffering grew. This led to strikes and riots there from 1935 to 1938 which resulted in the appointment of the Moyne Commission.

Working conditions

In 1938 the Colonial Office appointed Major St John Orde-Browne to head a commission into labour conditions in the British West Indies. The Orde-Browne Report entitled 'Labour Conditions in the West Indies', noted the hard times and increasing unemployment. It advocated co-operation between trade unions and governments to produce better conditions by legislation. Trade union preoccupation with higher wages, it was felt, would only lead to further unemployment.

In theory, better working conditions could have been achieved by the trade union movement but, in 1938, labour leaders in the British West Indies were inexperienced and ineffective. There were very few trade unions and those that existed had relatively few members and lacked effective striking power because peaceful picketing was illegal and unions were liable for damage caused during strikes if court actions were brought against them.

Following the Passfield Memorandum in 1937 the British government again urged colonial governments to improve the conditions of workers in the colonies. It said that any improvement in the financial position of the colonies and business enterprises after the slump should be passed on to the workers in the form of better working conditions and social services. It recommended inspection and re-appraisal of working conditions by separate labour departments established in each colony. The British government pursued this policy because it recognised that social distress was leading to instability and was threatening Crown Colony government.

Instead of seeking higher wages, the trade unions should have concentrated on gaining secure employment for their members and better working conditions. The Minimum Wage Law was passed in Jamaica in 1938 but such a law was an admission of trade union failure to negotiate satisfactory wage agreements in particular industries.

Details of working conditions in the British West Indies as reported in the Moyne Commission Report came largely from the evidence of Orde-Browne. The following table compares wages of unskilled workers in the sugar industry in 1938 with those just after emancipation, one hundred years before. Note that wages in the sugar industry are a fair indication of all agricultural wages.

Territory	*1838*	*1938*
Antigua	1/- to 1/6	1/2 to 1/6
Barbados	9d to 10d	1/3
St Kitts	6d to 9d	1/4 to 1/6
St Vincent	8d	1/2
Grenada	8d	1/3 to 2/-
Jamaica	1/6	2/- to 2/6
British Guiana	2/-	1/7
Trinidad	2/- to 2/6	1/6
Average for the British West Indies	1/3	1/7

(N.B. Wages are given in shillings and pence).

The average rise in wages of the unskilled workers in the hundred years since emancipation was four pence! Two territories are of particular interest.

In Barbados, the wages of field workers were exactly the same in 1898 as they had been in 1838, that is about ninepence. In Trinidad wages for field workers had actually fallen by sixty per cent in the period covered by the table. The basic wage for an oilfield worker was higher, about 3/- per day, but it was still inadequate. Barbados was the territory where social distress was most acute, Trinidad the territory where agitation was the strongest.

In real wages, that is, in terms of what money can actually buy, the workers were far worse off in 1938 than they had been in 1838, because prices had risen steeply. A family of four, husband, wife and two children, were on the poverty line in 1938. In the small islands of the Eastern Caribbean food would probably take up all but a penny a day of the wages. The result was either running up debts which could not possibly be repaid, or stealing food. Even if all the money was spent on food, the food they could afford was so low in nutritional value that malnutrition was inevitable. Despair was widespread, and despair led to crime, disorder and violence.

Unemployment

It is hard to give accurate unemployment figures for the British West Indies in the late 1930s. There were no Labour Departments to collect such statistics until after the Moyne Commission. The population in the West Indies had roughly doubled in the nineteenth century, reaching about 1,700,000 by the end of the century. By the 1930s it had passed two million. In the same period, the number of jobs had not increased in the same proportion. The situation was aggravated by the virtual ending of emigration about 1925 and the repatriation of workers back to the West Indies, especially from Cuba.

Other factors make unemployment difficult to assess. Are subsistence farmers counted as unemployed? Either way there is a very thin line between a subsistence farmer, a subsistence farmer with some cash income and a small farmer with dependence on a cash income for food. Most of the labour in the British West Indies was 'casual'. There was little permanent, full-time employment in secondary and tertiary industry. In primary industry, especially sugar, most of the work was seasonal and on a casual basis. Therefore, an unemployment figure of twenty per cent does not convey the gravity of the situation. The figure is high, but if casual labour was excluded, the figure would probably be about fifty per cent. The difference between the two figures could be classed as 'underemployment'.

In 1938 the sugar industry was still by far the largest single employer. It provided permanent employment for about ten per cent of its unskilled labour and forty per cent of its skilled. The full complement of workers were only employed in crop time. For about fifteen weeks of the year three-quarters of all workers, skilled and unskilled, were laid off. Most sugar workers were not unemployed, but underemployed.

Rotational employment, a device to give more men work by making each man work for shorter periods, made unemployment appear lower than it really was. For example, instead of employing one man for five days, two men would be employed for two days each. The employer was paying for only four days' labour and thus cutting down on his wage bill. More men were classed as employed, in fact twice as many men, but each man was underemployed. This system was common in Grenada where a man often worked for two days per week. In Jamaica rotational employment often consisted of two weeks on, two weeks off.

Jamaica's unemployment figures were perhaps the most misleading. Jamaica claimed unemployment of about twelve per cent in 1937. However, Orde-Browne reported that fifty per cent of the employed labour force was only casual; the twelve per cent referred only to those without any kind of work at all. The true situation was also obscured by the fact that the thousands of unemployed in Kingston were involved in costly labour-intensive schemes to reduce unemployment.

The Norman Commission and the Olivier Commission had pointed to a solution to rural unemployment; namely land settlement schemes. By 1938 only British Guiana was operating such a scheme successfully. About 30,000 hectares had been distributed among 10,000 small farmers in lots of between two and four hectares. This made a small impression on the numbers unemployed. In Trinidad there were about 20,000 unemployed or underemployed, yet there were only about 5,000 small farmers in the two to four hectares category. Jamaica had a large number of small, independent farmers, but they had developed as a free peasantry in the nineteenth century and were not the result of a government land settlement policy. This obvious solution to unemployment and social distress had been resisted by the plantocracy but the riots and strikes, and the Moyne Commission's Report, changed the attitude to land settlement schemes.

Food

The dearth of small farmers was the reason for the small amount of locally-produced food in the British West Indies in the late 1930s. Most of the islands could have been self-sufficient in food if they had diversified and pursued land settlement policies but, in practice, all of them had to import food. Only the cheapest and nutritionally inferior foods could be imported at prices which the masses could afford. By the late 1930s a quarter of Jamaica's imports were foodstuffs and Jamaica produced more food than most of the islands. Trinidad imported three-quarters of its food. In Barbados, land outside the sugar estates was so scarce and the population so high that the majority of food was imported. However, staples like rice and maize from the United States were very cheap. The West Indies could not have competed in maize. British Guiana was beginning to supply rice to the other islands, but still imports from the United States were needed. An ideal compromise would have been to allow the cheap staples to continue to be imported and turn West Indian farms over to dairy, egg and a small amount of meat production.

The slaves' regular diet had been salt-fish and corn from North America. The poor tried to keep this diet after emancipation. Salt-fish was their highest protein food and corn was the main carbohydrate food. In the twentieth century rice was supplementing maize as the staple food of the poor. Variations in diet consisted of red beans, cassava, sweet potatoes and a little powdered or condensed milk. Most of the rural poor tasted fresh milk very rarely and went for months without meat. Typical meals of the rural labouring classes were:

Breakfast   black coffee or coffee with milk;

Lunch   salt-fish and rice;

Supper   beans and rice.

Health

In poor countries, such as the West Indies in the 1930s, there were three critical periods in life: infancy (covering the first four years of life); the early teens; and about forty years old. A very small percentage of the population survived all three critical periods.

The most critical time was infancy. In 1938 infant mortality was measured by deaths in the first year. Today it is measured over the first four years giving, of course, a higher figure. Figures calculated over the first four years of life would probably give an infant mortality figure of about thirty per cent for the West Indies in 1938. Another important omission in the 1938 table below is the number of still-born children. Still-birth was very common due to the poor health of the mothers.

Table of infant mortality, 1938

Island	Percentage
Trinidad	12
Jamaica	14
Antigua	17
St Kitts	19
Barbados	22
Average for British West Indies	17
Average for developed countries	6

The principal cause of high infant mortality was malnutrition. A diet of very low nutritional value was universal among the poor in the West Indies. The staple foods, maize, rice, cassava, sweet potatoes and red beans are very high in carbohydrates and very low in proteins and fats. Very little high-protein food was eaten by the poor. As the figures from the tables in this section suggest, the labourer in Barbados was the worst off in the British West Indies and his family was most likely to suffer from malnutrition.

Malnutrition lowered resistance to disease. Some diseases like hookworm and tuberculosis were a direct result of poor living conditions. Hookworm is a debilitating disease producing lethargy, even dropping off to sleep in a sedentary occupation. Therefore it leads to inefficiency and low productivity. It does not kill quickly, but can result in death over a long period and certainly lowers a person's resistance to other diseases. The incidence of hookworm varied throughout the West Indies from island to island and from age group to age group. An average incidence amongst the young in a bad area would be about seventy per cent. An average incidence of fifty per cent over the whole population in a rural area was likely in the late 1930s. It explains the lethargy and inefficiency amongst sugar estate labourers.

Tuberculosis accounted for fifteen per cent of all deaths in the West Indies in the 1930s, making it the biggest single cause of death. Other diseases like malaria and yellow fever were endemic in the tropics. Unbelievable as it may seem, every adult in the West Indies from the poorer classes was affected by some disease or other. The effect on productivity was catastrophic. A man of twenty only had a working life of twenty years ahead because malnutrition and diseases reduced his life expectancy. Thus the economy suffered because of the poor health of the mass of the population.

Poor housing led to poor health. Even at the end of the 1930s a high proportion of rural labourers still lived in labour 'lines' or 'barracks', especially in British Guiana and Trinidad where they had been built to house immigrant labourers. The rapidly expanding rural population was squeezed into the existing accommodation which became more and more overcrowded. It became impossible to meet the demand on sanitary services, especially running water and lavatories, and so health suffered.

Most houses were 'mud-and-wattle' constructions, but bamboo was the usual framework instead of wattle, so the houses were even flimsier. Often the roofs were coconut branches and only rarely corrugated iron. Windows were holes in the walls and doors were floor-to-ceiling openings with a curtain drawn across. Sometimes concrete floors were laid by the sugar companies, but usually the floors were dirt.

The lack of medical services was a very grave problem. In fact the Orde-Browne Report said that it was what was most needed to improve the social conditions of the labouring classes. The plantocracy and the medical profession opposed free or subsidised state medicine on the grounds that 'something for nothing' would demoralise the people. The doctors wanted a fee-paying medical service but, of course, that was beyond the means of the masses. The Moyne Commission of 1938 concluded, 'Barbados has to thank God for health, not the medical profession'. The few doctors in the West Indies stayed in the towns. They were accessible to people with money and transport, but inaccessible to the urban masses and still more inaccessible to the rural masses. Boards of Health had been set up in the second half of the nineteenth century in most islands, and they provided free or subsidised medical treatment, but the services were confined to the towns and by the 1930s were totally inadequate. Rural communities were supposed to be served by dispensaries, but they were few and far between and inadequately staffed. The harsh truth is that the labouring classes had no medical services at all.

Education

Basically it was the plantocracy which held back universal education in the British West Indies. They felt that there was no need for education in an agricultural community. There was also the fear that education would make the rural labourer discontented with his lot. When forced to yield to the demand for education, the planters agreed to a standard of proficiency in English and some basic knowledge of mensuration and arithmetic. Surprisingly the planters did not want even rudimentary agricultural science taught because they did not think it would help a labourer. They wanted a labourer to be able to understand orders and instructions and not to make mistakes with measurements and quantities.

Therefore illiteracy was very high in the British West Indies in the 1930s. Among the larger colonies it ranged from about thirty per cent in Barbados to about sixty per cent in British Guiana. In some of the small islands of the Grenadines it was as high as ninety per cent. Even in the colonies where primary education was compulsory, as it had been in British Guiana since the 1876 Education Ordinance, illiteracy was high. This shows that
a) compulsory education was not enforceable;
b) children could pass through school illiterate.
Planters wanted to employ children, but this was often illegal. Unfortunately some parents allowed them to break the law because they needed the money. In other colonies like Jamaica, there was no compulsory education. In Barbados employment of children under twelve was made illegal, but education was not made compulsory.

A boys' school in Jamaica, 1911

The quantity and quality of education was low because West Indian governments spent very little on education in the 1930s. British Guiana spent five per cent of its budget on education, Trinidad about ten per cent and Barbados about fifteen per cent. Even this expenditure was disproportionately allocated. The towns received more than the country districts, and boys received more than girls. One or two select secondary schools in places like Barbados and Trinidad were favoured over the primary schools. Once again the lack of services was most apparent in the rural areas.

In the 1930s parents saw education as a means by which their children might improve their social status. With the coming of Crown Colony government and increased emphasis on social services and the expansion of white-collar jobs, education was essential, but at both primary and secondary level the curricula were attacked. At primary level the three 'Rs' were of less importance to the rural labourers than basic instruction in hygiene, domestic science and agriculture.

Any discussion of secondary education and higher education in the British West Indies is largely irrelevant when considering the social conditions of the poor. They could not aspire to secondary education because

a) there were too few schools, especially in rural areas;
b) schools discriminated in favour of whites and coloureds;
c) blacks seldom reached the required entry standard.

Education in the 1930s failed to meet the needs of society. There was lack of opportunity, an unfair system based on colour, location and sex, and an irrelevant curriculum. Inadequate education tended to heighten social discontent in the British West Indies.

Conclusion

The 1938 Commission exposed all these appalling inter-related social conditions. The Commissioners realised that they made up a cycle of human misery which had to be broken. However, by the time the Moyne Commission was published, the Second World War had broken out, which radically altered the situation for the British West Indies.

The Moyne Commission

The Moyne Commission was a Royal Commission representing the British government. It took its name from its chairman, Lord Moyne. Walter Citrine, an important British trade unionist, was a member of the Commission and was influential in labour and social matters. Orde-Browne's evidence on working-class conditions was also very influential. He was appointed Labour Adviser to the West Indies about three weeks after the Moyne commission had been appointed. Its terms of reference were

> to investigate social and economic conditions in Barbados, British Guiana, British Honduras, Jamaica, the Leeward Islands, Trinidad and Tobago and the Windward Islands, and to make recommendations.

The Commission was very thorough and the compilation of facts and hearing of evidence took fifteen months between August, 1938 and November, 1939. It had interviewed nearly four hundred people and received communications from hundreds more. Significantly it took evidence from labour representatives and unofficial members of the legislative councils, as well as from Crown officials. The recommendations of the Commission were published in February, 1940, but the full report was not made public until 1945.

The Moyne Commission dealt most comprehensively with labour relations and social conditions, but the value of the report as a social document has tended to be obscured by its constitutional and political recommendations which consisted only of modifications to Crown Colony government and were dismissed by nationalist politicians as most unsatisfactory.

Social and economic recommendations of the Moyne Commission

1 *Strengthening trade unions* Trade unions in the British West Indies lacked essential powers. The Commission recommended peaceful picketing and protection for unions against actions brought for damages, noting that British Guiana was the only territory with such protection in 1938. It encouraged the recognition of trade unions in both the public and private sector, and urged trade unions to register. In particular it noted the lack of trade unions for agricultural workers who needed them most as they were in the most distress, and urged that this gap should be filled.

The Commission attributed the ineffectiveness of West Indian unions to the inexperience of their leaders and recommended that labour leaders should be sent to England for training in industrial relations and negotiation. It was also worried that some labour leaders had different aims and aspirations from the members whom they were meant to represent and stressed that labour leaders should be democratically elected and responsible to their members.

Out of these recommendations came such measures as:
a) Workmen's Compensation This was compensation for injury suffered at work under certain conditions. Usually it was withheld if the worker's own negligence was proved.
b) Holidays with Pay Previously such a benefit was not a right of workers, but was paid at the discretion of employers. Governors were empowered to decree holidays with pay in most colonies.
c) Severance Pay If a worker lost his job because his employer went out of business, he would be compensated.
d) Inspection of Factories and Conditions for Agricultural Labourers Factory inspection had been haphazard and conditions in the fields not regulated at all before the Moyne Commission.
2 *Labour Departments* The Moyne Commission recommended that the duties of the Labour Departments should be: 'regulation of wages, conciliation and arbitration, the gathering of statistics, inspection of the protective laws, the resgistration of trade unions and auditing accounts'. As a result the Jamaican Labour Department was set up in 1939 with F. A. Norman as its first adviser.

While trade unions were gaining in effectiveness, the Moyne Commission suggested minimum wage legislation as an interim measure. If this was unacceptable to a colonial government and the unions were unable to negotiate satisfactory wages for themselves, the Commission suggested Wage Boards. These would fix wages industry by industry, even company by company, until the trade unions were able to take over their own negotiations.

Croix Health Centre

3 *The West Indian Welfare Fund* The Moyne Commission recommended that a fund should be set up by the British government to provide £1,000,000 per year for twenty years for relief measures in the British West Indies. It would cover education, health, housing, land settlement, labour departments, and social welfare. This was aimed at what the Commission saw as the root causes of social distress.

In 1940 the British government passed the Colonial Development and Welfare Act which provided funds for the alleviation of distress and for economic development in British colonies throughout the world. The West Indies benefited more from this fund than the other colonies in proportion to their size and population. The fund had a permanent staff under a British Comptroller in Barbados. In 1958 the government of the West Indies Federation became responsible for adminstering the fund.

4 *Farming Reforms* The Moyne Commission criticised dependence on imported food. It suggested land settlement schemes which would help to alleviate unemployment and raise the standard of living in the rural areas and of the territories as a whole. They would also make possible a new trend in farming and marketing put forward by the Commissioners. Small farmers would become the backbone of efficient farming aimed at making the colonies self-sufficient in food and even creating surpluses which would turn them from being net importers to exporters of food. Each territory would have to look to other Caribbean islands for the foods it needed. A whole new Caribbean market would have to be set up. The Commission knew that the demand was there. It was also hoped that there would be an export market outside the Caribbean for any surplus. Distribution within the Caribbean would have to be organised through inter-island shipping lines. In recommending these projects, the Moyne Commission was anticipating some of the ideas of CARIFTA and CARICOM.

5 *Education* The Commission gave much attention to education, but showed little optimism for the future. It attacked the irrelevant curricula in the West Indies and recommended:

> an end of the illogical and wasteful system which permits the education of a community predominantly engaged in agriculture to be based upon a literary curriculum fitting pupils only for white-collar careers in which opportunities are comparatively limited.

However, the Commission doubted if there could be improvements in literacy until a general improvement in economic development and social conditions had been achieved. It noted the lack of secondary and higher education opportunities, but concluded that there were not yet enough students of sufficient calibre to justify expansion in education at these levels. This would only come when the social conditions of the blacks improved. Therefore the Commission recommended concentrating on the primary and elementary levels of education.

Conclusion

The Moyne Commission marked the end of an era. It was making recommendations for Crown Colonies. After the Second World War came decolonisation and the local independence movements. Nationalists were anxious to take affairs into their own hands and were impatient for economic, social and political changes. They dismissed the findings of the Moyne Commission because of its Crown Colony attitude, but in paractice put many of its recommendations into effect.

Comparison with Puerto Rico

As the smallest of the ex-Spanish islands, Puerto Rico can usefully be compared with Jamaica, the largest of the British islands, both in area and population.

Islands	Area (sq. kms.)	Population (000s) 1940	1960	1970
Jamaica	10,991	1,150	1,610	1,861
Puerto Rico	8,897	1,880	2,350	2,712

Before 1940 there had been parallels in the economic development of the two islands. However, it is in social conditions that the similarities between the two islands are most apparent.

In the 1930s

In the second half of the nineteenth century Puerto Rico, like the British islands, could not compete with Cuba in sugar production. Coffee took over from sugar and by the 1890s forty per cent of arable land was under coffee. However, annexation by the United States in 1898 led to the collapse of coffee and the recovery of sugar. By 1939 sugar made up forty per cent of Puerto Rico's exports. Other agricultural products were fruit, tobacco and coffee, the latter making up less than one per cent of exports. Thus her economy was roughly parallel to that of Jamaica.

In both islands social conditions for the rural poor were wretched. Both lacked small independent farmers and had large numbers of poorly paid agricultural labourers. In Puerto Rico the independent farmers, the *jibaros*, the backbone of the island's social and cultural system, numbered only 40,000 by the 1930s. Their decline was due to the spread of the giant sugar plantations. They grew fruit, tobacco and coffee, but very little food, because the money from their cash crops could buy them up to four times more food from the United States than they could grow themselves. Eighty per cent of Puerto Rico's food was imported from the United States in the 1930s. The *jibaros* earned between $100 and $300 per year, over half of which they had to spend on food. Puerto Rican nationalists, especially Luis Muñoz Marin and the Popular Democratic Party, wanted to re-create the *jibaro* class and improve its economic position, but they were opposed by the sugar interests who held the land the *jibaros* wanted. Luckily they were able to come to terms with them.

In the 1930s most of the rural population were *peones* or agricultural labourers. Over fifty per cent of them earned under $100 per year on which they had to support families which averaged six persons. The urban workers of San Juan were hardly better off and the city was full of ghettoes. Urban wages were about $300 per year on average, but urban prices, especially rents, were much higher.

The unemployment position was similar to

that of Jamaica. Full-time unemployment was about twelve per cent of the working population, but half the labour force employed in the sugar industry worked for between four and six months of the year only. Thus underemployment was as widespread as in Jamaica. The mechanisation of the sugar industry increased unemployment by a further fifteen per cent. Land settlement schemes seemed to be the answer, but these could not be achieved unless the United States sugar interests co-operated.

The other causes of social distress noted in the British islands, were also present in Puerto Rico. Malnutrition was particularly acute because of low earnings. It resulted in high infant mortality. The number of live births per 100 was only 12.6. Tuberculosis, malaria and hookworm were the major causes of poor health. Overcrowding in Puerto Rico was even a greater problem than in the British islands. In the poorer areas five people per sleeping room was common. Health services were totally inadequate, with the only doctors concentrated in the towns.

The United States had placed great emphasis on education since 1898 to hasten the 'americanisation' of Puerto Rico. However americanisation required English as the main language vehicle and up to sixty per cent of school time was devoted to the study of English to the neglect of subjects like agriculture and hygiene. Of course, the population pressure was felt in education and this handicapped the efforts of the United States government. As with health services, the rural children suffered most from lack of educational facilities, with not a single secondary school in the officially designated 'rural areas'.

Remedies for social distress

Puerto Rico was much better served by social reformers than the British islands. From being roughly on a par with Jamaica in 1938, Puerto Rico had made greater progress towards alleviating social distress by 1945. Luis Muñoz Marin was the man chiefly responsible for this.

In 1931 he returned to Puerto Rico from New York. He understood the hardships of the poor, especially the rural poor, and was determined to do something about them. He encouraged the formation of the Puerto Rico Reconstruction Administration and announced the programme, 'Bread, Land, Country'. At first he appealed directly to the *jibaros* and built up strong support in the rural areas. His aims were:

a) concentration, initially, on land settlement schemes by reducing the size of the sugar estates and settling small, independent farmers on the land acquired;

b) to strengthen and protect trade unions because the Puerto Rico Reconstruction Administration wanted to improve the wages and working conditions of labourers;

c) to improve and extend public services like water supply and sewerage, health, education, electricity and transport;

d) finally, after 1945, he turned to industrial development and set up an Industrial Development Company and a Development Bank. This part of his programme was known as 'Operation Bootstrap'.

There was no similar success story in the British West Indies. By 1960 the World Bank was classing Puerto Rico as a 'rich nation', the only one in the Caribbean. The *per capita* income was just over $1,000, whereas it it had been below $100 in 1938. However, when considering this success, one must remember the overriding importance of assistance from the United States and emigration.

These two factors were essential in bringing about the change from a poverty-stricken agricultural island to a wage-earning industrialized economy. In the period 1938 to 1960, emigration to the United States held down Puerto Rico's population growth rate to between 1 and 1.2 per cent per year. Without emigration it would have been about 2.5 per cent per year which would have placed an intolerable burden on resources and made social reforms very difficult, if not impossible. For example, the reduction in illiteracy from about 30 per cent in 1938 to under 10 per cent of the population in 1960 could not have been achieved without emigration taking the pressure off educational facilities. Since most of the emigrants were young men from the rural areas, emigration helped the land settlement schemes by reducing the demand for land and the rural birth rate.

Assistance from the United States can be seen clearly in 'Operation Bootstrap'. As was noted in Chapter 6, the Puerto Rican Industrial Development Company encouraged private investment from the United States. Individual investors and companies took advantage of 'tax holidays', low rates of taxation and relatively low costs in Puerto Rico. This turned Puerto Rico into a country of small industries.

The success of individual reforms varied. The eradication of malaria was very spectacular. The government allocated about twenty per cent of the budget to health and allied projects such as pure water supplies, modern sewage disposal and sewage systems in towns, as well as establishing more clinics in urban and rural areas. The least successful reforms were in housing and the elimination of unemployment. Population pressure put too big a strain on the low-income housing projects. Unemployment remained high, in fact the reforms hardly reduced it, and if it had not been for the safety-valve of emigration the problem would have been desperate. Unemployment remains at about twelve per cent of the working population to-day and is particularly high amongst the young. In periods of high unemployment emigration to the United States rises to about 1.5 per cent per year.

Thus the character of Puerto Rico's economy has changed from pre-World War II days and social conditions have improved dramatically. Nowadays the political parties struggle for power over constitutional and political matters, but they seldom disagree over the correctness of Muñoz Marin's development programme.

Reactions to poor social conditions

Popular movements

In the British islands the reformers concentrated on constitutional reforms and then the attainment of self-government. They could not improve working-class social conditions because of the continuation of the 'colonial economy' in which profits were made, but not retained in the islands. The funds provided by the Colonial Development and Welfare Act after 1940 could not match American investment in Puerto Rico.

Therefore social conditions in the British islands remained very poor compared with Puerto Rico. This has resulted in considerable bitterness on the part of the poor which has been channelled into racial movements like 'Black Power'. The Black Power movement in its American form does not exist in the Caribbean, but the slogan is used and the sentiment exists. In the British islands there was not a white majority oppressing a black minority but there were other similarities with the racial situation in the United States, especially deprivation and prejudice.

In their origin, black popular movements in the British islands and the United States both owe much to Marcus Garvey. In 1914 he tried to establish the 'Universal Negro Improvement Association' in Jamaica, but he had little support. He re-established it in New York in 1916 and by 1926 it was an outstanding success. Basically he instilled pride into the blacks in their 'blackness' and black culture. He taught that God was black and that blacks would always remain subservient while they worshipped a white God. He preached that 'black is beautiful'. This brings us to the basic point of contact between the popular movements of the two areas. Both wanted to break the 'imitative culture' and foster the 'evolved culture' in which blacks would extol their African heritage. In the French islands this movement was called *négritude*. In Jamaica the evolved culture was embraced by people as far apart in society as Bustamante and the Rastafarians. In the extreme form blacks rejected any contact with whites, but in a more moderate form blacks concentrated on their own culture, not on copying white models.

In the United States the black protest was taken up by Martin Luther King and the Black Churches. Until the 1960s the movement was non-violent. 'Black Power' was really born when blacks accepted violence as a legitimate means of helping them achieve their goal. In 1966 Stokeley Carmichael held that the blacks were not achieving anything through Christian love and passive resistance. They must use violence to achieve their ends. Even the Black Churches in the United States felt sympathetic towards this view. They argued that white racism was violent and was the cause of the retaliation.

These trends in the black popular movements in the United States were reflected in the 'angry young blacks' in the Caribbean. However, they could not vent their anger against white oppression and white majorities because there was no direct provocation. Their anger was more an expression of the bitterness caused by unemployment, social distress and the squalor and hopelessness of their futures. Violence has been common in Jamaica and other islands, but only as sporadic outbursts of social discontent, and not as part of a mass racial movement.

13
Art forms in the Caribbean

Petroglyph

Art and architecture

Archaeological discoveries

As we have seen from our historical studies, the Caribbean has been peopled for many thousands of years. Time, climate, volcanoes, earthquakes, fighting and economic change have destroyed most of the art and architecture of our ancestors. Nevertheless, sufficient remains to enliven and enlarge our knowledge of them.

Archaeologists have revealed much about the earliest settlers in the Caribbean. Sites dating from 5,000 to 3,000 B.C. have been found in Hispaniola, Antigua, St Thomas and Trinidad.

Petroglyphs or rock paintings, like the one above, have been found over a wide area. These are of varying styles but show a remarkable similarity of subject and teach us much about the life of the Ciboneys, Arawaks and Caribs. Those found in Cuba, Haiti, Puerto Rico, St John, Antigua, Guadeloupe, Martinique, St Lucia, Trinidad, Bonaire, Curaçao and Aruba are particularly good.

Zemis like the one on the opening page of Book 1 have been found in a number of places throughout the Caribbean, some dating back to about 200 A.D. Made of stone or conch shell, these little figures were worshipped by the Arawaks. Broken stone *zemis* found in later occupation layers in Guadeloupe and Antigua may have been destroyed by the Caribs. The painting by Aubrey Williams of Guyana on the cover of Book 1 is strongly influenced by Arawak rock painting.

In Puerto Rico, St Croix and Antigua, archaeologists have uncovered ball courts and balls made of rubber from Venezuela. Although these ball courts were unwalled, they indicate links with the Mayans whose walled ceremonial ball parks were used for religion and sport.

Quantities of pottery, artifacts and shell ornaments have also been dug up and these, together with many petroglyphs, can be seen in museums throughout the Caribbean. The museums at Utuado in Puerto Rico and White Marl in Jamaica are especially interesting.

Archaeologists have also made many later discoveries. Ships sunk by storms or pirates have been located and their contents retrieved. Among the most interesting discoveries, perhaps, were those made in the underwater excavations of Port Royal in the 1950s and 60s. This pirate stronghold, shown on page 67 of Book 2, was destroyed by an earthquake in 1692. Divers brought up monogrammed silver and pewter, furniture, fine imported glass and china, watches, jewelry and thousands of white clay pipes. This gives an indication of the enormous wealth of Port Royal in its heyday.

Art tradition in the Caribbean

Caribbean art has had a relatively short history. Apart from a few Amerindian rock drawings, sculpture and painting before the mid-twentieth century followed the artistic concepts of the colonial powers. Often executed by European artists, these early paintings showed family groups, landscapes and historical events. The highly realistic style in which many of them are painted helps to bring alive for us some of the people and events which make up Caribbean history.

The cover of Book 2 of Caribbean Certificate History shows a water colour by William Clark of Antigua in 1827. Some of the other water colours in this series are shown on pages 122 and 123 of Book 1. From these paintings we can learn a great deal about the cultivation of sugar cane and the process of sugar making. Another of Clark's paintings reproduced on page 9 of Book 2 shows English Harbour, Antigua. If you look at the illustrations in this series you will see that many of them are reproductions of early paintings. They are included to complement the text and, if studied carefully, provide a very useful learning aid.

The rich planters and merchants, who commissioned works of art, were European in outlook. They took their artistic standards from their home country, be it Spain, France, Holland or Britain, in the same way as they took their education and social life. This European influence was strengthened because there were no art schools or museums in the Caribbean. In order to study art, West Indians had to go to Europe or, later, America. There was little support or, indeed, opportunity for local artists. Those who did paint tended to do so in a European manner because this was what their patrons wanted and because it reflected the artistic training they had received.

Jean Michel Cazabon One of the most important early Caribbean painters was Jean Michel Cazabon. He was a Trinidadian of French extraction who went to study medicine in France. While there he became interested in art and gave up medicine in order to study it. His water colours, reproduced in two series of lithographs in Paris, show us what Port of Spain and other parts of Trinidad looked like in the mid-nineteenth century.

Twentieth-century developments In the second half of the twentieth century, Caribbean art is tending to lose much of its European imitativeness and is emerging as a strong local force. It shows a wide divergence of style, ranging from naturalist painting to abstract expressionism. This divergence is both its strength and weakness.

There is also a considerable local divergence and, as yet, it is impossible to discern a characteristic Caribbean style of painting. Work varies from island to island and from artist to artist. What is evident is an increasing interest in and awareness of art. This is accompanied by ever increasing opportunities for talented people from all walks of life to receive training in art and art education both at amateur and professional level. Governments throughout the Caribbean are encouraging art by establishing art galleries, buying works of art, giving scholarships abroad, extending art teaching and sponsoring exhibitions.

As the colonial period began to draw to an end

in the mid-1930s West Indian desire for independence became increasingly strong. This was reflected in the arts. West Indians became interested in their own poetry, music and art, especially in Jamaica and Trinidad.

The brief outlines of developments in art in Trinidad and Jamaica which follow are typical of the Caribbean as a whole.

Art in Trinidad

Artists like Hugh Stollmeyer and Amy Leong Pang produced work which broke away from tradition and began to reflect the social and political changes taking place in the 1930s. Their work, although commonplace today, appeared revolutionary at the time and provided the foundation on which future Trinidadians could build.

Interest in art did not seem widespread until after the Second World War. The reasons for this were mainly social and political and can be found elsewhere in this book. This growing interest led to the establishment of the Trinidad Art Society in 1943. It was the first of a number of art societies and among its members were many well known Trinidadian artists including Mildred Faulkner, Sybil Atteck, Albert Gomes and Andrew Carr. Its annual exhibition, held for the first time in 1944, became one of the artistic highlights of the year. Boscoe Holder, still regarded as one of Trinidad's outstanding painters, exhibited there until he gave up painting in favour of dancing and emigrated to the United States. Besides providing a means by which artists could exhibit their work, the society provided training for young artists and encouraged general interest in art. Abstract painting was introduced into Trinidad in the late

National Museum and Art Gallery, Port of Spain

1940s and 1950s, notably by Nina Lamming Squires who had studied in England. This was not very popular and later, in the 1950s, a number of artists sought to establish a Trinidadian style of painting. Among these were P. Alladin, Noel Vaucresson and Joseph Cromwell.

The British Council also encouraged art by awarding scholarships to talented artists to study art in Britain. Art and Art Education became more widely taught in colleges of education and in schools. As a result an increasing number of creative artists have emerged who are showing strong independence of thought both stylistically and in choice of subject.

With the coming of independence in 1962, a National Museum and Art Gallery was established. This provides a permanent display of works of art, mainly by local artists, and also a changing exhibition area. The latter stages one-man shows by leading local artists, exhibitions by art societies or schools and exhibitions of reproductions and original paintings loaned by foreign governments.

The Department of Culture awards scholarships and sponsors artists who wish to exhibit abroad. It buys original works for display in government offices and public buildings, and also for the National Museum and Art Gallery.

The Extra-Mural Department of the University of the West Indies organises art courses for amateur artists. Increasingly, tourists are buying works of art, and although standards vary enormously, many of the talented artists who have emerged have found a market for their work. There are, however, very few professional artists. Even the most successful find it necessary to teach or work as commercial artists to supplement their income.

Art in Jamaica

Jamaica had no real painting tradition. What little there was came second-hand from Europe. Interest in the arts in Jamaica was awakened at much the same time as Trinidad, and for much the same reasons. The ways in which artists were encouraged and an interest in art stimulated were also similar. Among the most influential pioneers were Edna Manley, the sculptress wife of the founder of the People's National Party who later became Prime Minister of Jamaica, Sir Philip Sherlock and the Institute of Jamaica.

Edna Manley had a profound influence on Jamaican art for two reasons: firstly her own artistic ability and development, and secondly her interest in and encouragement of art in Jamaica. Although British by birth and training, she was one of the first Jamaican artists to be influenced by traditional African art rather than traditional European art.

One of her most famous sculptures is 'Negro Aroused' which appears on the cover of this book. It typifies the Negro struggle for independence and a fuller, more satisfying way of life. The sculpture shows a preoccupation with social and political problems typical of her work at that time and reveals her close involvement in Jamaican politics. Her carving shows great virility and focuses on Jamaica rather than overseas.

She held one-woman exhibitions in Jamaica in 1931 and 1937 and also exhibited abroad, establishing herself as a sculptress of international repute at a time when few Caribbean artists were known outside their own countries. Her success encouraged other artists to follow her example.

Apart from her own work, she was very influential in spreading interest in painting and sculpture. She taught art herself and was closely connected with the Institute of Jamaica which provided opportunities for many talented Jamaicans to study art. In addition, it held exhibitions and encouraged public interest in art.

In 1940 the First All Jamaican Exhibition of Painting was held, which proved the forerunner of a series of successful exhibitions. Another great step forward was made in 1950 with the establishment of the Jamaican School of Art. This was the first school of art to be established in the Commonwealth Caribbean.

As in Trinidad, there were three main categories of artist in Jamaica.

1 *The Primitives* who were self-taught and non-professional but whose work was very individual and evocative. Among these were John Dunkley, Henry Daley, Mallica Reynolds (KAPO), Ras Dizzy and David Miller senior and junior.

John Dunkley, a barber by trade, began painting in the late thirties. His subjects consisted mainly of exotic animals against weird, dark landscapes, painted in the sombrest of colour schemes. They record the nightmare scenes that haunted him until his death in the late 1940s. He worked in house paint, filling in the

Old Richmond – Kapo

foreground with heavily accented foliage and animals. Neither he nor his fellow primitive Henry Daley had any followers.

It was another outstanding primitive painter who was to establish a new school of painting. This was Mallica Reynolds, more often known as KAPO, who began painting in the late 1960s. He established himself as the foremost of the Jamaican primitives, concentrating on the African side of Jamaica's heritage.

2 *The Representationalists* whose work ranges from the post-impressionism of Albert Huie to the surrealism of Osmond Watson. This category was made up of professional artists, trained either in Jamaica or abroad. Among them were Albert Huie, Edna Manley, Earl Abrahams, Karl Parboosingh, Barrington Watson, Osmond Watson, Alvin Marriot and Christopher Gonzales.

One of the most important artists of the earlier period was Albert Huie, considered by many to be Jamaica's outstanding painter. He is best known for his landscapes with figures like the one below which reveals the influence of Cezanne in composition and use of light.

Karl Parboosingh's work is very varied in both style and subject, ranging from Mexican realism to North American abstract expressionism. He shares Edna Manley's preoccupation with social and political problems and all his work shows a keen interest in everday Jamaican life, as can be seen in this picture of a cement factory.

Among the younger artists perhaps the best known is Barrington Watson who has studied and travelled widely abroad.

Apart from Edna Manley, the other important Jamaican sculptors are Leslie Clerk, Dorothy

Portrait of a Girl – Albert Huie
Revival Kingdom – Osmond Watson
Cement Factory – Karl Parboosingh

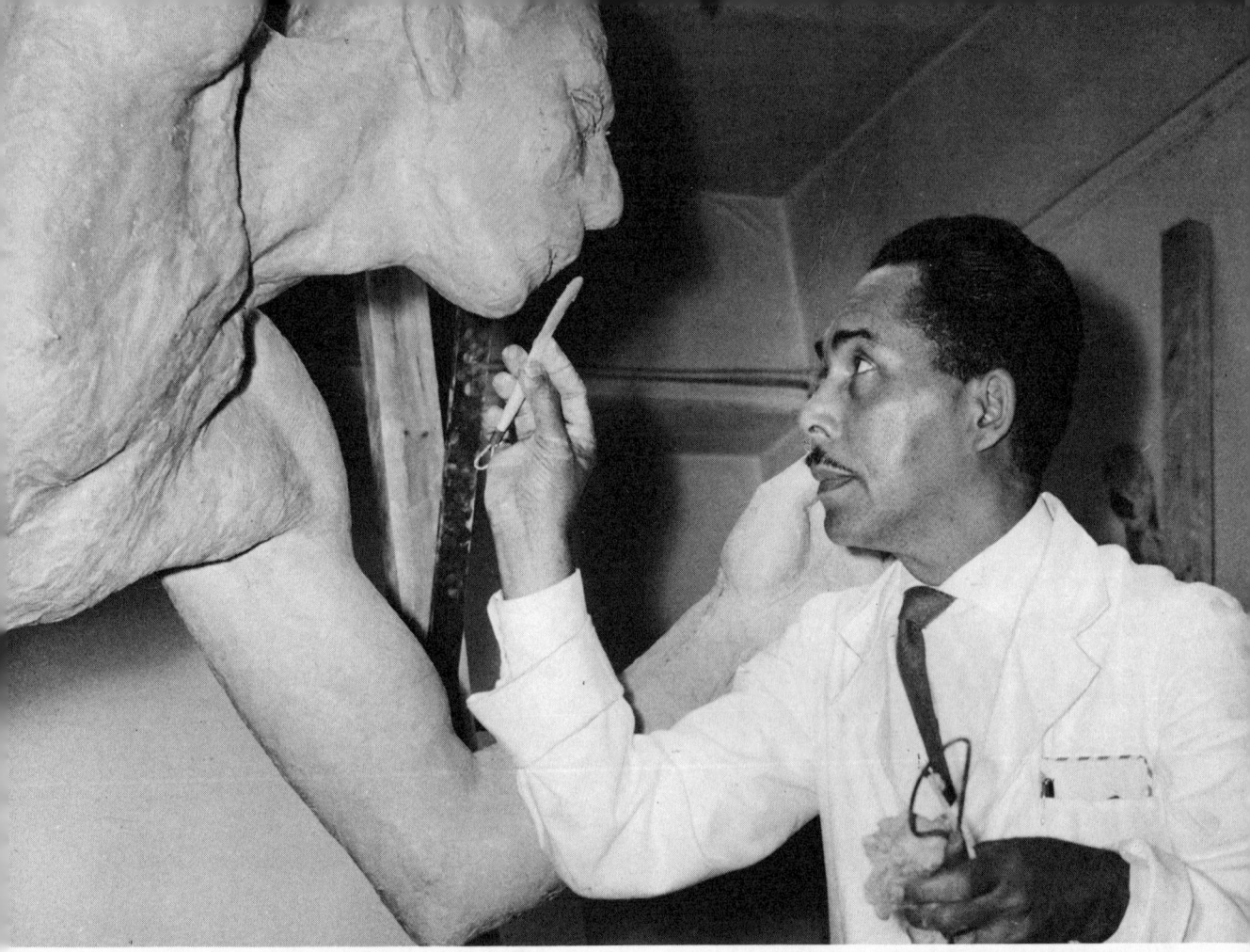

Alvin Marriot at work

Payne and Alvin Marriot. The latter is best known for his commemorative sculptures, among them the Jamaican National Monument.

3 *The Abstractionists* who are concerned less with pictorial art and more with formal and technical problems. Among them are Eugene Hyde, Milton Harley and Leonard Ferguson. They feel little involvement with the Caribbean and are more internationally orientated. They are painters before all else, and are not influenced by social and national problems.

Art in Haiti

No survey of art in the Caribbean would be complete without some mention of Haiti. The renaissance of art there since 1944 has placed Haiti second only to Mexico in artistic reputation among the countries of Latin America.

Revival of art in Haiti owed much to an American artist, De Witt Peters, who opened the *Centre d'Art* in Port-au-Prince in 1944. Until this time there had been little encouragement for artists and the few artists there were self-taught. The centre opened with a nucleus of ten artists including Hector Hyppolite and Philomené Obin. Peters searched out local artists and encouraged them to paint in their own style. Many talented and aspiring artists were attracted to the centre. Their success can be measured by the great impact that Haitian art made on the UNESCO international exhibition in Paris in 1947.

Other outstanding painters are Prefete Duffaut, Philippe Vieux, Jean Baptiste Jacques, Louines Mestor and Saint-Brice. They have been shown and bought all over the world and their works form part of the permanent collections of many famous museums. Haitian paintings always show plenty of people and animals. The overwhelming influence is African but they portray a colourful dramatic world divided between visions of the Garden of Eden and Voodoo magic.

Another great boost to Haitian painting was the commissioning of 'primitive' murals for the Episcopal Cathedral of St Trinité in Port-au-Prince. These have been called 'the crowning achievement of Haitian art'. Among the outstanding contributors are Obin, Wilson Bigaud and Castera Bazile.

In 1950 a group of painters broke away from the *Centre* to establish their own gallery, the *Foyer des Arts Plastiques*. Among them were Max Pinchinat, Roland Dorcély and Luce Tournier.

Two sculptors stand out from the older generation. These were Louis Laforesterie who exhibited in Paris in 1867 and Normil Charles, best known for his sculptures of Toussaint L'Ouverture and Dessalines.

Others were to emerge from the revival of sculpture and woodwork initiated by the *Centre d'Art*. Prominent among these were Odilon Duperier and Jasmin Joseph. The latter is best known for his imaginative terracotta sculptures and the choir screen in St Trinité Cathedral.

Haitian painting

Architecture

There are many architectural styles in the Caribbean. The men who built here were Europeans who followed the building and furnishing styles current in their home countries. Furniture and fittings were imported or copied. Houses designed for northern countries were modified to suit the local climate. However, no distinctive Caribbean style of architecture emerged. Spanish, Dutch, French and British influence is evident in different islands at different periods. Indeed, architecture shows how often islands changed hands in the seventeenth and eighteenth centuries. Unfortunately many of the early buildings have been destroyed but enough remains on most islands to give us a glimpse of the past.

Spanish architecture

Although the early Spanish settlers tended to build more solidly than the English or Dutch settlers, little remains of their building except in Cuba, Santo Domingo and Puerto Rico where they were not superseded by other European powers.

Spanish towns were built very much to a set pattern. There was always a cathedral with its plaza, a mission, a rectory, smaller chapels and other religious buildings, and houses belonging to government officials and merchants. These buildings were built of large stone blocks or a mixture of crushed stone and earth called 'tapia'.

The first town to be built by the Spaniards in the New World was Santo Domingo de Guzman founded in 1498 by Bartholemew Columbus. Its beautiful cathedral of Santa Maria de Menor, shown on page 98, where the remains of Christopher Columbus are thought to be buried, was begun in 1514. A mixture of gothic and baroque architecture, it is today one of the sights of Santo Domingo.

The Spanish settlers built tall airy houses with thick walls to keep out the heat. Floors were tiled

153

for coolness and the houses were built around a central patio and garden, giving a cool green vista to the rooms overlooking it. Ceilings were high and arched, and the many windows were placed in such a way as to give maximum ventilation. These windows had heavy wooden shutters which could be closed against storm or attack. Placed inside the window were pairs of triangular stone seats where Spanish ladies could sit and view life in the street below.

Since 1960 many buildings and neighbourhoods have been restored, among them the *Casa de Tostado*, a superb sixteenth century mansion, now a museum, the *Casa del Cordón* built in 1503, and the *Alcazar*, originally built by Diego Columbus and rebuilt by Ovando after it had been destroyed in an earthquake in 1502.

The buildings in San Juan, the capital of Puerto Rico, with the exception of El Morro, were not as grand as those of Santo Domingo. Nevertheless, a number of beautiful buildings remain. An imaginative restoration programme, encompassing not just individual buildings but whole areas, has shown us what the original city was like.

The Dominican Convent begun in 1523 is a delightful building with arched loggias on all four sides of a central courtyard. It is now the headquarters of the Institute of Puerto Rican Culture. Another well restored building is the *Casa de Callejón*, an eighteenth-century mansion which houses a museum. The sixteenth-century home of the Ponce family, Casa Blanca, was traditionally the home of the governors. It is now a cultural complex and museum.

By far the most outstanding building is the fortress of El Morro overlooking the harbour of San Juan. It was built in 1584 and added to throughout the following two centuries. In spite of this, it presents a very harmonious impression with well planned arches and courtyards. A castle rising above the top tier of guns about 40 metres above the sea gives a panoramic view of the harbour as well as the northern and eastern approaches of Puerto Rico.

Another great Spanish citadel is the fortress of El Morro at Havana, the rendezvous of the treasure fleets returning to Spain.

British architecture

In the years when sugar brought great wealth to the islands, the British were the dominant

El Morro

colonial power. They were responsible for building many of the great plantation houses, although they did not by any means have a monopoly, as can be seen from the rest of this chapter.

These houses are the most outstanding feature of Caribbean architectural heritage. Although showing signs of the owner's nationality in detail and decoration, they were designed primarily for the Caribbean, to keep out the heat and humidity and take advantage of the cool north-east trade winds. Most of these houses were rectangular or octagonal, built of cut stone with wood or brick. New wings were often added to the main building as the family fortune increased.

The ground floor was paved with stone or tiles and was used mainly for storage. A central or twin flight of stone steps led from the plantation drive to the main floor of the house. Inside the hall, corridors with arched and louvred interior windows looked on to reception rooms, a large dining room and possibly the main bedroom. The remaining bedrooms were on the floor above. The woodwork in many of these houses was superb. Floors, doors, lintels, panelling and dramatic curving staircases were made of mahogany or fruitwood, often beautifully carved. Rugs and carpets were seldom used because polished floors were cooler.

Although the plans for the popular Georgian or Palladian architectural styles in which many of these houses were built came from Europe, they were adapted and executed by island workmen. These craftsmen also made much of the elegant furniture including the huge four-poster bedsteads with their intricate carving. The china, crystal and other luxuries which graced these houses was usually imported.

The houses were very large because in an age when travelling was difficult, hotels unknown and domestic staff unlimited, hospitality was on a grand scale. Guests might stay on other plantations for weeks on end. They were entertained with balls, garden parties, hunting parties, as well as numerous luncheon and dinner parties.

It is, therefore, surprising to discover that the kitchens were very primitive and small. Except in the Spanish islands, they were sited away from the main house because of the heat and food smells. There was a brick oven for bread and another for meat, a smoke-house and a 'buttery' for perishable goods.

The huts where the slaves lived were also sited well away from the great house. These plantations were self-contained so that there was often a hospital, a cemetery and everything needed to keep the estate running. The sugar factory was often built with even more care than the great house. After all, sugar was the source of their wealth. This can be seen in the photograph below. It consisted of a grinding mill, a boiling house with a high chimney, a curing house, a rum distillery and a cooperage for repairing equipment and making hogsheads. See the pictures on page 122 and 123 of Book 1. Power was provided by huge water wheels or windmills, many of which can be seen throughout the islands. Although almost all these buildings are in ruins today, paintings and descriptions of sugar factories, like that of the Kenilworth Plantation in Jamaica, reveal the care and planning that went into their construction.

A number of important houses were built before the eighteenth century. These include Porters and Holders House in St James, Barbados. A photograph of the latter can be seen on page 87 of Book 1. Other outstanding early houses were Colbeck Castle and Stokes Hall, Jamaica. The former was built towards the end of

A Jamaican sugar estate 1892

the seventeenth century in stone walling with red and brick quoins. It was probably one of the largest houses on the island. Like Stokes Hall, only the shell of the building remains today.

The majority of the great plantation houses were built in the eighteenth century and one can find examples in almost every island. In Antigua there is the beautiful Clarence House, built in 1787 for William, Duke of Clarence, with particularly fine exterior ironwork, and in Nevis, Montpelier, where the wedding reception of Fanny Nesbit and Horatio Nelson took place. In Barbados there are Drax Hall, Farley Hill and Codrington College. Farley Hill is a large two-storey house built in stone with arched windows. It was rebuilt in 1861 but partially destroyed by fire in the early 1970s.

Jamaica, the largest and richest of the sugar islands, has more great houses than anywhere else. One of the most beautiful is Rose Hall. Built in 1760, it was an architectural gem with magnificent mahogany panelled reception rooms and staircase. Special building materials and much of the elegant furniture for this house were imported from England. Like many other plantation houses, Rose Hall was almost derelict but has recently been very well restored.

At Orange Valley is probably the most complete group of eighteenth-century sugar estate buildings to be seen in Jamaica today. These include an H-shaped great house with loop-holes for defence on all sides, a stone-built factory, a boiling house, a lime kiln and a hospital for slaves.

The British, like their colonial rivals, built many forts to defend their Caribbean possessions. Brimstone Hill, St Kitts, was begun in 1736 but not completed until nearly a hundred years later. It was built on a vast scale and included the Prince of Wales bastion, Fort George, Fort Charlotte, officers' mess, barracks, parade ground, hospital and many other buildings, all connected with roads and walls of stone and brick.

Only one battle was fought there, in 1782, when it fell to the French after prolonged fighting. Much damage was done to the fort by two hurricanes in the nineteenth century and by the twentieth century it was a ruin. Restoration work began on the Prince of Wales bastion but further damage was inflicted by the earthquake of 1974.

Rosehall before restoration

Rosehall after restoration

Naturally the fleet needed extensive dockyards and repair buildings. The dockyards at English Harbour, Antigua, which were named after Nelson, were damaged in an earthquake in 1843. Restoration work began in 1951 and many of the buildings have been restored to their original purpose using eighteenth-century building techniques.

The attractive wooden town of St John, dating

from the late eighteenth century, is laid out in broad avenues, intersected at right angles by narrow streets. Many of the eighteenth- and nineteenth-century wooden houses remain. They are noteworthy for their slim wooden columns and elegant wrought-iron handrails.

A few buildings were constructed in stone, among them Parham Church, Court House, Government House and St John's Cathedral. Parham Church was designed by Thomas Weeke and built in 1840 in the classical style. St John's Cathedral, with its twin towers, is wood panelled inside. After being damaged by repeated hurricanes it was restored, but was damaged again in the earthquake of 1974.

Bridgetown, Barbados, is noteworthy for the pink coral stone from which much of it was built. Founded in 1628, it has been damaged many times by fire and earthquake. One of the few early buildings to survive is St Anne's Fort with its clock-towered guardhouse built in 1702. Another is St John's Church which is an exact replica of many English country churches.

St George's, Grenada, has many eighteenth century houses with characteristic red tiled roofs. It is one of the most beautifully sited towns in the West Indies. Among its attractive features are the old spiked cannon along the Carenage to which yachts and schooners tie up.

Basseterre in St Kitts also has a number of attactive Georgian town houses, mostly in The Circus and Pall Mall. Built of stone or brick, with small gardens in front, they have arched overhanging upper storeys decorated with carved wood.

The architecture of Trinidad's capital, Port of Spain, has been more influenced by the French and Spanish than by the British. The exceptions to this are the Town Hall, St James' Barracks and the Deanery. Trinidad and Guyana are the only territories in the Caribbean which have a number of Moslem mosques and Hindu temples. Typical is the one shown on page 101 of Book 2. Georgetown has many elegant wooden houses and its Anglican Cathedral is the largest wooden building in the world.

Anglican Cathedral in Georgetown

New Providence in the Bahamas was first occupied by the British in 1666 and by the end of the century Nassau was a thriving town. One of the oldest buildings still remaining is The Deanery, built in 1710. It is three storeys high, with chamfered quoins and verandas on the east, west and north sides. These quoins or corner stones are typical of Bahamian architecture, as are louvred shutters, high peaked roofs, dormer windows and wooden handrails. Among its fine churches are St Matthew's Church built in 1802 and Christ Church Cathedral built between 1837 and 1840.

Montego Bay and Kingston in Jamaica have been too extensively modernised to have much of architectural interest. Although, like many other Jamaican towns, they still have many pitched shingled roofs, louvred windows and interesting colonnades and balconies with attractive wooden decoration. One of the most attractive nineteenth-century buildings remaining in Kingston is Devon House, now restored, which houses the National Gallery of Art.

Spanish Town, Jamaica's first capital, has a number of attractive Georgian public buildings, among them the House of Assembly and the Hall of Records.

Perhaps the most attractive town is Falmouth, built largely in the nineteenth century. All the houses are different but they add up to a unified whole. Their outstanding characteristic is the raised horizontal band which divides the two storeys emphasising their length rather than their height. Many of the houses have balconies with elegant iron or wood fretwork and cedar shingled roofs.

Devon House

French architecture

As in their other colonies, the French left a strong imprint on the Caribbean in architecture as in everything else. This was heightened by the fact that in the seventeenth and eighteenth centuries, French cultural influence was particularly strong throughout Europe.

One of the earliest and most prosperous of their settlements was Cap Français in St Domingue (now Cap Haitien in Haiti). This had such magnificent streets and buildings that it became known as the 'Paris of the Antilles'. This nickname was later given to Pointe-à-Pitre in Guadeloupe. It is typically French with its three-storied shuttered houses topped by steeply pitched roofs, many of which still remain today. Its eighteenth-century cathedral has a yellow and white stucco facade which hides an iron framework to protect it from earthquakes and hurricanes. It had decorative panels which alternate with columns, stained glass arched windows and an arched portico. The harbour was guarded by *Fort de la Fleur d'Epeé* of which only the moat and extensive dungeons remain, although the grounds are well kept.

The French settlers built many great plantation houses. One of the earliest was Fountain Estate in St Kitts built by De Poincy in 1640. Little of this remains, apart from the foundations and cellars on which the present great house is built.

Chateau Murat in Marie Galante is one of the few French houses in good repair. Built by Dominique Emmanuel Murat, it is a rectangular building with a classical facade. It has a three arched portico divided by columns with Ionic capitals. The original floors were said to be encrusted with gold *louis d'or*. It was surrounded by formal gardens in the French style. Chateau Murat has been recently restored using eighteenth century methods and materials.

Similar houses, now mostly in ruins, can be found in St Lucia and Martinique. Among those in the latter was La Pagerie, home of Josephine de la Pagerie who became the wife of Napoleon Bonaparte and thus Empress of France.

The French also built many forts. Among them was Fort St Louis in Martinique. Begun by Jacques du Parquet in 1640, it was further extended at the beginning of the eighteenth century. Built like a mediaeval castle with a moat

Chateau Murat

and underground passages, much of it remains today, although the moat has been filled in.

Another fort begun by the French in the mid-eighteenth century was Morne Fortune in St Lucia. Later additions were made by the British. Most of the buildings are two storeys high with arched galleries on the lower floor. Above, slim posts support the pitched roofs which extend over railed balconies to the edge of the galleries.

The exterior has been restored to its original design. The interior has been adapted for use as a school and a branch of the University of the West Indies.

Dutch architecture

An interesting feature of the Dutch islands is that much of the early architecture remains. They present a distinctive appearance, quite different from the other islands. The town houses are usually rectangular, three or four storeys high with dormer windows and steep tiled roofs. Many are decorated with elaborate scroll facings and mansard roofs. In Bonaire, Aruba and Curaçao window frames and shutters are painted in bright or deep contrasting colours to the painted walls which gives an attractive effect.

Curaçao

Curaçao has some of the oldest and best preserved buildings in the Caribbean. Many of them are in the capital, Willemstad. The Civil Service Registration Office is housed in a restored pre-1740 house which illustrates many of the architectural features mentioned above. An arched colonnade was added at a later date.

Its oldest building is Fort Amsterdam, begun by Peter Stuyvesant before 1642. Its churches too are old. St Anna's Catholic Church dates from 1751 and the Ismel Synagogue from 1730, the oldest synagogue in the West Indies.

Stream View is an interesting late eighteenth-century octagonal house with steps leading to a projected main storey. The Curaçao liqueur distillery is housed in a beautiful seventeenth-century plantation house named Chobolobo. Many of the town houses are painted in pink, yellow or beige, which gives a very harmonious effect.

St Eustatius was heavily fortified by the Dutch. At one time it had seventeen forts and batteries guarding its shore. The most important of these was Fort Oranje on the south-west coast overlooking Oranjestad. Begun in 1736 on the foundation of a 1729 French fort, it consists of a commander's house, a town hall, prison cells, barracks, a cistern, a powder magazine and gun emplacements overlooking the port. Although used for a variety of modern purposes, it looks much the same today as it did in the eighteenth century.

On the shore below are the ruins of warehouses, forts, cisterns and other buildings, many of which can no longer be identified. Recent underwater excavations have shown traces of other buildings as well as the sea wall which protected the shore from erosion. We can see from this something of the vast scale of Fort Oranje.

Haiti

The people of Haiti still build in their own traditional way showing distinct African influence. Their one-roomed huts are built of daub-and-wattle with dirt floors and thatch or tin roofs. These tiny houses are seen everywhere in Haiti.

Cap Haitien, originally built by the French in the seventeenth and eighteenth centuries, looks today much as it did when it was rebuilt after an earthquake in the 1840s. The facade of the Cathedral facing the Place d'Armes and part of 2, Place Toussaint L'Ouverture including the seal of the Marquis de Beauharnais, is all that remains from colonial times.

Port-au-Prince dates mainly from the nineteenth century. Many of its large town houses, built of wood or stone with dormers and balconies decorated with iron or wooden scrollwork, are still in a good state of repair. Another feature of Port-au-Prince is the Iron Market, with its superb iron roof. The original Cathedral, St Ann's, built in 1720, still exists but has been replaced by a nineteenth-century church. Particularly interesting is the St Trinité Episcopal Cathedral built in 1928. It has a series of biblical murals commissioned in the 1950s and executed by then unknown primitive artists.

Most famous of Haiti's buildings are the palace and fortress built by Henri Christophe at Milot. Sans Souci was a magnificent palace built in the style of Louis XV. Its walls were lined with tapestries, its windows silk hung and its floors, woodwork and panelling were in gleaming mahogany. Everything about it was grandiose. Christophe aimed at rivalling the court of France and as the picture on page 26 of Book 2 shows, he succeeded. The castle was destroyed by an earthquake in 1842.

Built 1,000 metres above it at the top of a steep winding trail is the fortress of La Citadelle. Designed by a French engineer, La Ferrière, it covers 80,000 square metres. Work began in 1804 and was still continuing when Christophe committed suicide in 1818. Everything needed to build and maintain the fortress had to be hauled up the precipitous rocky track by man or donkey.

La Citadelle

It was designed to house a garrison of 15,000 men able to withstand a siege of three years, with arms and provisions stored behind walls forty metres high and three metres thick. It was a vast structure with countless rooms, gun emplacements, storage vaults, etc. It was a folly which could only have been built by an absolute ruler.

Music

Today Caribbean music is the most distinctive of all Caribbean cultural arts. We know that the Arawaks and Caribs had music, but it had little influence on later musical forms. It was from European, African and Asian music that the present day Caribbean forms emerged.

The dominant influence is African. The African slaves brought their own music from West Africa. The drum rhythms were retained in the memories of the slaves although there was little opportunity to perform them and there were few proper instruments. The authorities also tried to suppress what they considered pagan rhythms, but they could not. Evenings and Sundays were the chief occasions for the slaves to recall their tribal musical traditions. The beats and rhythms of Africa proved more able to survive slavery than language and other tribal customs. In Haiti, African music was retained most successfully and completely. There the distinctive character of African music can easily be traced. Some African characteristics are

a) close relationship between melody and speech tone;
b) spontaneous creation of rhythm and melody;
c) willingness and ability of performers to extemporise within the main forms of the rhythms and melody;
d) emphasis on many voices and many parts in music, known as 'polyphony';
e) bringing these voices and parts together in harmony;
f) combination of polyphony and harmony in the same musical performance;
g) arrangement of complicated rhythms.

The complicated rhythms and the offbeat style of Yoruba drumming and even the syncopated rhythms of modern 'High Life' from Nigeria can be traced in Haitian music. The drumming is following one rhythm until the accent is suddenly placed on another beat, or the first rhythm is broken and another rhythm is taken up. This style is also found in some of the reggae of Bob Marley. Indeed, the reggae 'purists' rely heavily on syncopated rhythms in the African style. The early calypsoes of the Mighty Sparrow show the African traditions. Speech tone is very important in them, as is the displacing beats and accents in the melodies which is known as syncopation. This can be seen in his calypsoes, 'Old Man and Donkey' and 'The Village Ram'.

African influence is definitely the strongest on Caribbean music, but European and Asian elements are also present. Distinctive Caribbean music forms have resulted from the blending of African and European traditions. This is where we find the creative genius of Caribbean musicians.

Instruments

As with forms, so with instruments. Caribbean rhythms rely heavily on percussion instruments which are part of their African tradition. However, European instruments such as the guitar, clarinet and saxophone have been adopted too. East Indian drums have been experimented with by African drummers. Recently the sitar has also been borrowed from Indian music. From the Chinese have come the cymbals. In instrumentation, the genius for blending and adaptation is maintained. Perhaps the combination of traditions is most equally achieved in Afro-Cuban music. For example, the rhumba, 'La Cumparsita', owes much to slave rhythms and European instrumentation.

West African percussion instruments survived in the Caribbean. Sometimes they could not be copied in exactly their original form because the skins and other materials were not available. Then modifications on the original were made. With the passage of time Caribbean variants for African instruments emerged.

1 *Drums* In Africa they were usually cow or goat skin stretched over a wooden framework. In the Caribbean these were still used, but often the slaves improvised.

2 *Xylophones* The slaves adopted the African type, which consisted of strips of resonant wood of different lengths laid across two parallel struts. The most unusual variant of this in the Caribbean was the 'tamboo-bamboo' in Trinidad which consisted of bamboo poles being stuck in the

ground in a line. They were struck from a sitting or standing position, depending on how far they stretched.

3 *Claves* These are percussion sticks which are hollow. They are an essential part of the music of Cuba and Haiti. In Trinidad they were usually bamboo canes of the 'tamboo-bamboo' type cut to various lengths and struck together as the performers marched or danced along.

4 *Clappers* These Yoruba instruments were very common in Cuba.

5 *Rattles* These are common throughout the Caribbean and Latin America. Most of them are made from gourds. When the seeds are left in they are commonly known as 'maracas' and are probably native to America. However, other gourd-percussion instruments which rely on external striking or striking gourds together, probably derive from Africa. Gourds with liquid inside are played in Cuba and they are definitely of African origin.

6 *Scrapers* There are African and native Caribbean examples of these. A gourd with its natural stem forming a handle with notches cut in its surface and scraped with a stick, is an African instrument. A turtle shell cut into ridges and scraped is Caribbean.

7 *Thumb Pianos* These are known throughout Africa and were copied by the slaves in the West Indies, but their use is limited today. They are made of strips of metal of different lengths fixed to a sound board and twanged with the fingers. The Cuban name for them is 'marimbula' which shows their association with xylophones.

8 *Bones* Striking of bones was common amongst the slaves throughout the Americas. It has died out because of its pagan and primitive connotations.

Other musical instruments, mainly European in origin, have been incorporated into Caribbean music. The chief ones are the trumpet, trombone, clarinet, saxophone, piano, guitar, violin, cello and double bass.

The importance of carnival

The tradition of carnival in Roman Catholic countries is that it is the final merry-making before the forty days of Lent during which people abstain from pleasure to remember Christ's suffering and sacrifices for mankind. Most merry-making centred around music and dancing and thus carnival played a very important role in the development of these arts. This is definitely true of carnival in Trinidad.

The carnival season is long. In the church calendar it should begin at Epiphany (6 January) and end at Shrove Tuesday, the day before Ash Wednesday which is the start of Lent. In practice in Trinidad, carnival begins at Christmas and lasts until Shrove Tuesday. The culmination of the festival, however, is the last four days, that is from Saturday to Tuesday. Shrove Tuesday itself is the climax.

Every evening during the season people are on the streets of the towns of Trinidad 'jumping up', dancing and singing to the favourite current melodies and, occasionally, recalling old ones. They dress up in costumes at any time, although carnival costumes are usually reserved for the last four days. Then all work stops in Port of Spain. Calypsoes, written and composed for carnival have been whittled down to about fifty favourites for the final competition, and the winner will receive the title of 'King', or 'Queen' Calypsonian. Steel bands have also been competing to select the best in Trinidad. Thus by the choice of leading singer and leading band, carnival dictates popular taste for the coming year.

For the musicians of Trinidad carnival means more than just the season. Their minds have to be on carnival throughout the year. Their compositions and practices are undertaken with carnival in view. The professionals must maintain pitches or tents on or near the carnival streets because carnival is important not only for the pure considerations of Caribbean musical forms, but also for the commercial market.

Steel band music

Origins

Steel bands originated in the hard times of the late 1930s and the war years. After the disturbances of June 1937, in Trinidad, the police banned the use of 'tamboo-bamboo' canes because they could become offensive weapons. Street musicians turned to other sources for their 'beat' and most of them were made of metal. Oil drums became a common source of beat as they were so common in Trinidad. However, they could not be carried

Carnival in Port of Spain

along in parades, so they were dragged to areas of waste ground where musicians gathered and the steel bands were born. The empty spaces of the city were taken over in the evenings by groups of musicians. These spaces were known thenceforth as 'panyards'. One was occupied by the 'Invaders', a very famous early band. The names of the panyards became famous too; for example, the 'Hell-Yard' and the 'Lime Grove' just outside Port of Spain.

The development of the steel drum as a musical instrument is typical of the creative use to which West Indians can put discarded objects. The oil drum was not the first 'pan' that was beaten to make music. Some say that an empty biscuit tin was the first; but an old petrol tank of a car; a garbage-bin lid; a steel rod for reinforcing concrete; an aluminium milk pail; or an old hubcap – all of these have been recorded as the primitive musical instruments in the history of the steel band. However, the creative genius of the musicians gradually turned these pieces of scrap into regular musical instruments. The development of the steel drum is the most important.

The forty-four gallon oil drum was a common sight disfiguring Trinidad city streets. Brought into the panyards they were turned into musical instruments. Struck in their original empty state they produced a deep 'boom'. Then they were cut in cross-sections. By cutting them shorter and shorter, higher and higher notes were produced. Thus the bass-pan, or 'boom', is the oil drum with the bung end cut off. The next in size, the 'cellopan' is cut 30 to 37 centimetres from the bung end. Then comes the 'guitar-pan' which is about 50 centimetres deep. The highest note is produced by the 'ping-pong' which is the top 15 to 20 centimetres of the drum.

The discovery that these pans could be tuned is attributed to Ellie Manette. So the tuning is called 'Ellie's Technique'. It seems that the first pan he tuned was a shallow 20 centimetre pan which was subsequently called the 'ping-pong'. He hammered from the inside to give the striking surface a convex shape. On this surface he marked small circles round the circumference and then seamed them with a cold chisel. These he hammered from the inside to make them into domes or bosses which produced notes of different pitches when struck. The pans could be then tuned by tapping these domes until the desired pitch was achieved. The steel was then tempered by the primitive method of pouring oil over it and setting it alight. Ellie Manette was probably the first also to wrap rubber round his drumsticks to strike the pan.

Ellie's technique was then applied to all the four sizes of pan. Rafael 'Boy Blue' Samuel of the Casablanca Steel Orchestra is thought to have been the first to use a 'tuned-boom' pan. The number of notes on each size pan was regularised. The boom was given between three and four notes; the cellopan, between five and six; the guitar-pan, about fourteen; and the ping-pong, between twenty-six and thirty-two. The Invaders Steel Band was probably the first to combine the four standard sizes of pan and their range of notes into a regular band. Then other bands began to adopt the same pattern and the standard steel band had a range of about thirty-six notes which produced the famous 'liquid sound' of steel band music. In larger combinations the 'organ sound' was produced, and the sound from a very large ensemble could be made to resemble a giant theatre organ.

History of the bands

The first regular steel bands were known by the end of 1945. They emerged from the Victory celebrations for the Allied triumph over Germany in the Second World War. On 8 May, musicians 'jumping up' and beating pan came out of the 'Hell-Yard' in 'Across-the-bridge Port of Spain' and marched through the streets. The release of joy was even greater because the people had not experienced a carnival for over five years. After the success of this parade, musicians spent the rest of the year forming bands, improving techniques and developing their own beats and sounds. Apart from 'Hell-Yard', the most famous band of 1945 was 'Bar-29' under Scribo Maloney. They practised hard and developed their famous 'cut-and-tumble' beat.

For the next five years the steel bands had to struggle against an unsavoury reputation because hooligans congregated in the panyards and fought the rival gangs associated with other bands. However, by 1950–51 the true musicians were shaking off this reputation and becoming regarded as respectable performers. Indeed, in 1950 Ellie Manette's Invaders performed before the Governor at the Little Carib night club. In the

Ellie Manette

A steel band orchestra

same year the first steel band competition was held at the Trinidad Turf Club. The Casablanca Steel Orchestra stole the show by playing 'The Bells of St Mary's' with the hub-cap as solo instrument, and followed that by rendering Chopin's Nocturne in E-flat, arranged by their leader, Russell Manning. This was the first public peformance of a classical piece of music by a steel band. It demonstrated to a large audience the versatility of the steel band which ranged over ballads, calypsoes, marches and finally classics. The latter highlighted a characteristic of steel-bandsmen: they cannot read music, but play by ear and learn by heart.

Respectability led to the spread of steel bands throughout Trinidad and across into Tobago. By 1951 they had even attracted an international reputation. This was undoubtedly helped by the West Indies' successful cricket tour of England in 1950 which produced the calypso; 'Who are the devils of spin? Valentine and Ramadhin', accompanied of course, by a steel band.

After 1951 steel band music went from strength to strength. The number of bands multiplied and so did their size. In modern times there are full-scale steel orchestras of one hundred instruments. The Catelli Trinidad All Stars Steel Orchestra can give a full length concert with Schubert's 'Unfinished' Symphony and the first movement of a Mozart piano concerto in their repertoire. However, most bands are of a conventional size of three to six booms, two to three pairs of cellopans, two to four guitar-pans and one to two ping-pongs. The combinations of these instruments vary from band to band and this makes steel bands so adaptable to different forms and different occasions.

Other Caribbean musical forms

The Calypso

Of all the musical forms in the Caribbean, the calypso best illustrates the blending of African and European traditions. Sometimes it is like the English ballad in that it is a simple song with an accompaniment which is merely subordinate. At other times the calypso owes more to African tradition. As African melodies follow speech tones, so calypso melodies follow local speech patterns. In style and content, calypso lyrics can be traced to African patterns. They are imaginative, witty, poking fun at leading figures in society, having one meaning for devotees and another for outsiders.

The calypso dates from the time when the slaves were preparing for liberation. They made up songs about local and topical events and figures to do with the emancipation movement and their oppressors. In Trinidad groups of slaves led by singer-composers known as 'shatwell', who often made up their songs as they went along, paraded through the streets in carnival season.

The centre for calypso remained Trinidad. Carnival dictated the forms of the calypso and the conventions of its performance, whether the singer should follow the conventional calypso melody or invent one of his own. Carnival produced the convention that calypso singers should adopt popular names like 'the Mighty Spoiler', 'Lord Melody', 'Attila the Hun' and 'the Mighty Sparrow'. Language conventions also come from Trinidad where Spanish, Yoruba, Ashanti and Creole words have been remembered and incorporated in calypso lyrics. In the nineteenth century, calypsoes were accompanied by favourite instruments like the 'shak-shak' (maracas), the guitar and the 'cuatre', another stringed instrument. The 'tamboo-bamboo' was perhaps the most popular accompaniment until the steel pans took over. Today calypsoes are well known abroad and can be accompanied by full-scale bands.

In modern times the calypso has been dominated by 'the Mighty Sparrow'. With his manager, Syl Taylor, they led the 'Original Young Brigade' in Trinidad from 1956 to 1979. At carnival time their calypso tent on Wrightson Road, Port of Spain, was the 'mecca' of calypsonians. Then in 1979 'Calypso Rose' emerged as the new 'Queen of Calypso'.

'The Mighty Sparrow'

Reggae, Cadence, Soca

Almost every territory in the Caribbean has its own distinctive music form. The Bahamas and Turks and Caicos have 'Junkanoo'; Bermuda has 'Goombay'; Haiti has 'Merengue'; Martinique has 'Beguine'; and Puerto Rico has 'Plenas'. The 'Rhumba' from Cuba has become so international that it is forgotten that it is a Caribbean form. However, three recent Caribbean forms need special mention. They are 'Reggae' from Jamaica, 'Cadence' from Guadeloupe and Martinique and 'Soca' from Trinidad.

Reggae This has strong links in its lyrics with Black Power and Rastafarianism. In this sense reggae is a form of protest music. However, it can also deal with happy themes, and when these are local and topical to Jamaica, reggae is Jamaican folk music, parallel to calypso in Trinidad.

The pure reggae artists are Jamaican and so are the lyrics and the distinctive style of the music. However, modern reggae has its commercial side in which the lyrics can be universally understood. This is much resented by the purists. A famous reggae performer who has managed to reconcile musical integrity with commercial success, is Bob Marley. His residence in Hope Road, Kingston, reflects his commercial success as a reggae superstar. His music and lyrics, however, reflect pure reggae.

Cadence This dominates the middle of the Eastern Caribbean chain. The chief exponents of Cadence are the Dominican bands performing in Guadeloupe. Socially it is linked with the unemployed youth of the islands, but has gained some appeal with fashionable society in Paris and London. At present it is too early to say whether it is merely a temporary phenomenon, or will rank with reggae as an established Caribbean music form.

Soca This experimental music from Trinidad is made up from 'Soul' and 'Calypso' and is interesting because it represents a typical Caribbean blending of cultures. It combines the jazz of the blacks of the southern United States with the calypso and uses East Indian instruments like the sitar, the mandolin and the tabla.

Bob Marley

Revision questions

N.B. Students are not expected to answer the questions marked with an * without the help of the book. For objective-type questions please refer to *Multiple Choice and Objective Questions* by Robert Greenwood (Macmillan).

Chapter 1

*1 When and why did the United States become interested in the Caribbean in the nineteenth century? How was this related to United States foreign policy in general?

*2 Describe the United States policy towards Cuba and relations with her to 1902.

3 Study the picture on page 8 and answer the following questions.
   a) What sort of ship was it? Why had it been sent on this mission?
   b) What were the explanations offered for the cause of the event depicted in this picture?
   c) What was the ultimatum delivered by the owners of the vessel and what was the reply given to them?
   d) Outline the course of the war which followed.
   e) What were the results of the war for the defeated country?
   f) What were the results of the war for the island it was fought over?

Chapter 2

1 Trace the history of the Panama Canal project to 1914.

*2 What is meant by 'Dollar Diplomacy'? Show when, where and how it was used by the United States in the Caribbean in the twentieth century.

3 Describe American involvement in Cuba from 1902 to 1934. Why did their policy towards Cuba change about 1934, and what were their relations with Cuba thereafter as far as 1959?

4 Study the picture on page 13 and answer the following questions:
   a) What was the strategic importance of the Panama Canal to the United States?
   b) How did the United States secure the withdrawal of the European countries from the Isthmian Canal project?
   c) What part did Theodore Roosevelt take in the canal negotiations?
   d) Under what conditions could other countries' ships use the canal?
   e) What effect did the canal have on United States policy in the Caribbean?

5 On the map of the Caribbean below the letters 'A' to 'J' point to places of United States involvement in the Caribbean. Place the correct letter in the space provided on the left of the clues below.
   1 Involved some dishonest diplomacy with Colombia.
   2 Purchased from Denmark.
   3 Well known U.S. naval base.
   4 Popular during 'prohibition'.
   5 Shares dual citizenship with U.S.
   6 Border dispute attracted U.S.
   7 Scene of brutality in 1915.
   8 First target of dollar diplomacy (1905).
   9 A tax haven.
   10 Another possible canal route.

Chapter 3

*1 Discuss the development of trade unions in the British Caribbean before 1930. What were the difficulties faced by these early unions?

2 Make a timeline of the riots and strikes of the period, 1935 to 1938, in the British Caribbean.

3 Write a biography of any *one* labour leader in the British Caribbean.

*4 What part have trade unions played in politics in the British West Indies since 1938? Illustrate your answer from *one* trade union – political party link.

5 Refer to the portrait on page 22 and answer the following questions:
   a) What made him adopt the name 'Bustamante'?

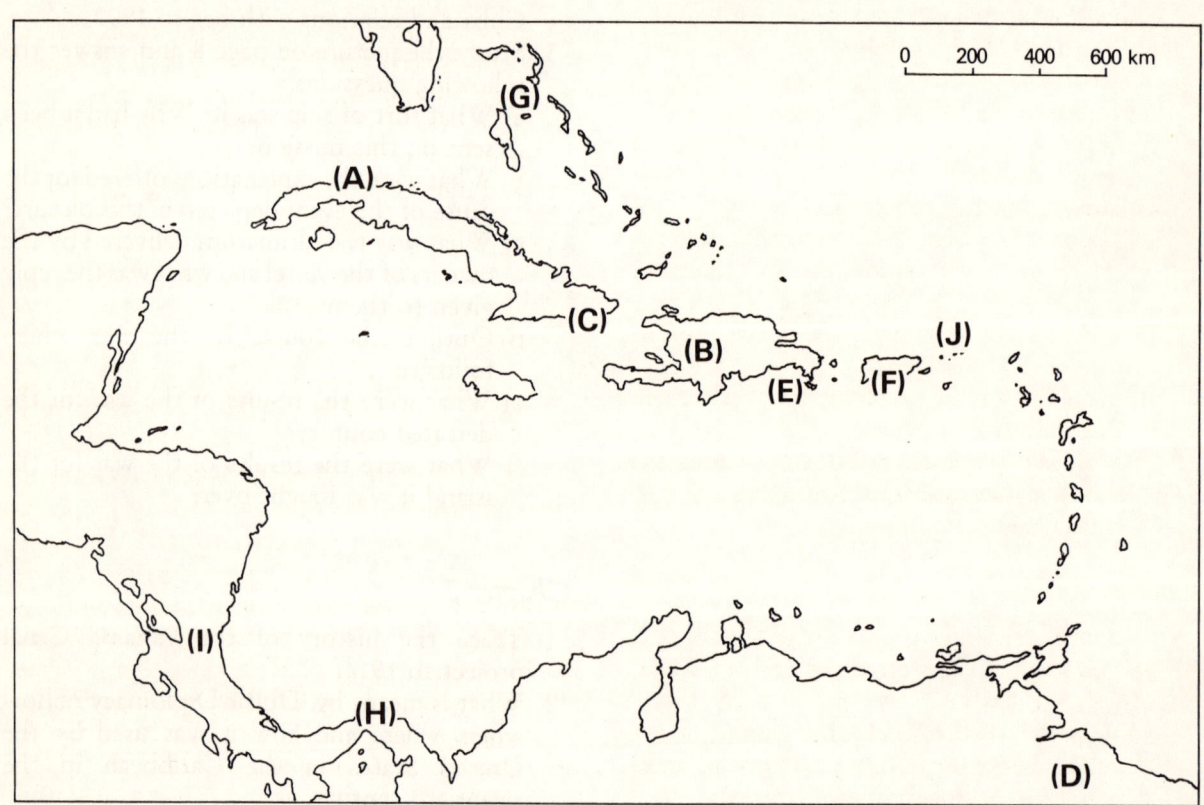

b) How did he use his colour to best effect in winning working class support?
  c) Why was he twice imprisoned between 1938 and 1942?
  d) When and why did he enter politics?
  e) Give examples of his flamboyant and emotional approach in public meetings.
  f) How did he turn the failure of the British West Indies Federation to his political advantage?

Chapter 4

*1 Describe the representative system of government as it operated in the British Caribbean from 1639 to 1865. Why was this system unsatisfactory to the British government by 1865?

2 What were the causes of the Morant Bay Rebellion in 1865?

3 Discuss the importance of the Morant Bay Rebellion in British West Indian history.

4 Examine the conflict between Governor Eyre and George William Gordon from the point of view of a personality clash and in the light of the events of the time.

*5 Describe Crown Colony government and show how it was operated in the British West Indies from 1866 to 1944.

6 Refer to the picture of Paul Bogle on page 42 and answer the following questions:
  a) What was he i) by colour ii) by religious denomination?
  b) What was his relationship with George William Gordon? When and how did they differ in their approach to Jamaica's problems?
  c) In what part of Jamaica did he have special influence and why?
  d) How far was he to blame for the Morant Bay Rebellion?
  e) Why is he regarded as one of the heroes of modern Jamaica? Do you agree that he should be so honoured?

Chapter 5

1 Why did Britain give up most of her colonies in the twenty years after the Second World War?

*2 Outline the stages in the constitutional development from Crown Colony to independence in a typical British territory.

3 Choose any one of the following territories and describe how it progressed to independence: Barbados, Guyana, Jamaica, Trinidad.

4 Explain why Guyana's path to independence was so troubled.

*5 How did Associated Statehood arise? What were the Associated States of the British Caribbean? Give an account of the Associated States' constitutions, explaining their links with Britain. What states ended their association with Britain in the 1970s and under what circumstances did they do so?

6 Refer to the picture on page 50 and answer the following questions:
  a) When was this organisation formed? What was its chief object?
  b) What was the attitude of this organisation towards colonisation? What did its Charter say on this subject?
  c) What effect did independence for former colonies have on its membership? How did this influence the organisation's attitude to colonialism?
  d) What happened in this organisation in 1960 and 1961 regarding colonialism? What was the immediate result of this development?
  e) What part does this organisation play in the external and internal affairs of independent Caribbean countries today?

7 What are the chief political and economic problems to be faced by newly-independent Commonwealth Caribbean countries?

Chapter 6

*1 Trace the history of the French colonies of Martinique and Guadeloupe showing how their constitutional and political position has reflected the changes in the constitution of metropolitan France.

*2 What do you understand by the term 'assimilation'? Show how it operates in the French Caribbean. Contrast this with its application in other parts of the Caribbean.

*3 How did the United States treat Puerto Rico constitutionally, politically and economically between 1917 and 1952?

*4 Examine and comment on the 1952 Commonwealth Constitution of Puerto Rico.

5 Refer to the picture on page 68 and answer the following questions.
   a) When did this man come to power in Puerto Rico? What party was he leading?
   b) What was his early programme i) constitutionally; ii) economically and socially?
   c) How and why did he please the United States administration during and just after the Second World War?
   d) When did his party's era of power come to an end? Which party took over? What is the essential difference between these two parties on the constitutional question?
   e) Make a brief assessment of this man's contribution to the progress of Puerto Rico.

Chapter 7

*1 Give an account of the attempts to federate the Leeward Islands and comment on the special problems they faced.
2 What were the forces making for West Indian unity in the nineteenth and twentieth centuries and what were the forces drawing the territories apart?
3 What bodies were responsible for inter-regional co-operation in the British West Indies between 1897 and 1947?
4 Refer to the map of the Leeward Islands on page 77 and answer the following questions:
   a) How large is the area over which the Leeward Islands are scattered?
   b) What new groups were created in the Leewards in 1816?
   c) What were the four Presidencies of 1871? Why was the term 'Presidency' introduced in 1871?
   d) When did St Kitts-Nevis-Anguilla become united? What problems has this group had in the 1970s?
   e) How has Dominica been associated with the Leeward Islands in the nineteenth and twentieth centuries?

Chapter 8

*1 Trace the movement to federation from 1945 to 1958.
2 Why was the Federation of the West Indies so weak?
3 Account for the collapse of the Federation of the West Indies after only four years.
4 What inter-regional bodies have been established in the Commonwealth Caribbean since 1962? What are their functions?
5 Refer to the picture on page 91 and answer the following questions:
   a) What was the density of population on this island at the time of the Federation?
   b) What measure did this island expect the Federation to introduce which would relieve its over-crowding?
   c) Why did Trinidad oppose this measure?
   d) Why did this island have a lot of political influence in the Federation?
   e) What part did this island play in the association known as the 'Little Eight'?

Chapter 9

*1 Describe the part played by the Dominicans in establishing Christianity in the Spanish Indies.
2 Compare the attitude of the Catholic Church to slavery with that of the Church of England. Why did it make little difference in practice?
3 Why did the Church of England have such a poor record in the West Indies before 1800?
4 What part did the Nonconformist churches play in the religion of the British islands before emancipation?
5 Study the picture on page 104 and answer the following questions:
   a) To what religious sect do these people belong? What is their i) proper name, ii) nickname?
   b) Comment on i) the dress, ii) the style of this meeting.
   c) Give three reasons why they were not popular with the planters in the British Islands.
   d) What was their attitude towards slavery? How did the movement adopt this attitude throughout the world?

Chapter 10

1 Describe the work of the Protestant Nonconformist churches amongst the slaves in the British West Indies.
2 Explain the role of the Church of England in the thirty years leading up to emancipation.

*3 What is the 'Third Force' in Christianity in the Caribbean to-day? What factors have determined its success or failure?
4 Assess the importance of Afro-Caribbean religions in the present-day West Indies. In your answer make particular reference to any ONE Afro-Caribbean religion.
5 Study the pie chart on page 111 and answer the following questions:
   a) Account for the low percentage of the Church of England.
   b) What percentage of the people attended the Baptist Church? Why is this figure comparatively high in Jamaica?
   c) What bearing did these figures have on the government's attitude to the Church of England in 1868?
   d) Outline the different classes of people attending i) the Church of England and ii) Nonconformist churches in the nineteenth century.
   e) What is the biggest single change you would make in a pie chart of religious denominations in Jamaica to-day? Account for the change you have made.

Chapter 11

1 Why did emancipation not turn West Indian society upside down?
2 What part did coloureds play in nineteenth-century West Indian society?
*3 Explain the major differences between Cuban society and British West Indian society in the nineteenth century.
4 Refer to the photograph on page 132 and answer the following questions:
   a) When did cricket develop in the British West Indies? When was the first inter-regional match?
   b) Why was Jamaica not able to take part in the early inter-regional matches?
   c) What cricketing body in the West Indies took control of inter-regional competition and organised overseas tours?
   d) What are the regions which contest the Shell Shield?
   e) Name a West Indian test cricketer from each region.
5 Visit your local library, museum and newspaper offices and collect material for a project on one of the following topics in your own territory over the past one hundred and fifty years: customs; recreation; dress. Try to illustrate your project with photographs etc.

Chapter 12

1 Describe briefly the chief causes of social distress in the British West Indies in the 1930s.
2 What could a) the employers and b) the governments have done to improve the social conditions of the labouring classes in the 1930s?
3 Why did the poorer classes in the British West Indies in the 1930s suffer from malnutrition? What were the effects of malnutrition on individuals and the country as a whole?
4 Outline the Moyne Commission's recommendations for strengthening the powers of organised labour in the British West Indies.
5 Refer to the picture on page 135 and answer the following questions.
   a) When and why was this method of housing frequently adopted in British Guiana and Trinidad?
   b) What was the usual size of the rooms in this type of housing? What did the furniture usually consist of? How many people were generally accommodated in these rooms and how did they manage?
   c) What were the hygiene and sanitation problems in this kind of living?
   d) Describe the typical diet of the people living in these quarters.
   e) What did the reformers propose as the best alternative to this sort of housing?
6 Compare and contrast the social conditions of the poor in Jamaica and Puerto Rico in the late 1930s

Chapter 13

1 How successful have West Indian artists been in developing Caribbean art forms? (In your answer you must refer to individual artists and their works.)
2 If you have visited an art gallery in the Caribbean, describe the works of local artists which you saw there, giving the names of the

artists and their works if possible. Say which works could be described as Caribbean art, and why; and which owed more to foreign influences.

3 Which West Indian town or city would you most like to visit for its architectural interest? (You must give reasons for your choice.)

4 Refer to the illustration on the front cover of this book and answer the following questions:
   a) What sort of art form is it?
   b) Who is the artist? What is the title of the work?
   c) Does this work belong to any special movement in Caribbean art? If so, say what movement. Or does it belong to a foreign movement? If so, say what movement.
   d) What is the social and political significance of this work?
   e) Write a short account of the artist's life and career.

*5 How much do Caribbean music forms owe to African models? In your answer you may like to refer to African rhythms, melodies, instruments and lyrics.

6 Give strong reasons for saying that steel band music is truly a Caribbean form.

7 Trace the development of steel band music from its origins to the present day.

8 What is the relationship between calypso and carnival in Trinidad?

9 Refer to the picture on page 168 and answer the following questions:
   a) What Caribbean form of music is this man associated with?
   b) What do you notice about his appearance? Suggest reasons why he favours this appearance.
   c) With what social or political movements might he be associated?
   d) Name other performers in his particular field.
   e) What is the conflict between 'purists' and commercial artists in the Caribbean?

Further reading

General texts

Augier, Gordon, Hall and Reckord, *The Making of the West Indies*, Longman, 1960

Edward Brathwaite, *The People Who Came*, Books 1–3, Longman

Sir Alan Burns, *History of the British West Indies*, George Allen and Unwin, 1954

E. H. Carter, G. W. Digby, R. N. Murray, *History of the West Indian Peoples*, Nelson

Isaac Dookhan, *A Pre-emancipation History of the West Indies*, Collins, 1971

Isaac Dookhan, *A Post-emancipation History of the West Indies*, Collins, 1975

Sheila Duncker, *A Visual History of the West Indies*, Evans, 1965

A. Garcia, *History of the West Indies*, Harrap, 1965

R. N. Murray, *Nelson's West Indian History*, Nelson, 1971

J. H. Parry and P. M. Sherlock, *A Short History of the West Indies*, Macmillan 3rd edition, 1971

P. M. Sherlock, *West Indian Nations*, Macmillan, 1973.

Eric Williams, *From Columbus to Castro*, Andre Deutsch, 1970

Island histories

Paul Albury, *The Story of the Bahamas*, Macmillan, 1975

Michael Anthony, *Profile Trinidad*, Macmillan, 1975

C. V. Black, *History of Jamaica*, Collins, 1965

C. V. Black, *A New History of Jamaica*, Collins-Sangster, 1973

Vere T. Daly, *The Making of Guyana*, Macmillan, 1974

Vere T. Daly, *A Short History of the Guyanese People*, Macmillan, 1975

Narda Dobson, *A History of Belize*, Longman, 1973

F. A. Hoyos, *Barbados–A History from the Amerindians to Independence*, Macmillan, 1978

C. Ottley, *The Story of Port of Spain*, Longman, 1970

Eric Williams, *History of the People of Trinidad and Tobago*, Andre Deutsch, 1974

W. S. Zuill, *The Story of Bermuda and her People*, Macmillan, 1973

Special texts

Chapters 1 and 2

Hofstadter, Miller and Aaron, *The American Republic*, Volumes 1 & 2, Prentice-Hall

Eric Williams, *From Columbus to Castro*, Chapters 23 to 25

J. H. Parry and P. M. Sherlock, *A Short History of the West Indies*, Chapter 17

Augier, Gordon, Hall and Reckord, *The Making of the West Indies*, Chapter 21

Chapter 3
J. Harrod, *Trade Union Foreign Policy*, Macmillan
Vere T. Daly, *A Short History of the Guyanese People*, Chapter 26
P. M. Sherlock, *West Indian Nations*, Chapters 22 & 23
F. A. Hoyos, *A History of Barbados*, Chapter 16

Chapters 4, 5 & 6
Sir Alan Burns, *History of the British West Indies*, Chapters 10 to 13, 15, 18 and 20 to 22
C. V. Black, *History of Jamaica*, Chapters 16 to 20
F. A. Hoyos, *A History of Barbados*, Chapters 12 to 18
Eric Williams, *From Columbus to Castro*, Chapter 27
Vere T. Daly, *A Short History of the Guyanese People*, Chapters 25 to 27
Eric Williams, *A History of the People of Trinidad and Tobago*, Chapters 10, 13, 15 & 16
P. M. Sherlock, *West Indian Nations*, Chapters 24 & 25
Augier, Gordon, Hall and Reckord, *The Making of the West Indies*, Chapters 23 & 24

Chapters 7 and 8
Augier, Gordon, Hall and Reckord, *The Making of the West Indies*, Chapter 25
J. H. Parry and P. M. Sherlock, *A Short History of the West Indies*, Chapter 18
Sir Alan Burns, *History of the British West Indies*, Chapters 12, 21 and 22
C. V. Black, *History of Jamaica*, Chapter 20

Chapters 9 and 10
J. H. Parry, *The Spanish Theory of Empire in the Sixteenth Century*, Cambridge, 1940
Eric Williams, *From Columbus to Castro*, Chapters 5 & 6
A. Caldecott, *The Church in the West Indies*, London, 1898
H. P. Thompson, *Into All Lands. The History of the Society for the Propagation of the Gospel in Foreign Parts, 1701-1950,* published 1951
Augier, Gordon, Hall and Reckord, *The Making of the West Indies*, Chapters 12 to 15

Chapters 11 and 12
Bridget Brereton, *Race Relations in Colonial Trinidad, 1870 to 1900,* Cambridge University Press, 1979

E. Clarke, *My Mother Who Fathered Me*, London 1957
D. Lowenthal, *West Indian Societies*, Oxford University Press, 1972
Eric Williams, *From Columbus to Castro*, Chapter 26
J. Arlott, *The Oxford Companion to Sports and Games*, Oxford, 1976

Chapter 13
A. W. Acworth, *Treasure in the Caribbean*, London, 1949
A. W. Acworth, *Buildings of Architectural Interest in the British West Indies,* London, 1957
M. Anthony and A. Carr, ed., *David Frost Introduces Trinidad and Tobago,* Andre Deutsch, 1975
M. Cargill, ed., *Ian Fleming Introduces Jamaica,* Andre Deutsch, 1965
T. A. L. Concannon, *Jamaica's Architectural Heritage,* Georgian Society of Jamaica, 1971
R. J. Devaux, *St Lucia Historical Sites,* St Lucia National Trust, 1975
J. Golding, *A Short History of Puerto Rico*, New American Library, 1973
R. F. Marx, *Port Royal Rediscovered*, Doubleday, New York, 1973
V. Radcliffe, *Caribbean Heritage*, Walker Publishing Company, 1976
A. Waugh, *A Family of Islands*, Doubleday, New York, 1964
N. A. Simmonds, *Pan–The Story of the Steel Band*

Index

Abrahams, Earl, 150
Adams, Grantley, 25, 31, 32, 51, 60, 61, 84, 87, 88, 92, 130
Adams, John, 3
Adams, John Quincy, 4, 5
Alladin, P., 149
American Civil War, 6, 7, 39, 41
Amerindian religion, 96–7, 118
Anguilla, 63, 77, 78, 80
Antigua, 37, 62, 63, 77, 78, 85, 92, 93, 105, 109, 122; tourism, 21, 63; trade unions, 26, 30; Assembly, 34, 36; Crown Colony, 45; elected members, 47; diocese, 111; archaeology, 146, 147
Antigua – Barbuda – Redonda, 61, 62
Arawaks, the, 101, 146; religion, 96–7; music, 162
Archaeology, 146–7
Archdiocese of the West Indies, 111
Architecture, 153–62; Spanish, 153–4; British, 154–8; French, 158; Dutch, 159–60; Haiti, 161–2
Arminius, Jacobus, 106
Aruba, 146, 159
Asbury, Francis, 109
Assemblies, 34–7, 39, 44
Associated States, 62
Associated West Indian Chambers of Commerce, 82–4
Atlantic Charter, 49
Atteck, Sybil, 148
Augustinians, the, 97

Bahamas, the, 20, 35, 80, 106, 168; tourism, 21; Assembly, 45
Baker, Moses, 106
Bank of Jamaica, 66
Baptists, 105–7; Missionary Society, 107, 109
Barbados, 20, 21, 24, 61, 62, 78, 81, 85, 92, 93, 109, 122, 126; tourism, 21, 67; trade unions, 25, 31–2; Assembly, 34, 45–6, 78; parishes, 38; Executive Council, 46; constitutional progress, 52–3; independence, 59–61; political parties, 60, 61; and Federation, 61, 87, 88; unemployment, 66; sugar, 67; and the Leeward Islands, 81; religion, 101, 104, 105, 107, 110, 113–14, 118; newspapers, 129, 130; cricket, 131; wages, 137; land shortage, 138; malnutrition, 138; education, 139, 140
Barbados Gazette, 129
Barbados Industrial Development Corporation, 66
Barbados Labour Party, 31, 32, 60, 61, 130
Barbados Progressive League, 25, 26, 31, 84
Barbados Workers Union, 31, 32, 60
Barbuda, 78
Barkly, Sir Henry, 36–7, 39
Barrow, Errol, 60, 61
Bascom, James, Sarsfield, 130
Basseterre, St. Kitts, Georgian buildings, 157

Batista, Fulgencio, 19
Bazile, Castera, 153
Beacon newspaper, 130
Belize, 61, 63
  See also British Honduras
Bell, Captain Philip, 101
Berkeley, Bishop George, 103
Bermuda, 20, 45, 168
Betances, Ramón, Emeterio, 72
Beveridge, Albert, 8
Bigaud, Wilson, 153
Birch, Vere, 63
'Black Power', 145, 168
Bogle, Paul, 42–4
Bonaire: archaeology, 146; houses, 159
Bradshaw, Robert, 63
Brahma and Brahmins, 114
Brathwaite, C. A., 130
Bridgetown, 127, 128; buildings, 157
Brimstone Hill, St. Kitts, fortifications, 156
British and Foreign Bible Society, 104, 108
British Caribbean Federation Act (1956), 87
British Guiana, 10, 24, 38–9, 81–2, 109, 123, 137; trade unions, 24, 26, 28; disturbances, 25, 26, 58, 59; constitutional progress, 52–3; independence, 58–9; political parties, 58, 59; racial divisions, 58, 59; rejects Federation, 85–6, 91; Indian immigrants, 114; white elite, 127; housing, 139; education, 139, 140; illiteracy, 139

177

See also Guyana
British Guiana and West Indian Labour Conference, 27, 83, 84
British Honduras, 61, 80, 93, 123; Crown Colony, 45, 80; elected members, 47; rejects Federation, 85–6, 91; diocese, 111
  See also Belize
British Virgin Islands, 61, 62, 78; rejects Federation, 86
Bryan, William J, 14
Bryan-Chamorro Treaty, 12
Buchanan, James, 6
Bulls of Donation, 98
Burchell, Thomas, 109
Burnham, Forbes, 58, 59; and Cuba, 65
Bustamante, Sir Alexander, 21, 26, 29–30, 56, 88, 90, 92, 145; and Industrial Trade Union, 26, 30, 32, 55
Butler, Uriah, 25, 28, 29, 56

Cabinet government, 54
'Cadence' music, 168
Calypso, 163, 166–8
'Calypso Rose', 167
Canadian Presbyterian Church, 114
Canning, George, 4, 6
Cap Haitien, Haiti, buildings, 159, 161
Capildeo, Dr Rudranath, 57
Caribbean Development Bank, 66, 95
Caribs, the, 96, 146; music, 162
CARICOM (Caribbean Common Market), 93–5, 142
CARIFTA (Caribbean Free Trade Association), 93, 95, 142
Carlisle, Earl of, 76
Carmelites, the, 97
Carmichael, Stokeley, 145
Carnival, 163, 167
Carr, Andrew, 148
Castro, Fidel 18, 19, 64, 65, 75
Castro, Ramón Baldorioty de, 72
Catholicism, Spanish, 97–101; and the Indians, 97–8, 100; and slavery, 100–1
Cato, Milton, 62
Cayman Compass, 129
Cayman Islands, 61, 62, 80, 126, 129
Cazabon, Jean Michel, 147

Césaire, Aimé, 70
Cespedes, Carlos Manuel de, 19
Chaguaramas: naval base, 20–1, 87, 91–2; site for federal capital, 87, 91–2
Charles V, 100
Charles, Normil, 153
Château Murat, Marie Galante, 159
Chiapas, Guatemala, 97, 100
Chinese immigrants, 122, 133
Christophe, Henri, 161
Church Missionary Society, 104, 108
Church of England, 101–4 organisation, 102; missions, 104; and the slaves, 103, 109; evangelical groups, 108; reforms, 109–11; disestablishment, 113–14; and immigrant religions, 114
Churchill, (Sir) Winston, 49
Cipriani, Arthur, 24, 28–9, 47
Citrine, Walter (Lord Citrine), 141
Clapham Sect, 108
Clarence House, Antigua, 156
Clark, William, 147
Clayton-Bulwer Treaty (1850), 11, 12
Clerk, Leslie, 150
Cleveland, President Grover, 8, 10
Code noir (1685), 101
Codrington, Christopher, 37–8, 103
Codrington College, 103, 110, 113, 114, 156
Coke, Thomas, 105, 109
Colbeck Castle, Jamaica, 155–6
Coleridge, Bishop William Hart, 110, 113
Colombia, and the Panama Canal, 12, 13
Colonial Church Union, 107, 109
Colonial Development and Welfare Act and Organisation, 53, 65, 83, 87, 88, 142, 145
Colonist newspaper, 130
Colour, 121–2
Columbus, Bartholomew, 153
Columbus, Christopher, 97, 153
Columbus, Diego, 154
Compton, John, 62
Constantine, Learie (Lord Constantine), 131, 132

Constantine, Leburn, 131
Convention of Zanjon (1878), 6
Cooke, Rector of St. Thomas, 40
Coolidge, President Calvin, 16
Coombes, A.G.S., 26, 29
Crawford, W. A., 31
Creech Jones, Arthur, 85
Creole families, 125–6
Cricket, 130–3; inter-colonial matches, 131; Board of Control, 131; Shell Shield, 132
Critchlow, Hubert, 24, 27–8
Cromwell, Joseph, 149
Crowder, General, 19
Crown Colony government, 44–7
Cuba, 4, 17, 25, 71–2, 100, 116, 133, 137; and the United States, 5–10, 17–21; Ten Years War, 6, 71, 133; War of Independence, 7–10; U.S. investment. 7; U.S. occupation, 9; independence, 9, 48; Platt Amendment, 9–10, 17–19; influence in the Caribbean, 64–5; society, 133–4; tobacco, 133; sugar, 133, 134, 143; slavery, 133; Chinese immigrants, 133, 134; archaeology, 146; architecture, 153; music and musical instruments, 163, 168
Cummins, H. G., 31
Curaçao: archaeology, 146; architecture, 159–60

D'Aguiar, Peter Stanislaus, 58
Daley, Henry, 149, 150
Danish Virgin Islands, 16, 17
  See also United States Virgin Islands
Darling, C. H., 40
De Gaulle, General Charles, 69
Demerara Bauxite Company, nationalised, 65
Democratic Labour Party, Barbados, 32, 60, 61
Democratic Labour Party, Federal, 88
Democratic Labour Party, Jamaica, 90
Development Corporations, 66
Devon House, Kingston, 158
Diaz, Adolfo, 16
Diversification, 67

Dizzy, Ras, 149
Dominica, 61, 62, 67, 78, 82–3, 95; Assembly, 35; Crown Colony, 45; elected members, 47, 54; independence, 62
Dominican Friars, 97–100
Dominican Republic, 10, 14–17
Dorcély, Roland, 153
Drax Hall, Barbados, 156
Duffaut, Prefete, 152
Dunkley, John, 149–50
Duperier, Odilon, 153

Economic problems, 64–7
Economics of Undeveloped Countries, The (Bauer and Yamey), 66
Education, 139–40, 142; and self-government, 51
Elective principle, 54
Emancipation, 81, 120–1; and religion, 108–9
English Harbour, Antigua, dockyards, 156
Estenoz, Evaristo, 18
European Economic Community, 70, 94
Evangelicalism, 108
Everett, Edward, 6
Executive Councils, 37, 55
Eyre, Edward, John, 40–4; and Gordon, 40–1; and the Morant Bay Rebellion, 43

Factory inspection, 141
Falmouth, Jamaica, 158
Farley Hill, Barbados, 156
Farming reforms, 142
Faulkner, Mildred, 148
Federation of the West Indies, 56, 57, 60–2, 78, 80, 83, 85–92, 142; Montego Bay Conference, 85–8; conferences of 1955 and 1956, 86–7; 1956 Act, 87; Constitution, 87; federal elections, 88; finance, 88; constitutional revision (1959), 89–90; breakdown of Federation, 90–2
Ferdinand and Isabella, 49, 98, 100
Ferguson, Leonard, 152
FIDOM, 71
Finder, president of Codrington College, 114
Florida, 4
Food, 138

Foot, Sir Hugh, 56
Foraker Act (1900), 10, 72
Fort Orange, St Eustatius, 160
Fort St Louis, Martinique, 159
Fountain Estate, St Kitts, 159
Fox, George, 104
France, 38; and U.S.A., 1, 3; Louisiana Purchase, 4; and Panama Canal, 7, 12; and slavery, 101
Franciscans, the, 97, 100
French Caribbean, 68–71
representation in French Assembly, 69; departments of France, 69–70; Decentralisation Decrees (1960), 69; French system of justice, 69–70; political movements, 70; French aid, 71; *négritude*, 145
French Guiana (Guyane), 68–70
French Revolutionary and Napoleonic Wars, 3, 71

Gairy, Sir Eric, 62
Garvey, Marcus, 52, 119, 122, 145
Georgetown, 127; Anglican Cathedral, 157
Globe newspaper, 130
Goddard, J. D., 132
Goethals, Colonel George, 13
Gomes, Albert, 56, 148
Gomez, José Miguel, 18
Gonzales, Christopher, 150
Gordon, George William, 40–4, 107, 130; and Morant Bay Rebellion, 43; hanged, 43
Gorgas, Colonel W. C., 13
Grant, Sir John Peter, 46
Grenada, 61, 62, 67, 78, 85, 87, 92, 93, 119, 137; Assembly, 35; Crown Colony, 45; elected members, 47; independence, 62; left-wing coup, 65
Grenadines, the, 78; illiteracy, 139
Grey, Sir Charles, 121
Guadeloupe, 68–70; dependent islands, 68; archaeology, 146; 'Cadence', 168
Guatumala, 63
Guiana Chronicle, 130
Guiana, diocese of, 111
Guyana, 21, 59, 65, 93, 115, 116; mineral resources, 65, 67; animist religions, 118; East

Indian immigrants, 122, 133; cricket, 132
See also British Guiana
Guyana Development Corporation, 66

Haile Selassie, 119
Hailes, Lord, 87
Haiti, 10, 15–16, 116, 118, 133, 163; U.S. intervention, 15–17; Voodoo, 118; archaeology, 146; art, 152–3; architecture, 161–2; music, 168
Harley, Milton, 152
Harris, Lord, 121
Havana, 5, 9, 18, 19, 154; Inter-American Conference (1928), 17; Conference of Non-Aligned Nations (1979), 65
Hay, John, 12
Hay-Pauncefote Treaty, 12
Headley, George, 132
Health, 138–9
Hearst, William Randolph, 8
Herald newspaper, 130
Herran, Tomas, 12
Heureaux, Ulises, 14
Hinduism, 114–16, 118, 122; gods, 114; festivals, 115; caste system, 122; temples, 157
Hispaniola, 5, 10, 99, 100, 146
Holder, Boscoe, 148
Holidays with pay, 141
Holiness Churches, 116, 118
Hookworm, 138–9, 144
Hoover, President Herbert, 17
Housing, 139
Huie, Albert, 150
Hyde, Eugene, 152
Hyppolite, Hector, 152

Ice House restaurant, Barbados, 127
Illiteracy, 139
Immigrant religions, 114–16
Imperial College of Tropical Agriculture, 82, 94
Infant mortality, 138
Internal self-government, 54
International Monetary Fund, 94
Irvine Commission (1945), 94
Islam, 115–16, 118, 122; mosques, 157
Ivonet, Pedro, 18

Jackson, Andrew, 4
Jacques, Jean Baptiste, 152

179

Jagan, Dr Cheddi, 31, 58, 59
Jamaica, 11, 50, 85, 93, 102, 122, 126, 133, 139, 144, 145; tourism, 21; trade unions, 23, 24, 26, 30, 32; disturbances, 26; Assembly, 36–7, 40, 45; Crown Colony, 45, 46, 54; Legislative Council, 45–7, 84; elected members, 46–7, 54–5; constitutional progress, 52–3; independence, 55–6 and Cuba, 65; bauxite, 65, 67; alumina, 67; diversification, 67; sugar, 67; and Federation, 61, 87–92; religion, 101, 102, 105–7, 109–11, 116, 119; white elite, 127 newspapers, 129, 130; cricket, 132; bananas, 136; unemployment, 137, 143–4; Labour Department, 141; comparison with Puerto Rico, 143–4; art, 149–52, reggae, 168
Jamaica Courant, 129
Jamaica Disestablishment Act (1870), 113
Jamaica Labour Party, 30, 32, 55, 56
James II, 103
Jefferson, Thomas, 3–5
Jesuits, the, 97, 100
Jiménez, President of Dominican Republic, 15
Jiménez de Cisneros, Cardinal, 99, 100
John, Patrick R., 62
Jordon, Edward, 40, 130
Joseph, Jasmin, 153
Josephine, Empress, 159
Judiciary, the, 37–8

Ketelhodt, Baron von, 40
King, Martin Luther, 145
Kingston, 127–9, 137, 158
Kinship, 125
Knibb, William, 109
Kumina cult, 119

La Citadelle, Haiti, 161–2
La Ferrière, French engineer, 161
La Pagerie, Martinique, 159
Labour Departments, 27, 137, 141
Laforesterie, Louis, 153
Las Casas, Bartholomew de, 97–100; writings, 100
Laws of Burgos (1512), 98, 100

Leeward Islands, 62, 76–7; Crown Colony government, 45; Federation, 77–8; cricket, 132
Legislative Councils, 35
Lesseps, Ferdinand de, 12
Liberal newspaper, 130
Liguanea club, Kingston, 127
Lima, diocese of, 97
Lipscomb, Bishop Christopher, 110
Lisle, George, 106
Lloyd, Clive, 132
Local government, 38
Louis XVIII, 68
Louisiana Purchase, 4
Lucas, R. Slade, 131

Machado, Geraldo, 19
McKinley, President William, 8
Macleod, Iain, 60
Magoon, Charles, 18
Mahan, Admiral A. T., 7
Maine, U.S.S. loss of, 8, 9
Malnutrition, 138–9, 144
Maloney, Scribo, 165
Manette, Ellie, 165
Manley, Edna, 149, 150
Manley, Michael, and Cuban aid, 65
Manley, Norman, 26, 30, 32, 51, 84, 87, 88, 90; and Trade Union Advisory Council, 29, 30; and National Workers' Union, 30, 32, 56
Manning, Russell, 166
Marley, Bob, 162, 168
Maroons, the, 43, 119
Marriage, 123–4
Marriot, Alvin, 150, 152
Marryshow, T., 82–4
Martinique, 68–70; archaeology, 146; music, 168
Mason, John, 6
Matri-focal families, 124–5
Mayans, the, 147
Menocal, President of Cuba, 18, 19
Mestor, Louines, 152
Metcalfe, Sir Charles, 36
Methodist Missionary Society, 105, 109
'Mighty Sparrow', the, 167
Miller, David, 149
Ministerial system, 54
Monroe Doctrine, 4, 6, 10, 21; Roosevelt-Corollary, 14, 15

Monroe, President James, 4, 6
Montego Bay, 158; Conference (1947), 85–8
Montesinos, Dominican Friar, 97, 99–100
Montpelier, Nevis, 156
Montserrat, 47, 61, 62, 77, 78, 85, 87, 92, 93
Morant Bay Rebellion, 39–43, 47, 78
Moravians, 105
Mordecai, John, 87
Morne Fortune fort, St Lucia, 159
Moslems, *see* Islam
Moyne Commission and Report (1938), 26, 52–3, 82, 83, 136, 137, 139–43; social and economic recommendations, 141–3
Muñoz Marin, Luis, 72–5, 143–5
Music, 162–8; African influence, 162; instruments, 162–3; carnival, 163, 167; steel bands, 163–6; calypso, 166–7

Napoleon I, 68, 159
Napoleon III, 68
Nassau: diocese, 111; buildings, 158
Nationalisation, 65
Negro Education Grant, 111
Nelson, Horatio, 156
Nevis, 45, 77, 78, 80, 81, 101 *See also* St Kitts – Nevis
New Mexico, diocese of, 97
New Orleans, 2–4
New Progressive Party, Puerto Rico, 75
Newspapers, 129–30; and party politics, 130
Nicaragua: Maritime Canal Company, 12; U.S. intervention, 16
Non-alignment, 64–5
Noncomformists, 101, 104–7; persecution, 107; missions, 109; and slaves, 109
Norman Commission (1897), 82, 135, 137
Norman, F. A., 141

Obeah magic, 119
Obin, Philomène, 152, 153
Olivier Commission (1929), 135–7
O'Neal, Charles Duncan, 24

One-party states, 64
Orange Valley, Jamaica, Georgian buildings, 156
Orde-Browne, Major St John, and Orde-Browne Report (1938), 136, 137, 139, 141
Orders-in-Council, 82
Organisation of American States (O.A.S.), 21
Ostend Manifesto, 6

Palladium newspaper, 130
Palma, Estrada, 17, 18
Palmerston, Lord, 6
Panama Canal, 7, 11-14; New Panama Canal Company, 12; construction, 13
Pang, Amy Leong, 148
Parquet, Jacques du, 159
Parboosingh, Karl, 150
Parry, Bishop of Barbados, 114
Parti Progessiste (Martinique), 70
Passfield, Lord (Sidney Webb), and Passfield Memorandum, 135, 136
Payne, Clement, 25, 31
Payne, Dorothy, 150, 152
Pentecostal Churches, 116, 118
People's National Congress, British Guiana, 58, 59
People's National Movement, Trinidad, 56, 57
People's National Party, Jamaica, 30, 32, 56, 84
People's Progressive Party, British Guiana, 31, 58, 59
Per capita incomes, 67
Peters, De Witt, 152
Petroglyphs (rock paintings), 146, 147
Philip II, 98, 100
Phillippo, Rev. J. M., 109
Pierce, President Franklin, 6
Pinchinat, Max, 153
Pinckney's Treaty, 3
Piñero, Jesús T., 73
Platt Amendment (1901), 9-10, 18; withdrawal (1934), 17, 19
Pocamania, 119
Pointe à Pitre, Guadeloupe, 159
Polk, President James K., 6
Ponce de Leon, 71
Pope-Hennessy, Governor of Barbados, 46, 78
Popular Democratic Party, Puerto Rico, 72, 73, 75, 143
Port-au-Prince: Episcopal Cathedral, 153, 161; buildings, 161
Porteus, Bishop of London, 109-10
Port of Spain, 20, 28, 29, 87, 92, 127-9, 147, 163, 165; architecture, 157
Port of Spain Gazette, 130
Port Royal, 103; underwater discoveries, 147
Prescod, Samuel, 46, 130
Price, George, 63
Probyn, Sir Leslie, 23
Protestant Chruches, 101-7; Church of England, 101-4; Noncomformists, 104-7
Puerto Rico, 5, 9, 10, 71-5, 116, 133; ceded to U.S.A., 20, 71, 72, 143; sugar, 72, 143; political parties, 72, 75; Industrial Development Company, 73, 144; Development Bank, 73, 144; economic advances, 73, 74, 143-5; Commonwealth (1952), 73-4; Constitution, 73-4; pressures from Cuba, 75; comparison with Jamaica, 143-4; coffee, 143; unemployment, 143-5; U.S. investment and aid, 145; social reforms, 143-5; emigration to U.S.A., 144, 145; Reconstruction Administration, 144, 145; archaeology, 146, 147; architecture, 153; music, 168
Pulitzer, Joseph, 8

Quakers (Society of Friends), 101, 102, 104
Qualitative franchise, 54
Queen's Park Cricket Club, Trinidad, 131

Rada cult, 119
Ramadan, 116
Ramadhin, Sonny, 132, 166
Rastafarians, 119, 145, 168
Rawle, Principal of Codrington College, 114
Recorder newspaper, 130
Reeves, Conrad, 46
Reggae, 162, 168
Regional co-operation, 76-84
Representative system, 34-6
Responsible government, 54
Revivalism, American, 116, 118
Reynolds, Mellica (KAPO), 149, 150
Richards, Sir Arthur, 30
Rienzi, A. G., 28
Romero-Barcelo, Carlos, 75
Roosevelt, Franklin D., 17, 19, 49
Roosevelt, Theodore, 8, 14; and the Panama Canal, 12, 13; Corollary to Monroe Doctrine, 14, 15
Rose Hall, Jamaica, 156
Royal Commissions: (1883), 82; (1897), *see* Norman Commission; (1929), *see* Olivier Commission; (1938), *see* Moyne Commission
Royal Essequibo and Demerary Gazette, 130

Saint-Brice, 152
St Dominique, 123
St George's Grenada, Georgian houses, 157
St John's, Antigua, 127; buildings, 156-7
St Kitts, 77, 78, 80, 130; disturbances, 25; Workers' League, 30; Assembly, 34, 36, 37; Crown Colony, 45; and Nevis, 81; and Barbados, 81
St Kitts-Nevis, 47
St Kitts-Nevis-Anguilla, 61-3, 80, 85, 92, 93
St Lucia, 61, 62, 67, 78, 82, 85, 92, 93, 159; disturbances, 25; status, 38, elected members, 47; independence, 62; and Cuba, 65; archaeology, 146
St Thomas, archaeology, 146
St Vincent, 61-3, 78, 85, 92-8, 113; disturbances, 25; Assembly, 35; Crown Colony, 45; elected members, 47; newspapers, 130
Salvation Army, 116
San Fernando, Trinidad, 127
San Juan, Puerto Rico, 143; buildings, 154
Sandys, Duncan, 59
Sans Souci palace, Haiti, 161
Santiago, 9; diocese, 97
Santo Domingo, 97; diocese 97; architecture, 153-4
Santo Domingo de Guzman, 153
Segregation of the sexes, 125
Severance pay, 141
Shango cult, 119

181

Sherlock, Sir Philip, 149
Shrewsbury, William, 107
Singh, Dr. J. B., 58
Siva, Hindu god, 114
Smith, Rev. John, 109
Smith, Sir Lionel, 37
Sobers, Sir Garfield, 132, 133
Soca music, 168
Society for Promoting Christian Knowledge, 108
Society for the Propagation of the Gospel, 103, 104, 108, 111
Solomon, Dr Patrick, 56
Spain, 3; and U.S.A. 2, 4; and Cuba, 6–10; Spanish-American War, 8–9; and Puerto Rico, 10, 71–2; and Trinidad, 38; Catholicism, 97–101; and slavery, 100, 101
Spanish Town, Jamaica, public buildings, 158
Squires, Nina Lamming, 149
Stanley, Colonel Oliver, 84
Stapleton, Sir William, 77
Steel bands, 163–6
Stokes Hall, Jamaica, 155, 156
Stollmeyer, Hugh, 148
Stuyvesant, Peter, 160
Sugar Duties Equalisation Act (1848), 39, 82
Supreme Court of the West Indies, 88

Taft, William Howard, 14, 15
Taylor, Syl, 167
Teller Amendment, 9
Thorne, Alfred, 24
Times, The (Barbados), 130
Tobago, 78; Crown Colony, 45; joined to Trinidad, 80 *See also* Trinidad and Tobago
Tourism, 21, 67
Tournier, Luce, 153
Trade unions, 22–33, 141; and politics, 30–2; Education Institute, 32; achievements, 32–3; and disputes, 33
Treaty of Antigua (1968), 93
Treaty of Chaguaramas (1974), 93
Treaty of Paris (1783), 1; (1898), 9, 10, 72
Trinidad, 21, 24, 25, 39, 50, 78, 82, 93, 126, 147, 162, 163, 168; trade unions, 26, 28; Crown Colony, 38, 47; elected members, 47, 51, 56; constitutional progress, 52–3; asphalt, 67; oil, 67, 136; and Federation, 61, 86, 90–2; site for federal capital, 87, 91–2 diocese, 111; East Indian immigrants, 114, 122, 133; Roman Catholic Church, 118, 119; African cults, 119; white elite, 127; newspapers, 130; cricket, 131; cocoa, 135; wages, 137; unemployment, 137; housing, 139; education, 140; archaeology, 146; art, 148–9; carnival, 163, 167; steel bands, 163–6; calypso, 167, 168
Trinidad and Tobago, 62, 80, 82, 85; independence, 56–7; political parties, 56–7; and Federation, 87–90
Trinidad Art Society, 148
Trinidad Labour Party, 28, 29
Truman, President Harry S., 73
Tuberculosis, 138, 139, 144
Tufton, Sir William, 38
Turks and Caicos Islands, 61, 62, 84, 168

Underhill, Dr. Edward, 41–2
Unemployment, 66–7, 137–8, 143–5
Union Club, Trinidad, 127
United Nations, 49–50; and French Caribbean, 70
United Negro Improvement Association, 52, 145
United States, 1–21, 64–5; foreign policy, 1–4; 'Manifest Destiny', 4–6; Monroe Doctrine, 4, 6, 10, 14, 15, 21; and Cuba, 5–10, 17–21; Spanish-American War, 8–9; Panama Canal, 11–14, 16; 'Dollar Diplomacy', 14–17; 'Good Neighbour Policies', 17; naval bases, 19–20; tourism, 21, 67; black popular movements, 145
United States Virgin Islands, 86
University College of the West Indies (now University of the West Indies), 83, 88, 94–5, 159
Urban blacks, 127–9
Utuado museum, Puerto Rico, 147

Valentine, A., 132, 166
Vaucresson, Noel, 149
Venezuela, 4; border dispute (1895), 10; blockade (1902–3), 14
Vichy Government, 69
Victoria, Queen, 42
Vieux, Phillipe, 152
Vincent, Sténcio Joseph, 16
Vishnu and Vishnuites, 114
Voodoo, 118

Walcott, C. L., 131, 132
Walcott, Frank, 32, 60
Warner, Thomas, 76, 77
Washington, George, 3
Watchman newspaper, 41, 130
Watson, Barrington, 150
Watson, Osmond, 150
Weeke, Thomas, 157
Weekes, E. D., 131, 132
Wesley, Charles, 105
Wesley, John, 105, 109
Wesleyan Methodists, 105, 109
West India Committee, London, 81, 82
West India Regiment, 43, 83, 88
West Indian Press Association, 82
West Indian Prisons Act (1838), 36
West Indian Standing Conference on Federation, 82
West Indies Court of Appeal, 82
West Indies Federal Labour Party, 88
Western Intelligence, 130
'Westminster Pattern' of government, 64
Weyler, General Valeriano, 7, 8
Wheler, Sir Charles, 76–7
White élite, 125–7
White Marl museum, Jamaica, 147
Willemstad, Curaçao, buildings, 160
Williams, Aubrey, 147
Williams, Dr Eric, 20, 56, 57, 89, 91, 92
Willoughby, William, Lord, 76, 101
Wilson, President Woodrow, 13–15, 17
Windward Islands, 38, 62, 78; 'federal' assembly, 39; Crown Colony government, 45; diocese, 111; cricket, 132
Wood, Major E. F. L. (Lord Halifax) and Wood Report (1921), 47, 51, 82, 83
Workmen's compensation, 141
World Bank, 65, 144
Worell, F. M., 131–3

Zayas, President of Cuba, 19
Zemis, 146